Out of Office

Out of Office

The Big Problem and Bigger Promise
of Working from Home

Charlie Warzel **and**
Anne Helen Petersen

RANDOM HOUSE
LARGE PRINT

Cover illustration and design by
Tyler Comrie

The Library of Congress has established
a Cataloging-in-Publication record
for this title.

ISBN: 978-0-593-46038-2

www.penguinrandomhouse.com/
large-print-format-books

FIRST LARGE PRINT EDITION

Printed in the United States of America

1st Printing

This Large Print edition published in accord
with the standards of the N.A.V.H.

Contents

Contents

Out of Office

Introduction

Whatever you were doing during the pandemic and its stilted aftermath, it was not working from home.

"Bullshit," you might say, remembering all those times you sat in a makeshift office in your bedroom, haphazardly constructed so that it might look semiprofessional over Zoom calls. If you're one of the roughly 42 percent of Americans who were able to work remotely during the pandemic, you likely spent most of the time chained to a screen in your home clocking in each morning.[1] You were, quite literally, doing your job from home.

But you weren't working from home. You were laboring in confinement and under duress. Others have described it as living at work. You were frantically tapping out an email while trying to make lunch and supervise distance learning. You were stuck alone in a cramped apartment for weeks, unable to see friends or family, exhausted, and managing a level of stress you didn't know was possible. Work became life, and life became work. You weren't thriving. You were surviving.

Here's the nightmare scenario: this could be the "remote" future. Until recently, broad implementation of work from home seemed more like a thought experiment in the pages of **Harvard Business Review** than an idea that might work in practice. But the pandemic forced millions into remote work, and companies got curious. For a CFO, the prospect of getting that expensive downtown real estate off the balance sheet is enticing, especially if you factor in cost-of-living decreases when employees move out of high-cost cities. And then there's the efficiency: no more commutes means more time to answer emails! Some of the biggest companies in the world have already made remote work an option for the foreseeable future, which, as with almost any business decision, means they think it could be good for the bottom line. And their cost savings will be shouldered by you.

This is the dark truth of remote work as we know it now: it promises to liberate workers from the chains of the office, but in practice it capitalizes on the total collapse of work-life balance.

We know this from experience. In 2017, we made the case that we could do our jobs as reporters even better from outside the city. We packed our car in Brooklyn and made the transition to working from home in Montana after more than a decade of office life. Anne—more organized, a bit more introverted by nature—settled right in. Before journalism, she'd been an academic and a professor; going to the office always felt weirder, more compulsory, than working from your kitchen table. But the "flexibility" of academic life—and now journalistic life—really just meant flexibility to work **all the time.** Dreams of daily hikes in the mountains quickly evaporated. She was working just as much as, if not more than, she did in New York. The backdrop was just more beautiful.

Charlie loves to bullshit with people in the

office. He can't manage his calendar to save his life. He thrives on interaction. And he struggled immediately. The first few months were disorienting and grueling. He spent so much time frantically writing, emailing, and staying in constant contact via Slack messages from the couch that when he'd sit back down at night to unwind, he'd break into a cold sweat. Working relentlessly from home crossed his wires; his mind and body were unable to understand why he was both at the "office" and mainlining Netflix.

Charlie was absolutely convinced the move would hurt his career. He'd be isolated, invisible to superiors, and overlooked for assignments. He worried he was becoming untethered from his work, that he'd lost those spontaneous encounters and conversations that sparked new ideas. So he worked obsessively, with his bosses reaping the rewards, even if they didn't know it. Work on weekends? Why not? After all, he was already at the office. No commute didn't mean free time in the mornings and evenings; it meant rolling out of bed and grabbing the phone and punching the clock. He was writing more than ever, but he started burning out every few weeks, desperate for any activity that would help demarcate work from leisure.

Something had to change. In order to make working from home sustainable—years before the pandemic hit—we had to figure out a way to cultivate a rich home life and then fit our jobs into that space, not the other way around. That meant disconnecting more, but it also meant changing the rhythms of our days and doing away with the rigidity beaten into us by the modern workplace.

Once we made those changes, the lesson was immediately clear: offices can be bullies. They force us to orient our days around commutes. They commandeer our attention with (sometimes enjoyable!) unscheduled, drive-by meetings. They elevate the **feeling** of productivity over being productive. They're a breeding ground for microaggressions and toxic loops of hierarchical behavior. It's no surprise that people who thrive in the office are almost always the same people who have accumulated or were raised with a lot of identity-related privilege outside it.

Working from home can be a meaningful act of control and resistance. But it's also not a cure-all. It can't promise to fix the rot at the core of modern capitalism. All of the toxic dynamics listed above can be ported over to the remote work world. This is especially true if you or your company conceives of working from home as everything that used to happen at the office, only now you're the one paying the rent and utilities. The goal of this book, then, is to think through how we can liberate ourselves from the most toxic, alienating, and frustrating aspects of office work. Not just by shifting the location where the work is completed, but also by rethinking the work we do and the time we allot to it.

This book isn't a how-to manual. It isn't self-help, at least not in the traditional way we think of it. We don't profess to have anything "figured out." Balancing work and life continues to be a struggle for us, and we fail all the time, in part because we **do** find satisfaction in our jobs. This book is also specifically focused on and addressed to the 42 percent of workers whose jobs can be done remotely: far from universal. But for that 42 percent (and growing), we are trying to figure out what's broken about the thing that takes up so much of our waking hours and begin to try to fix it.

Which is why we think of this book as more of a road map. It'll show you how we got to our current broken relationship with work and the routes we can take from here. We can double back, reproducing the same soul-sucking, exploitative office dynamics as before, only doing it from home. Individuals can forge their own path off the main road, as they have for years, struggling to maintain balance in the face of corporate norms. Those with the confidence and privilege to go remote on their terms will reap the benefits, while others will become second-class office citizens. Or we can take a third route, in which the workday itself—and the expectations of workers—are reconceptualized. That doesn't just mean implementing Zoom happy hours, or making a company-wide announcement that it's okay if your kids pop into your conference call to ask for a snack. That's the sort of incrementalism that fixes nothing and exhausts everyone.

Reconceptualization means having honest conversations about how much people are working and how they think they could work **better.** Not longer. Not by taking on more projects, or being better delegators, or having more meetings. Not by creating "more value" for their employer at the expense of their mental and physical health. Instead, it means acknowledging that better work is, in fact, oftentimes **less work,** over fewer hours, which makes people happier, more creative, more invested in the work they do and the people they do it for. It entails thinking through how online communication tools function as surveillance and incentivize playacting your job instead of actually **doing** it. It will require organization based on employees' and managers' preferred and most effective work times, and consideration of child- and elder-care responsibilities, volunteering schedules, and time zones.

There's no easy endgame. There are no actionable checklists at the end of each chapter. The process is difficult and, if we're being honest, never ending. But we are at a societal inflection point. Parts of our lives that were once quietly annoying have become intolerable; social institutions that have long felt broken are now actively breaking us. So many things we've accepted as norms, from public health practices to public school schedules, have the potential to change. In the absence of visionary governmental leadership, the impetus for change has increasingly fallen on the individual, but from individuals we're also watching movements set in motion rooted in fairness, equality, and racial and economic justice.

The policy proposals guiding these movements are ambitious, and the particulars can feel complex. But the ideas behind them are elegant in their simplicity: when an institution is broken, it can't be reformed with incremental fixes that touch the contours of the problem but don't probe the heart. They must be reimagined. Not in some utopian fashion, but with a vigilant eye toward how power is accumulated and distributed.

This work will be difficult and different for each company. It might, at least in the beginning, feel radical. Capitalism is inherently exploitative, but it is also—at least for the immediate future—our guiding economic system. If we're going to live under it, how can we bend it to make that experience involve less suffering? Not only for "office" workers, but also for our immediate families, the societies we share, and the rest of the working world?

.   .   .

The thesis of this book is that remote work—not remote work during a pandemic, not remote work under duress—can change your life. It can remove you from the wheel of constant productivity. It can make **you** happier and healthier, but it can also make your community happier and healthier. It can make the labor in your home more equitable and can help you be a better friend, and parent, and partner. It can, somewhat ironically, actually increase worker solidarity. It can allow you to actually live the sort of life you pretend to live in your Instagram posts, liberating you to explore the nonwork corners of your life, from actual hobbies to civic involvement.

And it doesn't have to be full-time remote work either: no one is suggesting that we're completely done with offices. As JPMorgan's chief operating officer put it in February 2021, "Going back to the office with 100 percent of the people 100 percent of the time, I think there is zero chance of that. As for everyone working from home all the time, there is also zero chance of that."[2] For most people, traditional office space will commingle, in some form, with co-working spaces, coffee shops, our friends' kitchen tables, **and** our own home setups. Whatever your isolating, claustrophobic setup was during the pandemic, **that** is not what the future of work looks like.

We see a real chance to repair our relationship to work—something that's deeply broken, particularly here in America, but increasingly in other countries as well. Work, which has long been a source of inspiration, dignity, and the cherished prospect of upward mobility, has stagnated and trapped us. We don't mean to sound revisionist; that same work was also intermittently miserable. But for so many so-called knowledge workers, it's become an identity above all else, slowly eroding the other parts that make a rich, well-rounded human existence.

The good news is that we can change that, but only if we commit ourselves to refiguring the place of work in our lives. Right now, our priorities are backward. Instead of changing our **lives** to make ourselves better workers, we have to change our **work** to make our lives better.

To get at that potential for change, we've arranged the book around four overarching concepts. For each, we'll explore its shape leading up to the pandemic, what was breaking or long broken, and how remote work could shift, exacerbate, or, most optimistically, begin to mend existing problems moving forward.

Flexibility

For the last forty years, business books, financial publications, and industry leaders have fetishized the idea of corporate "flexibility." The obsession with "nimble" companies should theoretically imply a similar obsession with accommodation: of different schedules, different work styles, different locales. Instead, "flexibility" has been a code word for a company's ability to rapidly hire and lay off employees as needed. It's gradually became the guiding justification of the freelance and contract economy, which beguiled employees with the promise of unshackling them from the constraints of a traditional, 9:00-to-5:00 job.

The benefits of the flexible economy have

flowed almost entirely to corporations as workers grapple with unprecedented levels of instability in the workplace. Contingent workers can adapt their schedules to fit their needs, but they're also always in search of the next job, always wondering if they're working enough, always striving for something approximating the security of the full-time office job, instead of the precarious, ever-shifting **gig.**

The future of office work has to be guided by a new, genuine form of flexibility in which the **work,** not the workers themselves, becomes even more malleable. Genuine flexibility is the linchpin of this work renovation project: without it, you can't meaningfully shift work culture, your relationship to technology, or your dedication to your community. Free workers from their arbitrary schedules, and you create space for all sorts of changes: in our experience of everyday work, in our capacity to do our jobs, in our relationships with the people who make life worth living.

What does genuine flexibility look like in practice? It means reconceiving what sorts of tasks and collaborations need to be synchronous and what can actually be done asynchronously, and how many days we'd like people to be in an office, and for how long, and for what purpose. It includes broadening job descriptions to better meet the time and location needs of people who are disabled and juggle caregiving duties. And it will require the implementation of actual, respected boundaries to ensure that "flexible work" doesn't spread into all corners of the calendar.

Culture

There's how an organization defines itself publicly, and then there's how employees experience life with that organization on a daily basis. Somewhere in the space between those two understandings is **company culture,** which, once in place, can be incredibly difficult to change—save through something as dramatic as, well, a paradigm-shifting pandemic.

We'll look at how companies conceive of themselves—as a clubhouse, a group of hustlers, a collection of workaholics, a bunch of inflexible but reliable traditionalists, and, most commonly, a "family"—and what standards of behavior, exploitation, waste, productivity, hierarchies, respect, or lack thereof, flow from them.

When an office goes fully or partially remote, there's a potential to retrench existing culture, largely born out of fear. Companies implement more meetings and micromanagerial communication in an attempt to preserve existing hierarchies. But management for management's sake isn't skilled management—something the pandemic year has made abundantly clear. You **can** shift company culture. But it has to start not just with the CEO or individual workers but with a dramatic rethinking of what management actually looks like, in and outside the traditional office.

If your company culture is not just theoretically good, or good for management, but **actually** good, it'll still require planning and diligence to figure out how to integrate more flexible work. And if it's toxic, flexible work won't fix it. But it might provide the window to start rethinking what that culture might be moving forward.

Technologies of the Office

We often think of office technology in terms of our digital devices: our computers, our smartphones, and the programs and apps that run on them. But so much of office culture flows from the technology of design, which includes everything from the physical architecture that arranges workers within a building to the digital architecture that determines when and how you interact with your Slack messages. So much office tech, from the dreaded open office plan to business email, was designed with utopian hopes, only to collide with corporate imperatives and devolve, slowly, to make work **so** much worse. Same for the cool Silicon Valley campus, the Aeron chair, and Google Calendar: the cool stuff intended to solve problems created new ones, more massive and nightmarish than its creators could ever have imagined.

The question, then, is how do we break our current reliance on tech and design that creates more—and more mind-numbing—work? How do we reframe our technology away from the vague but ruthless notion of productivity? How do we create spaces for in-person work that adapt to more flexible use but don't feel like alienating, anonymous work hotels? These are challenges that demand more strategy than Inbox Zero, more vision than a behemoth like WeWork, and more nuance than tools that equate "time working" with "time your cursor is moving."

It is here, in our technology, tools, and design, that we can see the most profound changes the quickest. Changing the way we communicate about our work—and variability in the spaces we do it—can transform our daily schedules and reshape the contours of our days. In the past, office tech and design have been oriented toward figuring out how to compel employees to spend more time at work and/or working. Now the task is to use them to help us do the opposite.

Community

What would you do if you had more control of your life? Would you start each day with a walk? Would you finally establish that exercise routine? What about picking up new hobbies? What's stopping you right now? Turns out, it's your job.

Work will always be a major part of our lives. What we're suggesting, however, is that it should cease to be the primary organizing factor within it: the primary source of friendship, or personal worth, or community. Because when work envelops our lives, our intimate community shoulders the consequences. We give and receive **less:** less care, less intentionality, less communication. But genuinely flexible work—and the de-centering of our jobs that accompanies it—can liberate us to recultivate and restructure our relationships with ourselves **and** our community. Sure, you might not be as close with your colleagues. But if you have other areas of your life that make you feel loved, understood, valued, and essential, will it matter?

In practice, this de-centering might free up the time to actually equalize the distribution of labor in the home. It could allow you to figure out what you actually like to do in your spare time, when that time is not consumed with recovering from the sheer amount of work you're doing. It might mean figuring out an elder- or childcare scenario that feels less frazzling. It can't mean even more multitasking, more hats to wear when you're in the home, more pressure to be everything to everyone. When work becomes truly flexible to our needs, that's when we're able to carve meaningful, consistent, nourishing space from our days: for ourselves, but also for the people who make this life worth living.

And that means connecting with your greater community as well. Before the pandemic, our nation had arrived at one of the lowest rates of social cohesion in modern history. We're less invested and have less trust in each other. We're less willing to sacrifice for people we don't know. We're far more focused on the fate of the individual—**on me and mine**—than the fate of the societal whole. When our livelihoods feel threatened and precarious, we tend to behave as we're taught during moments of crisis: **place the oxygen mask on yourself first, before helping others around you.**

There are myriad reasons for this decline in social cohesion, most of them connected to unfettered capitalism, scarcity, and a general refusal to authentically address profound, enduring race- and gender-based inequalities. But as knowledge workers, we've both contributed to and reacted to this decline by **working more.** This strategy sometimes results in a (marginally) more stable income, but it also leads to alienation, loneliness, and markedly decreased feelings of belonging. When we work all the time, we volunteer less, we spend less time hanging out with people who are and aren't like us. We might love the place that we live, but we don't manifest that affection through actual involvement.

Flexible work, done right, means working less and directing far more time, investment, and intention into the greater community. In practice, that means more than just having the time to volunteer for the library board. It's making sure that the library board isn't just made up of people like you. It's more than signing up for the local CSA. It's devoting the time to figuring out solutions to food insecurity in your community. It's about finding time for yourself and then, once you've found it, using some of that time to make life better for everyone around you.

Which is why we'll also think about how a shift to genuinely flexible work can have meaningful effects on city planning, on public and private gathering spaces, and on ideas about everything from childcare to worker solidarity. Cities contract and expand all the time, but how do we resist the sort of transformation that limits reliable access to public transit, well-funded schools, and sources for fresh food? How do small cities and towns adjust to an influx of high-wage workers while local wages remain low? What plans need to be put in place, both on the governmental and on the corporate level, to actively combat even further stratification between those who can control the rhythms of their work and those who cannot?

The future health of the greater community demands we pay attention to these questions **now.** Because in the end, all of these changes will feel superficial and hollow if the community that surrounds you is suffering.

Knowledge work—the primary type of work that's done remotely—is, ultimately, privileged work. And the problems therein are, at times, gilded ones: few people struggling with working from home are also struggling to get food on the table. If the pandemic has shown us anything, it's that the compass that guides our ability to identify and reward essential work has been uncalibrated. Our obsession with productivity has distracted us from systemic inequalities, swallowing the sort of time and energy necessary to advocate for change. One of the refrains of the current moment is "I don't know how to make you care about other people." And one of the most straightforward solutions could be giving people the time and mental freedom to actually care about things that aren't themselves and their immediate families.

And then there's the secondary possibility of a wholesale shift in what and whom we value. If we shift our focus from relentless productivity, we may collectively rethink our societal metrics for success. A society obsessed with shareholder value, GDP, and corporate wealth creation will value and reward those who drive those metrics upward: bankers, venture capitalists, day traders. A society obsessed with quality of life, care, and societal health values and rewards a very different set of people. Before and during the pandemic, our most "essential" workers struggled to receive equitable pay and adequate protections, precisely because their work wasn't valued. But what if it was? And what if one of the key steps to getting there was for nonessential workers (like us!) to change the way we see ourselves?

For years, many of us have behaved as if our jobs trump everything else in our lives. We're loath to say it aloud, but our actions tell the true story: we value our work performance over our families, over personal growth and health, and over our communities. Part of that commitment is rooted in fear of instability. But part of it, too, stems from the ways in which we've convinced ourselves that our work is important in order to justify how much of ourselves, how many years and hours, we've devoted to it.

That sort of emotional devotion makes it harder to think of work as what it is: not a savior, not "a family," but a **job.** It also makes it harder to organize or demand better conditions for other employees, in your workplace and in others. It's paradoxical, but the ability to de-center work in your life—and separate it, however slightly, from your identity—actually makes you a better advocate for **other** workers.

Done wrong, flexible work will only exacerbate the class divide, further separating the actual essential workers from those who can labor from the safety of their homes. That's where we're headed if we don't make meaningful changes in the way we conceive of our labor and the way we advocate for others. But a deliberately conceived flexible future could also do something remarkable: it could liberate us, in meaningful and lasting ways, from work. We don't work from home because work is what matters most. We work from home to free ourselves to focus on what actually does.

1

Flexibility

If you've called the customer service line at Airbnb, Instacart, Amazon, Disney, Home Depot, Peloton, Virgin Atlantic, Walgreens, Apple, or AT&T, you've probably talked to an Arise "Service Partner" and had no idea. Service Partners are call center employees without the call center. They work from home, they buy their own equipment, they pay for an additional phone line and weeks of training. And then they compete for shifts. They're not employed by the companies whose customers they're speaking to. They're not even technically employed by Arise, which, like so many companies in the gig economy, conceives of its employees as "independent contractors." They don't have health insurance, paid time off, or benefits of any kind. What they do have is "flexibility."

"The Arise Platform is not necessarily a guarantee of success," the company told ProPublica. "The work can present challenges like any other, and it can be dependent on demand like many independent contractor arrangements—but it offers significant flexibility."[1] Freedom, as the Arise website puts it, to "be your own boss" and "make your own schedule" from the comfort of your home. But the benefits of this flexibility flow entirely to the companies, from Amazon to Airbnb, that secure Arise's services. Unlike call center employees, Arise "Service Partners" aren't paid for lunch, or breaks, or their training. As its former CEO told **Argyle Journal,** Arise helps companies "squeeze wastage out of a typical workday."[2]

This is the dark promise of flexibility today: it gives workers the "freedom" to work on their own schedule, for far less, with no labor protections. And even if you work for a company that seems very different from Arise, the ethos of "flexibility" has nonetheless worked its way into your organization's DNA. Because "flex," at least as it is currently defined, doesn't refer to the option to leave a bit early to pick your kids up at day care. It's the ability to expand and contract quickly: in size, in workforce, in real estate, in output. It's the capacity to produce more work—sometimes exponentially more—with a much smaller workforce. It's a rickety cost-saving measure dressed up as a benefit. And its meaning must change if we're actually going to change our relation to work.

This sort of flexibility is often known by its aliases: "scrappy," "lean," and "resourceful." It took its early form at some of the biggest, best-known corporations, but it manifests itself today in all manner of organizations, from the start-up to the nonprofit. And no matter what it's called or where you find it, the ethos remains the same: do more with far less. Less security, less support, and less rest. It primarily or predominantly benefits a company's bottom line and generally makes the workforce less resilient, more resentful, and worse at their jobs. As a corporate strategy, "flexibility" transformed so many workplaces into sites of anxiety where productivity-obsessed workers lived in anticipation of the next massive layoff. At the same time, it was repackaged, often to those same workers, as the future: **we laid you off, but we'll give you your job back, as a "flexible" subcontractor, only with fewer benefits and less stability, and you'll have little choice but to take it.**

The defining characteristic of the flexible workplace has never really been freedom, no matter how it's been sold. It's always been worker precarity. It's a hollow solution to the problem of the global marketplace, derived from desperation. But to leave that understanding behind—and arrive at a new conception of **genuine** flexibility, which manages to benefit employees while bolstering the organization as a whole—we have to recognize why so many corporations found it desirable, and how, in turn, it became the hallmark of a burned-out workforce. The future has always been some sort of "flexible" work configuration. But we have a rare chance to redefine its character and where its benefits will flow.

In the early 1970s, AT&T asked the celebrity architect Philip Johnson to design its new Madison Avenue headquarters. Their request, Johnson later recalled, was to make the building feel like "the front door into our empire."[3] To do so, Johnson's design evoked the grand buildings of Gilded Age New York and the palazzi of Renaissance Italy, including an arch at the entrance that rose seven stories high, swallowing all who entered, and a distinctive "Chippendale" notch at the top, which made it look as if someone had taken a big, circular bite out of the building.

Apart from suggesting an empire, the building was also intended to beguile AT&T employees. It would remind workers of their import—they worked for one of the most powerful companies in the world!—but also how small and insignificant they were compared with the size and scope of the company's history. That last bit was made clear before the company even moved in. In 1982, AT&T, which had long functioned as a telecommunications monopoly, lost a massive antitrust case and was forced to create a plan to divest itself of two-thirds of its assets. In practice, that meant laying off more than 107,000 employees.

With that knowledge, the company made the decision to rent out nearly half of its office space, and prepared the rest of the building for more changes. All ceilings had been designed with special grooves that made it easy to move walls, expanding and contracting the size of a given office space. The building, in other words, was flexible. But flexibility of physical space can do only so much. By 1992, the AT&T building was largely empty. Some workers were shipped to offices elsewhere in Manhattan and in New Jersey; others worked from home. AT&T agreed to lease the building, with an option to buy, to Sony, which would occupy the space until it was sold to developers in 2013, and once more, in 2016, to a Saudi conglomerate. AT&T was forced to become flexible—in its office space, in its organization, in the number of workers it employed, where they worked, and the sort of security they could expect from the company that employed them. But over the course of the 1980s, flexibility was embraced by hundreds of other companies seeking to compete on a global scale, to take larger business risks, to increase stockholder value, and to follow the advice of consultants aiming to cut the bloat of the typical American company.

The goal: a "lean" organization, where redundancies, inefficiencies, and other forms of waste are eliminated. AT&T had the right idea with its modular (and readily sublet) office space, but ideally that ethos would be applied across the company: "flexible" perks and benefits often meant less robust perks and benefits, with pensions, for example, turned into 401(k)s—with employer "matches" that could be gradually reduced or eliminated altogether; same for "flexible" staffing, which meant easily hireable and, more important, easily fireable. As the historian Louis Hyman writes in **Temp: How American Work, American Business, and the American Dream Became Temporary,** "In the place of long-term investment and stable workforces, the new ideal for American firms was short-term returns and flexible labor."[4]

Between 1979 and 1996, more than forty-three million jobs were eliminated from the U.S. economy. In the 1980s, the composite of laid-off workers tilted more heavily toward manufacturing and other "lower skilled" jobs, whose pay averaged under $50,000 a year.[5] Between 1990 and 1996, that number shifted: the majority of people who lost their jobs were "white collar," and they lost them at nearly double the rate that they had in the 1980s.

Over that same period, more than forty-three million jobs were added back to the economy. The difference, as would also be the case following the Great Recession, was the type of job that was added back. In 1972, if you were laid off from your job, the chances were high not only that you'd quickly find a new one but that it would pay just as well as the one you had before. By 1996, only around 35 percent of laid-off workers were able to find jobs that paid as well or better.[6]

The workplace had "fissured": the term the economist David Weil uses to describe the process whereby companies outsource significant layers of labor to freelancers, contractors, and entirely different companies.[7] The logic: Why should an insurance company employ and be responsible for a janitor, for example, when it can hire a company that specializes in janitorial services at a much reduced cost? Over the last forty-plus years, the same theory has spread up and down the organizational chart: payroll processors, IT specialists, executive assistants, manufacturers of your product, even members of HR could be outsourced, put on short-term contracts, or hired through temp agencies, all of which ultimately cost the company less than a full-time employee.

You don't have to pay for their health care, you don't have to provide a pension, you don't even have to consider them an employee. More flexibility meant less responsibility to the people who powered your workplace; less responsibility meant increased profits and increased stability for the company in the global marketplace. Who paid for this process? The worker. "The conundrum," Louis Uchitelle and N. R. Kleinfield pointed out in **The New York Times** in 1996, "is that what companies do to make themselves secure is precisely what makes their workers feel insecure."[8]

It didn't matter how long you'd been with a company or how many people you managed; if anything, middle managers, whose management work was less visible, were more susceptible to cuts. In his sprawling history of the office, **Cubed,** Nikil Saval quotes from the 1983 diary of an AT&T manager. "Stress is high in my life right now . . . [p]rincipally because of the job," the manager wrote. "In this era of ambiguity, uncertainty and inordinate turf battles, the manager who **really** cares may well kill himself with anxiety and worry and what those emotions generate—stress."[9]

Late in the first decade of the twenty-first century, the researcher Melissa Gregg started collecting business books, picking up old copies at second-hand stores. She began to notice patterns between the rhetoric of these texts, with their now-garish cover jackets and embarrassing titles, and the explosion of productivity apps in the wake of the Great Recession. There was the first flush in the 1970s and early 1980s, another in the early 1990s, and then again late in the first decade and into the second decade of the twenty-first century. Each spike roughly aligned with moments of mass anxiety over layoffs, downsizing, and generalized precarity in the workplace. For office and knowledge workers, that precarity translated into an increased need to demonstrate one's value—particularly to the consultants whom many companies called in to make decisions about whose job and labor was "essential" and whose was dead weight.

Workers attempted to manage their stress—and prove their worth—by transforming themselves into optimized, productive workers. But what does productivity look like? In the economic sense, it's the ratio of gross domestic product to overall hours worked: if everyone at a factory works forty hours a week and produces four thousand widgets a week one year, and five thousand widgets a week the next, then their productivity has increased. In the factory scenario, it's relatively straightforward to collect information of worker hours and the number of outputs and, by extension, measure their productivity. But how do you measure the productivity of a salaried mid-level manager? By the work of their subordinates, maybe. But even that could be difficult to calculate. You had to generate the perception that you were working a lot, producing a lot, just generally doing a lot. Enter: productivity culture.

Productivity culture is rooted in the **performance** of work: making a to-do list and crossing items off it, achieving in-box zero, writing and sending memos, or holding meetings, or completing tasks that transmute the intangible products of knowledge work into something tangible. Some of this work serves a purpose, some of it stinks of desperation, but all of it offers the worker the **feeling** that they're productive, so visible and undeniable that others feel it too.

Productivity culture has no room for creativity. It doesn't include thoughtful management or mentorship, the sort that actually makes your organization run more smoothly or actually facilitates the rollout of products. It's **getting things done.** Plowing through tasks, off-loading work, and, most important, exuding an aura of efficiency—becoming the person who's known for responding first to an email, even if that response is vapid and meaningless, or always being in the office, doing . . . **something,** who knows what, but it must be work. Efficiency and long hours might seem at cross-purposes, but they're the twin pillars of the ideal flexible worker: obsessed with productivity, but instead of trading that productivity for less work, they work all the time.

Again, this made a curious sort of sense: the most straightforward signal of the knowledge worker's commitment to the work is presence and correspondence. In the 1980s and 1990s, that meant presence in the office, early in the morning, late at night, and on the weekends; over the course of the last twenty years, that performance has expanded to include constant availability, no matter one's location, accompanied with evidence of work in that location. The middle-of-the-night email about an upcoming meeting, the Saturday afternoon notes on a slide deck—all of them were ways of evidencing just how much work is happening in off-hours.

Part of this attitude trickled down from the investment bankers and consultants who, over the course of the 1980s and 1990s, began to fill the C-suites at companies across the United States.[10] Their workplaces had developed cutthroat standards of work in which commitment was understood as more hours on the job; when they judged commitment in the companies they now helped run, they often based it, even if subconsciously, on those same factors—no matter that workers at these companies were compensated far less for their time in the office. Within this paradigm, so many of the ineffable attributes of quality work and effective management

naturally fell to the wayside. If you didn't write
a lot of memos, if you couldn't put in seventy-
hour weeks, if you did your best thinking on
a walk—that might all sound good in theory,
and might even produce better-quality work.
But it didn't **look** productive.

But fear of consultants can account for
only a portion of productivity culture. A significant amount of the obsession stems from
the basic challenge of absorbing the work of
colleagues whose jobs have been eliminated.
That could be the administrative and clerical
work of secretaries and administrative assistants, who handled typing and managed correspondence, calendars, and incoming calls,
or it could just be the accounts and responsibilities of a colleague who was deemed "redundant." But how do you optimize yourself
to do the work previously performed by two
people? Three? Four?

The books and apps and rhetoric of productivity culture promised an alluring fix:
here was a blueprint on how to make yourself
into a work computer with higher processing speeds, faster internet connections, larger
memory stores. Sometimes that just meant
more hours at work. And sometimes it meant

learning how to ignore the demands of others—in your workplace, in your community, in your family—so that your ostensible productivity could shine brightly.

Productivity bibles like **The Seven Habits of Highly Effective People** functioned, in Gregg's words, as "a form of training through which workers become capable of the ever more daring acts of solitude and ruthlessness necessary to produce career competence."[11] But the other thing they taught was satisfaction, or at least a demeanor that approximated it. Life at a flexible company might be unstable, with ever-shifting demands, goals, and expectations for future pay and benefits. But successful workers were the ones who could roll with it: make themselves flexible and remain mostly upbeat. The impetus wasn't on the company to provide stability but on the workers to amend their attitudes toward the absence of it.

The unhappy or unsatisfied worker, after all, is a more expensive worker. Every year, Gallup releases a wide-ranging study of the effects of "lack of engagement," which it measures through a twelve-question survey asking employees to gauge their agreement with various statements, from "I know what is expected of me at work" to "At work, my opinions seem to count." Within Gallup's conception, "engagement" is a measurement of how much employees themselves are invested in the work but also of how much their managers and leaders are investing in **them.** In 2019, Gallup found that 52 percent of U.S. workers were "not engaged" and an additional 18 percent were "actively disengaged" at work.[12] This sort of disengagement can cost companies millions of dollars every year: disengaged employees are less productive, but they're also more likely to steal from the company, "negatively influence" co-workers, and repel customers.[13] Which is why companies, frightened by stats like those in the Gallup survey, funnel money into wellness programs and internal comms, plan "team-building exercises," sponsor literal happy hours, and consult "happiness professionals," all in hopes of keeping workers "engaged," which is to say "productive" and "happy."

The sociologists Edgar Cabanas and Eva Illouz argue that these strategies aren't **actually** meant to increase worker happiness, which is already a deeply subjective designation.

Instead, they're used to "help individuals enhance performance and autonomy in competitive workplaces, cope with organizational changes and multitasking demands, increase flexible behavior, manage emotional expressions, pursue newer and more challenging goals, recognize promising opportunities, build rich and extensive social networks, or rationalize failures in a positive or productive way."[14] The ideal "happy" worker is defined, according to Cabanas and Illouz, by their "resilience": their ability to cast every setback, every cut in resources, every furlough or slight or request to do more with less, as a "stunning opportunity for self-development."

If that sounds totally normal and even unobjectionable, congratulations: you've successfully internalized the demands of flexible work culture, in which the problem is never structural, never corporate, never cultural, but individual. The "burdens" of flexibility "have been unequally distributed," the tech employment scholar Carrie M. Lane writes. "Employees are expected to become infinitely mutable while employers become increasingly rigid, demanding that workers ask nothing more than a paycheck—no benefits, no training, no personal accommodations, no promise of security or upward mobility."[15] Even the bare minimum employer responsibility (for example, paying workers for their labor) has been recast as a form of benevolence. Workers should not feel entitled to wages: they should, instead, be grateful.

Consider just how much work you've had to do, how disciplined you've had to remain, year in and year out, in order to achieve and maintain that ideal. There's no true allowance for sickness, or sadness, or caregiving. And, if you take time off, it's often just an opportunity for someone to prove they're more flexible—and thus more valuable—than you. There's no solidarity, only extractive networking; there's no resistance to corporate demands, only your ability to demonstrate malleability to them. It's an incredibly individualistic, quietly ruthless way of approaching the world. And it's exactly what flexibility demands of us.

The flexible ideal, embraced as a cost-cutting measure and competitive edge, has transformed us into workers more obsessed with the **performance** of work and happiness than with their actual achievement. Moving forward, how do we create a work culture that promotes real, genuine flexibility—the sort that actually benefits both employee and organization? Here are some places to start.

How Much Work Is There?

Before the pandemic, a friend used to reserve between 9:00 and 11:00 p.m.—after she'd put her kids to bed, while her husband watched television beside her—for what she called "actually getting my work done." Technically, she worked pretty standard hours, arriving at the office at 9:00 a.m. and leaving around 5:00 p.m. to pick up her oldest from day care. But those hours were almost always chockfull of meetings, some more essential than others. The only time she could do careful work, concentrated work, was at home during those extra two hours every night.

For salaried employees, working outside expected hours has long been a way of proving yourself. You came in early, you stayed late, you showed up on the weekends, or,

depending on the sort of work you performed, took it home with you. As we'll explore at length later in the book, the spread of
laptops, the internet, and smart devices made
work all the more portable. Work expands to
fill the time available to it, and digital technologies gradually and efficiently carved more
and more time out of our nonwork lives.

But instead of making us work efficiently—
and, by extension, less—all of this tech has
mostly just made us work more. With time,
that amount of output isn't considered above
and beyond. Spending an extra two hours
on work at home isn't a way to distinguish
yourself. It's just the norm. It's keeping up.
It's treading water. But it's also, in the vast
majority of cases, uncompensated labor.

A manager may or may not know just how
much time someone is putting in outside
established working hours. But many, even
most, don't think to ask. Maybe they don't
want to know how many hours assigned tasks
are taking, and most workers aren't transparent about just how many hours they're putting in. Part of the problem is that a lot of
the work that goes on during off-hours is
much harder to quantify: it's catching up

with emails, which shouldn't take that long but somehow always does. It's finding even thirty minutes to think uninterrupted. It's organizing documents in a way that you'll be able to find them later. It's proofreading a presentation for the fourth time and then rehearsing it.

In **Work's Intimacy,** Melissa Gregg studied the work lives of dozens of Australian workers in the aftermath of the Great Recession, when smartphones, cheaper and more portable laptops, and the continued spread of Wi-Fi made working from home easier than ever. She found that digital technologies not only were responsible for "consummating" the middle class obsession with work—something we'll talk about more in the pages to come—but also led to significant "function creep." "Workloads that may have been acceptable to begin with are shown to accumulate further expectations and responsibilities that aren't being recognized," Gregg writes, "and never will be, if home-based work continues to go unremarked."[16]

For many employees, the ability to take work home is tantamount to absorbing the work that could be allocated to an entirely separate part- or full-time employee. Which is appropriate, because following the Great Recession those who managed to keep their jobs were also called upon to fulfill the obligations of co-workers who'd been laid off. In both situations, few companies find reason to recalibrate. If the work is getting done with fewer people, why change what isn't broken?

The problem, of course, is that the worker is breaking. It might take several years for that breakage to have measurable ramifications, but it will. The recent shift to remote work has offered a unique opportunity to discern just how much work you're doing. Not "official" work done in the office versus furtive work done at home, but **total work.**

So pause for a moment and try doing this with your own work. You can think of it as a self-audit, or an inventory, or an analysis, but what matters most is actually being honest with yourself about the work that you're doing. How many hours do you spend performing "presence" on Slack? How much time is allocated to organizing your in-box? How many hours are spent in meetings—and what types of meetings—every week? The one blessing of having a digital calendar is that it's incredibly easy to track how much time you spent in meetings (and the character of those meetings) in a given week. So what if you actually went and did that? Here's one possible way to map it: Whatever the core of your job is, how much time do you allocate to that? "Core" can be tricky to define, but it might be the work that would come first if, say, you had only ten hours to complete all your tasks in a week. It could be sales numbers, it could be a presentation or a project, it could be a draft of a research grant. There are apps that can help track where you're spending time on your computer each day, but digital surveillance can tell you only so much. You have to figure out what you've been doing with your time, even if you think you'll be sheepish about the results.

For managers, whose jobs often have less visible outputs, this may feel especially hard, but it is crucially important. Think about how you spend your time each day. Are you calling meetings because you relish those moments where everyone's in the same space, or does each meeting have a specific goal? Are your meetings serving each employee, or are they simply the easiest way for you to download information? If the answer is that it primarily serves you, then chances are you are creating more work with tertiary, administrative tasks that you're passing along to others. It's not your fault. It's part of a classic trap where performative work begets more performative work.

When you figure out how much work you're actually doing, you can start to have productive conversations about where and how that work is completed. If you're a manager or executive, you can share the results with others on your team. In those scenarios, you have to make it incredibly clear that you're not trying to track productivity, and this is not an opportunity to eliminate positions, and then keep that promise. Failure to do so, on either end, will just encourage people fudging how much time they're actually dedicating to work, which is part of what led us to this scenario in the first place.

Once you've completed the self-audit, you can ask yourself some questions: Which work is actually most important? Which work feels secondary, superfluous, or totally wasteful? Which work could be more effectively performed by someone else on your team, and what work could you do more effectively than someone else? In our survey of roughly seven hundred workers, we asked respondents to do a super-informal version of this process. Many found that they spend only a portion of their week doing what they would classify as "their actual jobs." "There's sort of always something to be done, but honestly I could probably get away with thirty hours a week for most of my work," one data analyst from Seattle said. "I could do my job in less than thirty-five hours a week. Maybe a few hours in the morning and a few hours in the afternoon," an IT consultant in London agreed. A technical writer in Hawaii admitted he really had only "a few hours of focused, highly productive work" every week.

Your task, then, is to figure out how to bring the number of hours you're actually working closer and closer to that "actual job" number. To do so, you'll have to prioritize the work that you're doing. Not by whether it takes place during traditional office hours, not by whether it's performed in the presence of others, but by what is actually essential to completing your job.

From there, it's worth revisiting job descriptions and altering them so they actually match the work that is required—something we'll go further in depth on in the next chapter. If you're going through this reconsideration on your own, without explicit buy-in from co-workers or management, the job description could potentially offer a more neutral way to start the conversation about shifting your work habits to something more flexible. **Here's my job description,** you could say, **and here's where I've noticed I'm actually spending my time. Should we change my job description, or should we change my focus?**

For some, that might still be too difficult a conversation. But that doesn't mean you can't be more aware of how you're allocating your own time over the course of the day and which tasks to prioritize. Unless you're on the same page with yourself and/or your team about the work for which you're actually responsible, you can't change when and how it's performed.

What Work Should Be Rigid, and What Work Can Be Flexible?

Organizations are naturally resistant to change. That's what we have to remind ourselves: your company didn't struggle with remote work during the pandemic because you're all staid, boring sticks-in-the-mud. You struggled because even a fifteen-person company can be as difficult as an ocean steamer to change course. Most companies left their offices very quickly, with very little preparation or coaching on how to adapt their normal workflows. The result: people attempted to simply do what they did before, only virtually. And because everyone was dealing with a pandemic, and all the resultant stress and upheaval that accompanied it, there was little room for actually thinking through how work could change and why it should.

Once you figure out just how much work you're doing, it's time to figure out which types of work need to be rigid—synchronous, with others, at a specific time—and which types of work can become flexible to your needs. You had to actually be honest with yourself to arrive at the actual amount of discrete work that you really do over the course of the week, and now you have to be honest with yourself in a different way. What types of work are currently inflexible out of habit or ceremony? What do you actually miss about office interactions? What ideas about your work are you holding on to simply out of a lack of better options?

The best place to start: meetings, which form the very building blocks of the vast majority of office lives. Let's say, in pre-pandemic life, you worked in an office and wanted to run an idea by a colleague. It was too complicated for a Slack message or an email, so you stopped by their desk and asked for a moment of their time. Some people love these drive-by interactions; others find them enormously distracting.

But they're one of the main things that people say they miss about the office: unanticipated, organic interactions. But what people are actually missing is twofold. Some actually crave disruption and dynamism in their days, a symptom that they probably actually don't need to be in the office, in one place, as much as they are. But most want generative, collaborative conversations, the sort that make the work you're doing feel, well, alive. It's not the drive-by meeting itself that's essential. It's the space for authentic idea generation and human interaction. And that can be found in any number of places, if we actually allow ourselves to let go of our limited ideas of where it can happen.

So let's go back to the scenario where, in the past, you'd do a drive-by meeting. Maybe you'd do a loop by a colleague's desk and office and see they were busy talking to somebody. No problem, you'd check back later. Now it's more complicated. You could call your co-worker on the phone, but you don't know if they're busy with something else and can't be interrupted, which would be awkward, especially if they're senior to you. You decide, in office speak, to "put some time on their calendar." All that's available: a thirty-minute slot near the end of the day.

When you get to that appointed time, you turn on Zoom or Microsoft Teams, and one of you is three minutes late because a previous meeting ran over. You spend a few minutes on pleasantries, because you haven't spoken in a while and it would be rude not to. You remember the idea you needed to run past them, they respond with a few ideas, and you arrive at a crossroads: end the meeting quickly, and have twelve minutes to yourself before your next meeting, or keep talking about other projects, because, hey, you have this time on the calendar, and you want to make some of the work and thinking you've been doing from home evident. So you talk for another ten minutes, and then one of you awkwardly ends the call, and you're three minutes late to your next meeting, which someone slightly junior to you put on your calendar.

The problem: this shouldn't have been a meeting. That's not to say that the conversation didn't need to happen, but it didn't need to happen in the form of a synchronous, rigidly scheduled meeting devouring thirty minutes of your afternoon, smashed between other afternoon-devouring meetings.

"There's an entropy associated with meetings," Eric Porres, who runs the company MeetingScience, told us. "They take on a life of their own. We've been trained and conditioned to schedule meetings for half an hour to an hour. When we look at a company and they have all of their meetings in thirty-, sixty-, ninety-minute chunks, we say, wow, you have a big problem. You don't have any time to process. And when do you actually get any work done?"

MeetingScience gathers the wealth of information available through a company's digital calendars and analyzes it alongside a thirteen-question anonymized survey, sent to individuals after every meeting, about what just happened. Was there an agenda? Did **you** know what was expected of you? Were there clear next steps? Was the meeting satisfying? Was it important for me to be there? Did it start on time, or did it start late?

For the sheer amount of time companies devote to meetings, most have very little understanding of what's happening in them and their overall effect on employees. People are generally worse at making decisions in the afternoon, for example, but we jam meetings that require decision making in there anyway. We need time to process information and prepare ourselves for the next obligation, but often don't even build in enough space between meetings to go to the bathroom. One meeting that goes five minutes over in the morning can have a butterfly effect that goes on to affect five hundred employees over the course of the day. Five minutes might not seem like much, but that hustled feeling you have when you arrive late to a meeting accumulates over the course of the day into an overarching frustration.

"When people sign on with our company, and they first get their data back, there's always an expletive that comes out of their mouth," Porres said. "People have no idea they're in so many meetings. But you can't optimize what you don't measure. Until you actually see that 75 percent of your time in October was spent in meetings, then you can't process that. You realize, no wonder I was working late, and had no time, and didn't have space for my family. Other than sleep, the second most taxing thing on our time is meetings."

Some meetings really are important—usually about 20 percent of the ones you're asked to attend, according to MeetingScience. Some could be accomplished via an email or a phone call. Some should actually be a conversation between two people, instead of a conversation between two people with eight other people there as an audience. Some people see calling a meeting as a way to show they're important, when it's really a way to make everyone resent you. Some meetings—like so-called silent ones, which were gaining in popularity leading up to the pandemic—are really just blocking off time so that people can actually read a document, presentation, or report and talk very briefly about it, which they've previously failed to do because, again, their days are filled with too many meetings.

The tech company Hugo, which bundles meeting scheduling and notes, tracks the number of meetings per week among its clients. As you'd expect, the numbers over the course of the pandemic were telling: Between January and May, the average number of meetings climbed from 12 to around 15, before dipping to around 14.5 for most of the summer. But in early September, the number started climbing again; by November, users were averaging 16.5 meetings per week: more than 3 meetings a day, every day of the week. (Microsoft Teams data shows that this meeting surge was global: between February 2020 and February 2021, average Teams meeting time rose from thirty-five minutes to forty-five minutes.)[17]

Hugo's users began meeting more when

they hit remote, and then spiked again right as kids went back to school: the more stressed we became, the more meeting we called. In our heads, meetings are usually drawn up in an attempt at having more control over a project or a particular decision. As we imagine it, more deliberation means more control, which means less stress. But having more meetings doesn't decrease stress, because they rarely accomplish the things that would actually decrease your stress levels, like completing a task or having clear and cogent feedback about your completion of that task. Instead, we default to status meetings, brainstorming meetings where no one's ready to brainstorm, and meetings about future meetings, all of which leech the time out of our days, make us inflexible to people's needs, including our own, without actually doing much. They're rigid without reason.

Companies like Hugo and MeetingScience work to reflect back just how many meetings you're actually having as an organization and help you to get better at them. MeetingScience allows people to schedule meetings only in twenty- and fifty-minute chunks, for example, and can locate overload points in individual workers' schedules, when an abundance of meetings begins to have discernible effects on their own preparedness and stress levels. All of that's valuable.

But that doesn't mean that you need to cut them out altogether, or that a meeting that goes off the rails is the sign of the failure of the company as a whole. Some of the best, most generative meetings we've ever attended started in one place and ended somewhere completely unanticipated. Overanalysis and optimization always risk squeezing the vibrancy and serendipity out of work. Which is why you don't necessarily need a company to help you, but you do need perspective. Regular meetings should be held up to the light and examined, even the ones that have been on the books for years. It's not just figuring out the meeting's goal. It's figuring out whether a meeting is the best way to achieve it in the first place.

Many companies have become so reliant on meetings as their primary mode of accomplishment—and demonstration of busyness—that it's hard to imagine alternatives. Or, if they do, they feel too technically advanced for broad-scale adoption. You'd be

surprised, though, just how old-fashioned
some of these fixes feel.

Take the example of Loom. The premise
is pretty hokey: instead of emails and Slacks
and unnecessary Zoom meetings, Loom allows you to tape short videos of yourself
(Looms) and quickly send them to other
people. Described that way, it sounds like
office Snapchat: fun, but gimmicky. That's
definitely what we thought, at least until
we ended up on a call with Karina Parikh,
a content marketing manager for Loom. It
was meant to be a sort of pre-interview to the
actual interview with the CEO, but Parikh's
story was more compelling.

Before the pandemic, Parikh had worked at
a completely different company, supporting
animal shelters around the country as they
attempted to use the software that makes
adoption possible. A lot of the people who
run these shelters aren't the most tech savvy,
so the easiest way to show them how to fix
a problem with their software isn't over the
phone, or via email, but by making an actual video—a Loom—of someone like her
modeling how to fix it. The Loom is sent via
email; all users have to do is press play.

Then the pandemic hit, and by the end of March, Parikh's job had been eliminated. She took a break, played a bunch of video games, and then one day, while scrolling Twitter, she came across a tweet from Susannah Magers, the managing editor of Loom's blog. It was a job ad—in Loom form. Because Magers had recorded the job ad instead of just writing it as a paragraph, Parikh was able to get a sense of who she was, and what working for her might be like, before she even took the time to apply.

When Parikh got the job, she was welcomed via—what else—Loom. "It was the smoothest remote onboarding process I've ever had," Parikh explained. "At other companies I've worked for, usually they're like, here's a laptop, see you online!" The "welcome" Zooms were less intimidating than getting walked through the office and meeting a ton of people in a row, but more intimate than a bunch of people responding to an email announcement that you'd been hired. She could watch them on her schedule, taking notes in between. On her first day, she did icebreaker games with her team—again, via Loom, with everyone describing their phobias and random celebrity encounters. "It was very different than signing in, and then just having this static image of all of your co-workers on Slack," Parikh said.

Loom takes the intimacy of in-person interactions and makes them available for flexible application and consumption through the day. That quick idea you wanted to run by someone in the office? Make a Loom. Want to demonstrate how to update software or use a new tool? Make a Loom. You download an add-on for your browser, and anytime you want to record one, you press it. It automatically creates a file and, when integrated with your email or Slack, a prompt to send.

This isn't an advertisement for a specific piece of technology, but it is a full-throated endorsement for non-text-based conversations (especially ones where you don't also have to stare at yourself in a small box in the corner). Video can convey tone in a way that no number of emojis quite can. Our brains, after all, use visual and audio cues like facial expressions to add context to words. Visuals can clear up confusion, demonstrate seriousness, and, most important, help set our minds at ease. According to Roderick M.

Kramer, who studies organizational behavior, their absence while working from home can exacerbate uncertainty about status, which can lead to overprocessing information.[18] In short, we get paranoid about whether we're doing good work, about to be fired, annoying our managers, and so on.

But constant video meetings obviously aren't the solution either. Neither is simply going back to conference calls. Instead, you have to match the interaction to its appropriate need. Loom is great for onboarding and training, but it's not so great for a quick-fire communication. Ultimately, all of these apps matter less than what they represent: actual flexibility. A status morning meeting can be better served as a Slack check-in, where everyone lists not only what they're working on but what they need help with for the day. If you're more experimental, you can do team building in Oculus, which is precisely what Loom did, at the height of the pandemic, in lieu of their annual retreat, which involved collaboratively "sculpting" a pirate ship. (Bonuses of a VR retreat: spatial auditory awareness, being able to "walk up" to people and say hello. Drawbacks, at least in this iteration: a bunch of kids on the platform came and started throwing rocks at their pirate ship, which has now become a company-wide joke.)

Virtual reality workplaces might sound totally weird! But so is pretty much everything we've naturalized as part of office life, including meetings and the five-day workweek. Even before the pandemic, companies all over the world were experimenting with variations on the four-day week. The specifics of implementation vary from company to company, but the basics are the same: you get paid the same amount as you did before, only you work less. And this isn't some start-up, millennial-focused fringe benefit. One of the most public, and most successful, implementations of the four-day week is at Perpetual Guardian, a very staid, very old-fashioned company that manages trusts in New Zealand.

When Perpetual Guardian first implemented the program, some workers took off Mondays, some Fridays, others loved a day off in the middle of the workweek, but everyone took it, from the newest hires to the most senior managers. The effect was startling: at the end of a two-month trial, productivity had risen 20 percent, and "work-life" balance scores rose from 54 percent to 78 percent. After the change was made permanent, over-all revenue went up 6 percent, and profitability rose 12.5 percent. Other experiments have yielded similarly astounding results: at Microsoft Japan, a four-day workweek led to 40 percent gains in productivity; a 2019 study of 250 British companies with four-day weeks found that companies had saved an estimated £92 million, and 62 percent of companies reported that employees took fewer sick days.[19]

During the pandemic, Buffer—which creates social media campaign tools currently used by more than seventy-five thousand brands—made the dramatic decision to switch to a four-day workweek. In April 2020, they had surveyed their employees about their most significant barriers to family or self-care and how the company could eliminate or ease those barriers. Twelve percent wanted more paid time off, 24 percent preferred reduced work hours, and 40 percent wanted to try a four-day workweek.

So they launched a four-week pilot program. "This 4-day workweek period is about well-being, mental health, and placing us as humans and our families first," Buffer's CEO, Joel Gascoigne, explained. "It's about being able to pick a good time to go and do the groceries, now that it's a significantly larger task. It's about parents having more time with kids now that they're having to take on their education. This isn't about us trying to get the same productivity in fewer days."[20]

And yet productivity went up; employees felt as productive as during the five-day schedule, if not more so, and employee stress levels improved. And this included developers and engineers: actual coding days went down (3.4 to 2.7 for product; 3.2 to 2.9 for mobile and infrastructure), but "productive impact," a.k.a. how much they were actually getting done, increased significantly and in the case of infrastructure and mobile doubled.[21] Buffer opted to extend the trial another six months, to see if it was sustainable, and in February 2021 decided to officially adopt the schedule moving forward.

A four-day week is a slightly different

solution from companies figuring a mix of remote and in-person work, but the principle is ultimately the same. They figured out how to prioritize the work that mattered, with the promise that they would ultimately be able to do less of it. But it wasn't as simple as just telling people to try to be more productive. For the Microsoft Japan trial, all meetings were thirty minutes or less and limited to five people—the logic being that if more than five people needed to be there, it should be an announcement, not a meeting.

At Perpetual Guardian, the company installed little flags at work spaces (red, yellow, green) so that individuals could indicate whether they were available to chat, and reorganized the offices as a whole so that people would spend less time trekking up and down stairs. They provided lockers where employees could stash their phones—and, by extension, their distractions—and watched as internet surfing declined by 35 percent.[22] But the most significant change involved leadership: they had to get everyone, including managers, to buy into the project and collectively agree to waste less of each other's time. Otherwise, they understood, the entire scenario would fall apart: it takes just one thoughtless person to derail a meeting, clog your in-box, or continually interrupt your workflow. Which is why, when Perpetual Guardian first announced the plan for the four-day week, it tasked each team—led by a manager—with coming up with their own ideas and strategies for how the schedule could function for their particular corner of work. Not the CEO telling employees how it should work, but employees telling the CEO how they thought they could make it work.

The real innovation of the four-day week, like other flexible, intentional schedules, is the conscious exchange of faux productivity for genuine, organization-wide, collaborative work. For the four-day companies, that strategy was so effective that it opened up an entire day. For your company, that exchange might open up the mornings, or the middle of the day, or anytime after 2:00, depending on the rhythms of your business and your employees' lives. If that sounds like magic, it's not because it's actually mystical, or make-believe; it's a sign of how thoroughly you've internalized a rigid understanding of how work works.

The pandemic forced so many organizations to be more flexible than they ever had before. Suddenly crucial components of the office status quo—ideas about where and how work should be done—were revealed as arbitrary. But we also realized that some of the ways we did things before, whether in the office or in the physical presence of others, we did with good reason. The point, then, is cultivating the honesty, lack of preciousness, and imagination to see the difference between the two.

Establish Guardrails, Not Boundaries

When people find their way to Daisy Dowling's in-box, they're usually at the end of their ropes. She primarily works with people who are often, in Dowling's words, "super-ambitious, super-committed, very intense people who've always worked long hours but also want to be loving parents." Like so many of us, they're struggling to make everything happen all the time. And they come to Dowling for a parent-focused version of career coaching.

Since the pandemic, Dowling's noticed that her clients have a new, almost existential crisis. "People had seen working from home as a silver bullet for their problems," she said. "Like if they could get their boss to agree to let them work from home, all of their issues would be solved."

The reality of working from home—at least during a pandemic—has disabused them of that fantasy. But what they haven't learned is that working from home is a discrete, defined skill. "If you're going to give PowerPoint presentations, or draw blueprints, you see that as a skill, something you have to learn and apprentice at, get feedback on, and continue to learn," Dowling said. "But no one has really thought about working from home as a skill: it's not taught; it's not addressed. It's just sort of like, 'Be on your laptop at home.' And that's just not sufficient."

When someone walks into an office, they're immediately presented with models of what you should be doing: what work "looks like." You've been in workplaces before, or your parents have told you about workplaces. You immediately get a sense for the vibe and, with time, the culture. "You're not taught, but you do **learn**," Dowling told us. "Whereas when you work from home, you're totally isolated."

A big source of the problem, according to Dowling, is that managers haven't been doing this teaching. Many are also new to working from home themselves and likely struggling with the same issue with **their** managers. But the core of the issue remains the same: expectations either haven't been set or aren't clear, boundaries are blurry, and communication is poor. Employees have found themselves working and parenting sixteen to eighteen hours a day, turning into miserable, exhausted, unproductive versions of themselves.

Work first thing when you roll over in the morning? Why not? Work on a Friday night? What else is there to do? Work through the weekend? Sure, what's a weekend? This sounds like parody, but it's not. In 2020, a colleague requested time on one of our calendars on Thanksgiving Day. "Well, I know you're not traveling or celebrating with family," the person half joked. Some people were working these extended hours to compensate for time lost to childcare responsibilities during traditional work hours. And some were just beset by fear: that their company's finances would soon be in jeopardy and layoffs were around the corner. Others were merely bored or motivated to use the quarantine to get a leg up, oblivious to the expectations they were setting for their co-workers.

Over the course of the pandemic, some companies did furlough or fire office employees, and others instituted temporary pay cuts. But for plenty of organizations, the feared economic apocalypse never came to pass. Still, in those first heady months, everything—including the extent of the financial recession to come—was unclear. And the primary way we attempted to protect ourselves was to evidence our productivity and dedication. In previous recessions, both could be demonstrated by hours in the office. But how do you show everyone just how hard you're working when no one can see you?

One answer is completing delegated tasks with accuracy and submitting them on time. But that's too straightforward for a frazzled, anxious, pandemic brain. Instead, our stress makes it difficult to concentrate, and that difficulty is exacerbated by the growing number of meetings and emails and messages that other people's frazzled, anxious, pandemic brains are sending us. You feel as if you were not getting enough done, and compensate by working more hours, even if they're scattered, made inefficient by fatigue, alcohol, and other forms of distraction. It's so incredibly easy to enter the fugue state where you always feel as if you are half working, half not.

At night, your mind runs wild with all the things your manager could be thinking about you. When they asked a question in Teams, and it took you a while to respond because you were making lunch, did they think you were slacking off? You make plans to show greater investment tomorrow by sending more emails, or putting more time on other people's calendars, or participating more in your group's chat—effectively pushing your other work, yet again, into the corners of what used to be your nonwork life.

The bad news is that once these boundaries dissolve, they are incredibly difficult to build back up again. There's a reason some people never give out their personal cell phone number to anyone at work other than HR or keep work email off their phones. Once work takes up residency in a part of your life, it takes real, concerted effort to evict it. Boundaries are no longer up to the task. We need guardrails.

A guardrail is conceptually and crucially different from a boundary. Boundaries are easy to conceive of as a neutral, malleable demarcation, a property line: no match for the hulking semitruck that is the pressure to fill all of our time with work. Guardrails, by contrast, are designed with the understanding that we need protection. Not because we're fragile or undisciplined, but because the forces that undergird work today—especially the obsession with growth and productivity—are indiscriminate in their destruction. They flatten even our best intentions and find power in our precarity.

Boundaries are personal. But guardrails are **structural.** If you tell everyone "just work wherever you want, whenever you want," for example, including the office, there's a solid chance that the people who work in whatever way the management does, or who show up at the office more, will be perceived as more dedicated. As the Harvard Business School professor Prithwiraj Choudhury points out, "If the whole company is working remotely but the C-suite is working in an office, then middle managers will line up just to get face time."[23]

Without guardrails, the hierarchies of the old office will simply reproduce themselves: privileging people without caretaking responsibilities over those who share them, or people who thrive on more consistent in-person interaction over those who find it exhausting. Post-pandemic flexibility would just be the same big, amorphous blob of work, favoring the same people it always favored.

But there's a different way. Back in 1999, Kramer, the professor of organizational management at Stanford, surveyed how trust is created, maintained, and destroyed in organizations. When he looked at past studies, a pattern emerged: explicit rules about the way a workplace **worked** helped to foster high levels of "mutual trust" in an organization.[24] Clear rules, implemented fairly, become guardrails: not just ways to hold people accountable or penalize, but structural components of the company culture.

The problem, then, is when it comes to boundaries around work, those rules, guidelines, and "best practices" have been hollowed out entirely by years of corporate degradation. Companies that claimed to offer employees "work-life" balance often hired and promoted with the exact opposite ideal in mind. The fewer nonwork obligations, the better. But no one would dare say as much in company messaging. Instead, the words "balance" and "boundaries" become part of the lie a company tells itself about its own culture, thrown around in emails and all hands until they lose meaning altogether.

This is toxic company culture, of course—something we'll talk about at length in the next chapter. Some version of it goes on at most companies, and it happens when a company declares a value and then doesn't actually enact or enforce the policies that would make it a reality. In this case, the job of resisting the erosion of boundaries falls entirely on the employee: it is your task, and yours alone, to maintain the guardrails on work's incursion into your life. If you fail, the blame isn't on the culture, or your manager, but on you:

---

you failed to set and abide by a set of rules, even though no one else is following them.

But let's say you do manage to keep those hard-won boundaries in place. Let's say you have no problem with saying no. If you're in a place of seniority and privilege in your workplace, you **might** get away with it, and if you're not taking advantage of that opportunity, you're a sucker. That's what Tim Ferriss suggested in **The 4-Hour Workweek,** which has sold more than 2.1 million copies since its initial publication in 2007.

The message Ferriss preached in the book, building on the vivid, brazen example of his own life, was intoxicating. In short, he argues that life does not have to be this hard. He offers some helpful instructions on how to remove "work for work's sake" from your life and fill that time with things that give your life meaning. (In conceit, it is not all that dissimilar from this book!) But the tactics he suggests in order to attain his luxurious new lifestyle are treacherous, at best, without the right social capital or status within an organization. He encourages readers to embrace selfishness and cultivate the skill of grooming your boss to get what you want; at several points in the book, he evokes the image of a savvy, spoiled child who knows just how to pester their parents to get them to agree to their demands.

"Learn to be difficult when it counts," Ferriss wrote. "Think back to your days on the playground. There was always a big bully and countless victims, but there was also that one small kid who fought like hell, thrashing and swinging for the fences. He or she might not have won, but after one or two exhausting exchanges, the bully chose not to bother him or her. It was easier to find someone else. Be that kid."[25]

Reading Ferriss's book can feel cathartic, especially if you find yourself burned out or frustrated by your work situation. When he suggests strategically withholding productivity so that you get more done on days where you propose a "trial" work-from-home situation, it's easy to smile at the puckish manipulation. But you can achieve Ferriss's level of productivity only by ruthlessly off-loading tasks onto others (Ferriss has a whole section about outsourcing menial tasks to cheap virtual personal assistants based overseas) and constantly toeing the line of appropriate behavior—a strategy almost exclusively available to white men.

Boundaries **can,** theoretically, work, but only for a privileged subset of your organization. They're simply not a sustainable option for the vast majority of workers, especially those who aren't in senior positions, who are women, who are people of color, or who are disabled. For those groups, attempting to maintain them can lead to an office reputation as difficult, aloof, unresponsive, or the dreaded "such a millennial" or "not a team player." It might mean getting passed over for promotions or, eventually, getting fired. You can't **4-Hour Workweek** your way out of this problem. You need something structural.

Back in 2016, France passed a piece of legislation, known as the El Khomri law, discouraging anyone who works for a company with more than 50 employees from sending or replying to email after official working hours. The French, like those in many other European countries, have long resisted the fetishization of the work ethic endemic to America.

They've resisted it through their daily schedules, with ample time, midday, for a meal and
to rest; they've resisted it with their weekly
schedules, capped at thirty-five hours; they've
resisted it with their yearly schedules, with
five weeks of paid vacation. All of these policies are in place—and held in place, through
union efforts—not because the workers of
these countries are lazy but because they are
stalwart in their belief that one's job is not the
same as one's life. The policies are guardrails:
when you don't respect them, it's not just a
social faux pas but an actionable offense.

When it became clear that emails and digital contact were hopping over those guardrails, leaders recognized that they could not
depend on individual companies—or the individuals within them—to accomplish what
was, in truth, a national goal. Legislation can
slow the inertia of capitalist growth, but it
cannot counteract it entirely. If you're an "executive," you're allowed to violate the thirty-
five-hour weekly cap. And non-executives
break it all the time: a 2016 study found that
71.6 percent of French employees worked
more than thirty-five hours a week.[26] The
El Khomri law, at least in its current form,

has no teeth. A 2018 study of more than one hundred workers in companies with more than fifty employees found that 97 percent of the participants had seen no relevant changes since the law went into effect in January 2017.[27] It's ultimately a **code du travail**—a labor code—but there are no real penalties for violating it, if companies adhere to it at all.

As with many attempts to regulate the French business world, the legislation also fails to understand France as part of a rapidly expanding global marketplace. There's no accounting for obligations that multinational companies might need to take place outside established business hours. A rigid daily cutoff for work emails, such as 6:00 p.m., also reifies the standard work schedule, which has long privileged people who aren't caregivers. As one French employee put it, "If I had kids, I would prefer to leave work early and pick them up from school, spend time with them, and start working again later during the day. How can you do that if you're not supposed to access your emails after 6:00 pm?"[28]

The law is meant to provide a new guardrail between life and work, but it is at once too weak and too inflexible for the realities of the contemporary workplace. Still, it's an instructive failure. You can't protect employees by simply trying to reinstate the old mode of work, and you can't change any practice simply by announcing a policy. Real guardrails need to be built from the ground up for the new flexible reality. They're not incredibly difficult to construct, but they're **enormously** difficult to maintain. And that maintenance depends on respect.

In the workplace, we often start a conversation, a meeting, an email, or a request with "I want to be respectful of your time." Most of us authentically do want to be respectful of our colleagues and their time. But we usually conceive of showing respect purely in terms of brevity, as if it were somehow significantly more respectful to take up five minutes of someone's time with an unnecessary meeting or bcc on an email instead of ten.

Respect for others' time demands care, knowledge, and thoughtful implementation of policies and practices. Many team status meetings were set years ago, by someone who might not even be your manager anymore, often at a somewhat arbitrary time. Maybe it worked for everyone on the team then. But it has little relation to the needs of your team now, or when people's schedules become even more flexible.

Exercising respect means continual consideration of a meeting's utility, its place in the day, and its form. Same for email: Does this need to be an email? Do I need to send it now? How would I feel if I received this email right now? How can I make it so that it arrives in my colleague's in-box at a time that will be more respectful of their time?

The tech company Front was founded by a Frenchwoman, Mathilde Collin, who realized that you can't just kill email, but you can fundamentally change the way that other people think about emailing you. Front allows users to integrate workflows, chat, and "next steps" into email; in companies dealing with tens of thousands of customer service emails, for example, it allows workers to delegate responsibility, action, and follow-up on each one. The system can limit the number of "assignments" that a given worker has at one time and ensure that no future assignments are given after a certain time (say, fifteen minutes before the official end of their workday).

It's a useful customer service work-flow tool. More interesting, though, is how Front is using its own app across the company. Employees can essentially close off their in-boxes so that an "Out of Office" diverts incoming mail directly to a delegated recipient. "It's totally changed the way I think about being unavailable," Heather MacKinnon, Front's head of communications, explained. "I know that someone else is actually going to pick up any emails that arrive."

A lot of people turn on "Out of Office" auto-responders when they're on vacation or leave. But you can still watch the emails roll in. You can still be on the receiving end of texts and calls and messages asking "just a quick question." You can still feel the pressure to remain in-box vigilant, because you're terrified of just how much work will be waiting when you come back. But Front functions as a force field, bouncing others' lack of respect for the lines you've drawn around work back before they even reach you.

Many of us tell ourselves stories, in our work

and nonwork lives, that if we don't do something, then it just won't get done. But that's often a self-fulfilling narrative: when you never actually allow others to do something, there's no room to develop trust that it'll actually happen. When you think of yourself as essential to a process, you become so.

But so much of that mindset is simply a long-running coping mechanism for workplace precarity. To be essential, at least in this office job capacity, is to build a protective shell around yourself during times of economic insecurity. It's a survival strategy, built on fear and desperation. And it makes everyone miserable, no one more so than yourself. Front's real utility is its ability to transform email from a personal burden into a collective, collaborative task. To do that, however, you have to actually trust your colleagues and be less precious about your own essential role in the process.

There's a secondary effect to this process as well: a greater understanding of where your work travels and how it impacts others. Say an entire company adopts a force-field approach to email. A culture begins to develop around time off. Those taking time off will be more aware of who will pick up their work burden. They'll be more appreciative—and ideally more respectful—of others' time. There might be more coordination, more care, and more respect involved in handing over responsibilities. More important, colleagues in a force-field situation might be more mindful that their requests will fall to others. At its best, it could trigger others to inventory their demands on others' time.

As we'll discuss below, trust cannot be built without adequate resources. And it cannot be maintained unless we get rid of the boundaries we've long been rewarded for breaking and put company-wide guardrails in their place. Hopping the guardrails cannot be seen as a means to distinguish oneself, and respecting them must be a quality that is continuously and authentically praised.

How do you start the process of rebuilding these structures of respect? If you're a manager or run your own company, it can't just be you coming up with ideas that you think might work. You need to start talking with your team—large or small—to build the sorts of guardrails that will actually protect them. That might change from team to team, depending on the nature of the work and the people on it. One team might want to make it physically impossible to set meetings after 4:00 p.m. on Google Calendar. Another might decide that they're fine with people who do their concentrated communication during off-hours, but you absolutely must schedule emails to arrive during established work hours. If someone tries to work during a break, chiding them and letting it happen just further normalizes the behavior. When an employee takes time off, **not working** becomes their job. So how can your team actively set expectations to take that job as seriously as their everyday one? Whatever the policies are, they have to be more than mealymouthed "suggestions" and arrive in collaboration with workers themselves.

To be clear, this is yet another really difficult change in a list of really difficult changes. Maintaining guardrails is hard, continuous work, especially when so many of your old habits and ideas about work are trying to erode them. But actual flexibility—in work, in life—demands them.

Don't Leave a Generation Behind

Kiersten R. graduated from college straight into the middle of a pandemic and a precarious job market. She managed to find an entry-level job with a government contractor that allowed her to work from the safety of her home. There was no fanfare on her first day; she simply opened her laptop and began an endless series of Zoom training sessions. The sessions were helpful, Kiersten recalls, but very formal, with little room for socializing. Even among her fellow new hires, Kiersten felt at a remove. "I just stared at their Zoom boxes and willed us to be friends," she told us. "But we never had the opportunity to interact."

With time, she grew accustomed to the daily cadences of her job. But she still felt like a stranger in her own company, whose remote policies were haphazard at best. To send chats, employees used an outdated version of Skype; in Zoom meetings, almost all co-workers left their cameras off. Months into her job, she could identify co-workers only by their chat avatars and voices. At one point, she says, she began "obsessively stalking" her company's Glassdoor reviews, just to try to get a sense of the company culture. She was, by her own admission, unmoored, totally unmentored, and insecure, with no way to learn from her colleagues. It's one thing to start a new job remotely. It's another to start your entire career that way.

"I was shocked at how all the skills I had learned on how to navigate this type of environment in person evaporated remotely," Kiersten said. "They feel entirely inaccessible to me now." She's not alone. While reporting this book, we heard similar stories from young career workers who've felt adrift during the pandemic. All were grateful to be employed, but many felt left behind, invisible, and, in some cases, unsure about how to actually do their jobs. While their companies adapted their workflows to work outside the office, few spent the time to craft policies to mentor young professionals, many of whom found themselves stuck on their couches, attempting to decipher cryptic emails and emojis sent over Slack.

Like any newcomer, most are terrified of screwing up and hesitant to ask questions that might make them sound naive. Which, of course, means that they're also scared that they're already failing. "I think I'm missing out on a lot of the soft skills that one picks up in the first few years of working," Haziq, a twenty-two-year-old living in Ireland, told us. He's found it nearly impossible to socialize with colleagues and lacks the confidence to casually ask a question of his manager or teammates. "If I was sitting next to my manager, I could just have a quick chat and move on," he said. "But I'm much less likely to Slack my manager and ask something, because I don't know what they're up to at the moment. The amount of on-the-job learning has reduced dramatically."

For Kiersten, who has never set foot in her office, her professional life has come to feel like an abstraction—to the point that she's sometimes not even sure if she's employed (she is). Worse, her job feels almost completely transactional, with her conversations limited, in her words, to "exchanging information in pursuit of an immediate, work-related goal."

You could chalk up some of these experiences to the harried nature of the pandemic, which required many organizations to build a work-from-home plane, as it were, while also trying to fly it. But many of the perks of truly flexible work—a self-directed schedule, distance from overly chatty co-workers, remove from office gossip and politics—could also work **against** younger employees. If companies don't create intentional, structured mentorship programs to help younger and remote colleagues with on-the-job learning, we risk leaving a generation behind.

We spend a lot of time in this book arguing that the spontaneous watercooler interactions of the office are often romanticized, but that doesn't mean we don't recognize the ways in which gossip, after-work drinks, and even body language come together to teach new employees the standards of behavior in the office. Small talk, passing conversations, even just observing your manager's pathways through the office, may seem trivial, but in the aggregate they're far more valuable than any form of company handbook. But that doesn't mean they can't be translated into the remote or flexible work environment.

Almost every story we heard from adrift and isolated employees had the same root cause: well-intentioned but frazzled managers working inside systems that adapted to the pandemic by trying to cram office work into the home. "When I joined, my manager was like, 'Oh, if we were in the office, I would've taken you out to lunch and gotten to know you,'" Kiersten said. "She realized that things were missing but didn't have any strategies to replicate that type of experience." But Kiersten didn't blame her manager for not doing more; it was clear she didn't have any support or practice in remotely onboarding employees.

For Joe, a mid-career lawyer who started a government fellowship right before the end of the pandemic, remote work meant his already distant manager disappeared fully. Pre-pandemic, he described his supervisor as "one of those people that was visibly very busy and constantly apologizing for it." Things only got worse when they left the office. "I can't emphasize the extent to which I felt like I fell off the face of the earth to her," he said. Like Kiersten, Joe doesn't blame or have any ill will toward his supervisor, who he says clearly struggled during the early parts of the pandemic with childcare issues. But because Joe's office made no formal plans to adapt schedules or workflows for remote work when the pandemic started, his supervisor's struggles trickled down to him.

The first week of remote work, Joe's supervisor canceled their check-in without rescheduling a new one. "We went months without emailing over the rest of the fellowship, and we only spoke on the phone once over that time, and weren't in any meetings together," he said. On his last day, there was no exit interview or procedure at all. "I sent out a goodbye email to about two dozen people right before leaving my laptop in the office on my last day, and cc'd my personal email, but only one person wrote back," he recalled.

This is a classic example of how flexible work—absent intentionally designed support systems—can hurt the most inexperienced employees in an organization. Had Joe's office implemented a remote plan, it's possible his supervisor could have changed her schedule to fit her needs or delegated portions of her work across other employees and departments. If she'd felt more supported, perhaps she might not have felt the need to juggle direct reports she didn't have time to mentor. Perhaps the organization could have crafted clear HR policies and procedures so that employees lacking guidance could feel comfortable coming forward. Something, anything, would have been better than nothing.

We asked early career workers what resources they wished they could have had during those early pandemic months, and the responses were full of helpful ideas for any company. Most important, they wanted a clearly delineated mentor who—crucially—was not also their supervisor or in charge of evaluating their performance. One suggested a dual mentor program that paired new employees with a co-worker in a similar position in the company who could offer advice on more quotidian concerns, as well as a more senior employee who could provide longer-term career advice.

Others wanted more scheduled sessions for employees to come together and bond. "Zoom meetings are not enough," Joe told us, though he struggled to articulate exactly what kind of bonding might work. "Maybe take something that people already do and bring it into the workplace—pub quizzes, pen pals, video games, a book or movie club. I feel stupid writing those! But you have to try something." Kiersten, for her part, eventually found camaraderie in her company's diversity, equity, and inclusion, or DEI, initiatives. "We just spent most of the first session doing introductions and talking about quarantine work-life balance," she said. "But it was still really nice to have a dedicated time and space to meet people not from my project team and learn about them personally and not just via their deliverable output." Importantly, these sessions were presented as safe, off-the-record opportunities to connect but also to vent and commiserate, which is often the primary (if unacknowledged) value of in-person co-worker interactions.

But that early professional hunger for structure extended far beyond Zoom meetups. They wanted opportunities to sit on calls with senior members of different teams—the equivalent of silently sitting in on an in-person meeting—if only to get a better sense of what others' jobs entailed. They wanted access to email templates for specific kinds of intra- and out-of-office outreach. They wanted to know what time it was normal to reply to emails. In short, they wanted to be told what it is they were supposed to be doing at work and how to do it successfully. Even those who admitted that such guidance could quickly become stifling agreed that it was better than flailing around with vague expectations and zero guidance.

Speaking to those who feel left behind by remote work, we realized there's no one template for creating mentorship opportunities and support. For organizations with a hybrid approach, where employees split time between home and the office, some of these problems may quickly abate. A few days in the office won't fix these larger issues. But intentional design could. Truly flexible work may **seem** breezy and carefree, but it's actually the product of careful planning and clear communication. It requires peering around corners and attempting to identify needs and problems before they fester. It may seem onerous at first, especially when "let's just go back to the way things were before" seems like such a clear option.

But it's not. We've moved past that point. If we're serious about building a sustainable future of work, we can't leave a whole swath of employees behind. They'll just develop bad habits and waste endless hours trying to piece together the rules of the game when someone could've just **told them.** You have to decide: Are you going to pretend the problem doesn't exist, allowing it to tax your organization in all sorts of tangible and intangible ways, or are you going to invest in the sort of intentional mentorship and structure that will yield dividends down the road?

Allocate the Resources to Make This Happen. No, Really.

Boundaries are cheap and flimsy or purely theoretical. Solid guardrails demand time and funding. Without them, the work will simply fall back on—and eventually overload—the individual. We cannot say this loud enough: **If you don't fund these changes in some capacity, they will fall apart.**

Take the example of Front, discussed above, and the potential to liberate workers from their in-boxes in a way that actually allows them to go on vacation, take time to care for others, or recover from an illness or operation. If a company doesn't have enough employees to absorb the labor of someone taking time off—whether short or long term—you'll end up in a stew of resentment and overwork.

Let's say you need to take a week off to recover from an operation. You're assured that others will pick up your slack and handle your correspondence. But your colleagues are already operating at full capacity and can't take on the additional labor. Your emails go unanswered or inadequately answered. When you come back from recovery, you spend days picking up the pieces. You might as well have just kept checking your email from the hospital: at least there'd be less of a mess and you wouldn't be left with passive-aggressive frustration at your co-workers' incompetence. But the fault is neither yours nor your co-workers'. It's your team's—or the company's—for failing to adequately resource time off.

There are two ways to fund time off. You can temporarily and authentically lower productivity expectations. Or you hire slightly more than enough people, thereby building in the expectation that a percentage of your workforce could be taking time off at any moment, and it wouldn't overload the system. Many companies are theoretically set up this way: an average employee's baseline of assigned tasks should take up, say, 80–85 percent of their day, leaving them available to take on 15 to 20 percent more work when a colleague is sick, on vacation, or on leave. As many of our survey respondents confessed, they usually do their core work over a short period of time anyhow.

But so many companies, especially those that have recently gone through a "re-org"—frequently code for "cost-cutting efficiency measures"—are set up so that an employee works at anywhere between 100 and 200 percent of their capacity. It's the office version of just-in-time scheduling, a strategy adopted by retail chains so that they'll never be paying for "excess" labor. An algorithm looks at historical customer levels throughout the day and week and determines how many employees need to be present to provide "just enough" labor. In practice, this type of scheduling wreaks havoc on retail workers' mental health: it's just not sustainable to operate at full capacity for an entire shift. And when a rush of customers, unanticipated by the algorithm, arrives, customers wait longer and get crankier, quality plummets, and stress goes through the roof. Everything goes to shit.

This example from the retail world should be instructive: if you have only enough employees to barely get the work done as is, you've engineered a scenario in which employees may have theoretical permission to take time off, but understand that they'll shoulder the burden of that time off in some way. Either they try to keep doing part of their work while on leave, a colleague takes on an even larger work burden, or a portion of essential work goes undone, slowing everyone on a team.

We saw this strategy at work in our previous workplace. The organization had expanded too quickly, overextending its funding, and needed to contract. Cuts were made across the board, including departments that were already overtaxed, like art, design, and copyediting. Instead of cutting the expectations for the number of articles we published, we upped the expectations for how fast, and how many articles, each designer and copy editor was responsible for. The result was a company-wide bottleneck, general frustration, and burnout. At one point, there were only two copy editors checking for typos and weirdly written sentences for the entire news side of the website. If one took even a day of much-needed time off—or became ill—they were essentially placing the weight of the entire website on their colleague's shoulders. It was no way to work, and certainly no way for them to live.

Our previous employer was operating in classic lean start-up style: we were often told that we were "scrappy," which is another way of saying "under-resourced." But how does a company tread the fine line between under- and over-hiring? What's the difference between "running a tight ship" and asking twenty employees to do the work previously divided among twenty-five? As will become clear in the next chapter, companies spend millions of dollars on consultants every year trying to hit that sweet spot, and historically it usually means cutting middle management and support staff. The end result: employees are increasingly forced to self-manage and do the essential support work of those who were let go, often quite poorly, instead of what they were actually hired to do. Cue:

ever-expanding work hours, and the message that if you're not getting your work done during traditional hours, the failure, again, is yours, for poor prioritizing.

In America, particularly in non-unionized workplaces, this sort of chronic understaffing acquires a logic all its own. If you can stand to lose employee weight, you should; if you don't, you're leaving profits on the table. Appropriately staffing isn't a way to create a better work environment; it's "bloat." Workplaces attempt to counter the negative effects of understaffing with professional development, bonuses, perks, snacks, therapy dogs, subsidized gym memberships, swag, happy hours, access to meditation apps; the list is truly endless. One HR person told us that she was always amazed that employees complained about stress and overwork but then never took advantage of the perks. It makes sense, though. They don't have the time. What would really make their lives better isn't a meditation app, but adding a few more employees without also adding the expectation of more work.

Understaffing might be cheaper in the short term, but it has real ramifications on

morale, creativity, production quality, and retention. It affects the way employees interact
with each other and with the outside world.
It is reflected, in however diffuse a way, in a
company's overall reputation and its ability
to attract and recruit job applicants. And if
that's not convincing enough, when you have
high turnover and burnout rates, you end up
spending a whole lot of money on hiring, on
training, and on medical bills. You're also just
a shitty company that nobody really likes. Or,
if you're a nonprofit, you might have a vision
that people on the outside of your organization respect and cherish, but you're treating
your employees in a way that's the direct in-
verse of your values as an organization.

Actually funding flexibility is one way to
fix that. Not by holding a mandatory professional development day about self-care, but
by actually hiring enough employees so that
self-care is possible.

"Growth works if you're growing with
the company," Russ Armstrong, who runs
business development for a fast-growing
Canadian finance start-up, told us. He argued
that a hyper focus on growth or productivity
isn't a bad thing per se, so long as a company

actually supports it with staff. "How do you make sure people aren't working too hard and going crazy and going in over their head? You have to understand what your employees are actually doing. Where are the gaps in work-flow? What is causing their frustration? What can alleviate them? If the answer is more work, then you need to know what key hires to put in place to make it manageable. It's often hiring a specialist that takes some of the load off and solves the pain point."

In other words, it's going to come not from mandating an after-work happy hour as a morale boost but from actually supporting your organization with resources so that mo-rale doesn't need to be boosted.

A work system isn't actually flexible if it's not universally accessible. David Perry, a senior academic adviser in the history department of the University of Minnesota, knows this firsthand. As a working parent, Perry con-siders himself lucky that his employers have always allowed him ample flexibility to help raise his son, who has Down syndrome. But taking time away for therapy appointments and other necessities highlighted just how inequitable most leave policies remain.

"Even the best work environments are accommodation based," Perry told us. "We identify certain needs we think are virtuous and valid, and we support those needs." In Perry's case, having a son with a disability was a sufficiently "virtuous" cause to trigger a flexible work schedule. But would HR offer similar leave for a childless employee with a sick pet? Or what about an older relative who recently moved in and needed more care? Or an ostensibly "healthy" worker who was deeply burned out?

Perry started thinking about what an equitable, flexible, simple, and intuitive system for leave and benefits would look like. It would have to be transparent but also have tolerance for error and even, theoretically, misuse. He called it "universal design for work-life balance."

"Universal design" is the term for the movement to create spaces, tools, and lived environments that are accessible to all, regardless of age or ability. The thing about universal design is that its benefits are not simply for those who need it most. A curb cut in the sidewalk, for example, makes the sidewalk accessible for wheelchair users, but it also makes navigating the space infinitely easier for people on bikes or pushing strollers.

For something like workplace leave, universal design means creating policies that allow set time for leave, no questions asked—whether it's for something that others deem virtuous and necessary, like taking home a newborn or a medical emergency, or whether you just need it for . . . something else. According to Perry, the vagueness around "something else" is the most important part of the policy. "Taking some of every Tuesday afternoon to play Spanish guitar isn't the same as caring for a baby," he said. "But in a truly just workplace, you'd make exceptions for each."

Perry realizes the idea is provocative; it is, of course, understandable for companies to design HR policies that offer rules and exceptions. But he also argues that in a diverse workplace employees will have different needs at different points in their lives, some more readily appealing to HR than others. Is it fair to give generous leave to new parents and never offer a sabbatical to those who opt not to have kids? Not if you don't want to breed resentment. "Over the course of a career, a worker will need different things," he said. "Middle-aged employees with parents dying need one thing, while hyper-ambitious young people burning out need another. Why aren't we taking care of employees through their whole careers?"

A universal design for work-life balance is naturally more inclusive, meaning companies would be catering to accessibility levels from first principles, rather than hastily instituting carve-out policies when employees with additional needs, whatever that might mean, are hired. And Perry, who has spent the last three years presenting on universal design for work-life balance to companies like Hulu and human resources departments at places like Northwestern University, believes such systems could ultimately lead to happier, more productive workforces, even though his end goal isn't really productivity at all. Instead he's advocating for workers to be able to access the time they truly need to keep their lives afloat.

But policies like universal design for human

resources require trust: something, again, most companies are not used to cultivating. From his own experience navigating disability benefits networks, Perry knows just how complicated many human resources departments have made accessing time off, and he knows many disabled people who've been unable to access support because of draconian antifraud measures, engineered to combat an imagined manipulative worker who wants to endlessly exploit their employer's goodwill.

Sure, a handful of people might work the system this way—by taking exorbitant amounts of time off or abusing an honor system for expenses on non-work expenditures—but when you design HR benefits to combat that small handful, you're essentially engineering a system to protect against a sliver of bad actors, instead of one that will engender authentic trust and respect. "We are constantly trying to build systems that resist abuse, rather than help max out the amount of people they help," he said. "When we build universal systems, we can discover fringe benefits we didn't know we'd find, and that means for everyone."

That's the sort of revelation at the heart of all of this rethinking: it's going to take a lot of intentional work, but the benefits will ripple out for years. But if you don't explicitly make it someone's job to figure all of this out, it's either not going to happen or it's not going to stick. During the pandemic, several large corporations hired a director of remote work and tasked them with the work of constantly thinking and rethinking how to make remote work sustainable.

Maybe this becomes their full-time job. Maybe it becomes half of their job description. But you can't just add this task to a person's existing job responsibilities. If you do that, you're already underlining how unseriously you take this task. Nor can you simply tell every manager to start thinking in this way; they must be given the training and tools to do so. As we'll talk about in the next chapter, remote work is going to require substantive changes in the way that we actually manage each other, and if you simply load "flexible work coordinator" onto every manager's job description, they will fail.

But flexibility will fail, too, if workers

don't feel secure enough to experiment with it. For years, employees have performed an unsustainable kind of flexibility: they became whatever was asked of them, even if it meant spreading themselves increasingly thin in order to find security. They've bent and bent, and now they're breaking. Flexibility was a coping strategy, made from the defensive crouch of desperation. It'll take time and dedication—on the part of everyone involved—in order to start thinking of it as something whose benefits do not simply flow toward the company.

That process doesn't have to mean adopting a bunch of new apps or tools. We highlighted some potential options, but less is always more when it comes to work-flow gadgetry. It doesn't have to mean getting rid of your office. And it certainly doesn't mean you'll never see your colleagues again. But it does demand something that we've shied from for so long: extended honesty about the sheer amount of work we perform, how unsustainable it's become, and how actual flexibility could sustain us moving forward.

For so long, flexibility has meant approaching work as a tsunami that will inevitably engulf even the most sacred parts of your life. Combating that destruction doesn't just mean actively redefining that word. It means remembering that those long-submerged parts of our lives and selves are worth saving.

2

Culture

S. C. Allyn, chairman of National Cash Register, would often tell a story about his company's early days. He had survived World War II and, in 1945, became one of the first civilians allowed back into Germany to check on his factories. Upon arrival, he found that one of the factories had been obliterated. His employees were there, sifting through the rubble in tattered clothes, but when they saw Allyn, they smiled and hugged—at least according to Allyn's telling—and immediately got the work of rebuilding. The moral of the story, and the reason the chairman so often repeated it, was that company culture was uniquely resilient: the war had torn through the country, leaving destruction and death in its wake, but NCR's employees remained loyal, dedicated. A shell-shocked but productive family.

This is the lead anecdote of **Corporate Cultures,** a seminal 1982 book by the consultants Terrence Deal and Allan Kennedy. The book was designed for executives and fellow consultants who coveted employee devotion, with stories like Allyn's functioning as a sort of secular parable. But what are the rest of us supposed to take from this story? That NCR has such a durable corporate culture that it can survive **literal airstrikes?** Or is it that NCR's employees are so dedicated that amid unspeakable death and destruction they feel the need—not to be with or tend to family—but to help rebuild a factory?

Deal and Kennedy seem to acknowledge the outlandishness of the anecdote. But that doesn't keep them from arguing that it remains one of the pantheon of "myths and legends of American business." They insist these types of stories create an environment "in which employees could be secure and thereby do the work necessary to make the business a success."[1] It's true: the actions companies and their leaders take—coupled with the stories

they recount or invent—become the framework for a company's work environment,
which is to say, its **culture.** But like any story,
its moral can be corrupted or leveraged for
ill—in service of productivity, profitability,
or shareholder value.

At best, company culture is a clear mission
statement about the organization's goals: for
its product, but also for how it treats its employees. Procter & Gamble's company culture
statement begins, for example, with this sentence: "P&G is driven to make life better—
not just within the company, but across the
globe." Netflix claims, "We value integrity,
excellence, respect, inclusion, and collaboration." Deloitte's "shared beliefs" include "lead
the way," "serve with integrity," "take care of
each other," and "foster inclusion."

All of these sound good in theory. But in
most organizations, there's long been a disconnect between the **stated** company culture
and the way employees experience that culture on an everyday basis. **Actual** corporate
culture is the ineffable feeling you get working at a place. It can be "everyone is expected
to show up on weekends" or "no one is expected to show up on weekends"; "going to

HR will help change things" or "going to HR means you'll never get promoted again." It can take the form of unwritten rules, passed down in hushed office chats or via after-work drinks or text messages, and manifest itself in the cornucopia of company reviews on Glassdoor.

Sometimes, bad culture is explicit, and it's no secret that employees are expected to grind themselves into the ground in service of profits. But sometimes a cheery paragraph on a website functions as a smoke screen for exploitation, exclusion, and generally shitty workplace practices. If your organization is "family friendly" and you quietly encourage female managers to limit the number of childbearing-age women on their team, you have bad company culture. If one of your values is "inclusion" but making an office fully accessible feels too expensive, you have bad company culture. If you're a law firm with a month's paid time off and no one taking more than a week or two, you have bad company culture.

Company cultures solidify slowly, taking form over years and decades. But they're often treated as intractable, even though there's nothing natural, or obligatory, about culture: it's just as much a construct as the need for corner offices or time cards. Still, we should be prepared that any attempt to actually de-center work's place in our lives, or make work more flexible, will feel like a threat to that culture—because it is.

This will be the recurring question, from leaders, managers, and employees alike. **Sure, we'd love to have people have more flexibility with where and how they work,** they'll say. **But what about our company culture?** This reaction elides an uncomfortable truth: in so many organizations, that culture sucks. It is toxic or repressive or stultifying, even if no one dares say it aloud. And while executives set the tone and parameters for that culture, it is enforced and reproduced, up and down the organizational structure, by managers.

Early in our interviews for this book, we spoke with Adam Segal, the CEO of Cove, a company that helps coordinate shared desk and conference space. "The future of work," he said, "is actually having to manage people." He was referring to the fact that in the past most management took place in person and now managers would need to figure out how to have conversations, and judge performance, from afar.

But the comment stuck with us. It's not just that managers will need to modify their existing tactics. Instead, organizations will need to rethink the purpose that management has served over the years and all the largely impossible roles it's asked to fulfill today. The role of the manager has become hopelessly overdetermined: in pop culture, they're at once useless and overly powerful; in practice, they're usually overworked and under-trained. But you cannot build a new work culture—for yourself, for your team, or for the entire company—without them.

We have so few models of good management, let alone good company culture, in our past or our present. The reason is pretty straightforward: the stated and unstated goals of an organization have rarely aligned with the health or stability of the employee, creating a chasm that no amount of management can correct. It's not that the organization wants profits so much as the organization wants as much profit as possible, with little regard to the effect of that demand on the employee.

What follows, then, is a parable of our own:

of what becomes of company culture when profits and optimization begin to preclude all else, the feelings of alienation and precarity that follow, and how to begin the slow but essential process of bridging that divide. Flexible work won't fix your work culture. But the management practices, trust, and accountability that accumulate around it have the real potential to transform it.

Manage Your Productivity

Read enough books on the history of work, and you'll see the same theme emerge again and again. Humans crave meaning and dignity, and one way some of them find it was through the completion of necessary tasks— a.k.a. **work.** But these same meaning-craving humans also bristle at the idea of modern work: the hauling of oneself to a location, then toiling for someone else for a set number of hours. Work can be satisfying, in other words, but who wants to do it all the time and on someone else's schedule?

This was the problem that early management was designed to solve. It did not go over well with the rank and file. "I found the utmost distaste . . . on the part of the men, to any regular hours or regular habits," a nineteenth-century English hosiery manufacturer wrote. "The men themselves were considerably dissatisfied, because they could not go in and out as they pleased, and have what holidays they pleased, and go on just as they had been used to do."[2] And why wouldn't they be dissatisfied? Preindustrial labor was by no means easy, but much of it could be done on a worker's own terms.

Forced into formalized, factory-like arrangements, laborers viewed six-hour workdays as onerous and perhaps only temporary until desired productivity had been achieved. Attendance was poor. Something had to be done to condition the workforce to perform strenuous labor on behalf of others. Owners began to impose fines and strict oversight because, as the social psychologist Shoshana Zuboff points out, "workers submitted to the physical rigors of factory discipline only when other alternatives had been exhausted."[3] Early factory designs were modeled after workhouses and prisons.[4] Positive reinforcement was attempted, but the carrot was usually abandoned for the stick, even when it came to the children who increasingly filled the workforce.

Early corporate culture, in other words, was built on a foundation of intimidation, paired with punitive measures used to condition the human body to submit to repetitive tasks, day in and day out. This culture of physical coercion is still prevalent in exploitative workplaces today, from shipping warehouses to sweatshops, but it's a blunt, unpredictable mode of enforcing productivity. The development of modern capitalism, as we'll explain, required something more surgical.

That form of management arrived at the turn of the twentieth century, from the mind of a mechanical engineer named Frederick Winslow Taylor. As an employee for Bethlehem Steel, Taylor lamented that workers were naturally lazy, and in order to counter their slovenly attitudes, he began to closely study their movements. He realized that coal shovelers with standardized shovel sizes could haul more weight without getting tired quickly. He timed others' movements on the factory floor with a stopwatch, looking for extraneous movements to shave off their routines. He was often brazenly manipulative: while monitoring pig iron haulers, he experimented with daring the strongest loaders to load as fast as they could. When they finished the task quickly, he concluded that "first class" men could be hauling far more per day, provided they just worked faster and without as much rest.[5]

Taylor believed that perfect productivity was possible: redundancies were everywhere, and there was always room for optimization. This should all sound familiar, even if we're far from the floor of Bethlehem Steel. And just as with today, it made employees miserable. "We don't want to work as fast as we are able to," one machinist, debating Taylor in 1914, declared. "We want to work as fast as we think it's comfortable for us to work. We haven't come into existence for the purpose of seeing how great a task we can perform through a lifetime. We are trying to regulate our work so as to make it auxiliary to our lives."[6]

Over time, Taylor's theories were dubbed "scientific management," a moniker that helped rationalize the cold, unforgiving, unemotional treatment of subordinates with an aura of empirical credibility. His ideas continued to spread, with little regard to critics who argued he was making up or misinterpreting his own data. For managers, the prospect of applying science to the world of industry was simply too intoxicating, especially when it forced laborers' goals to align with the company's. And like so many business theories to come, Taylorism was taught and codified through the academy. "Taylor is the mortar . . . of every American business school," the historian Jill Lepore wrote in 2009.[7] Devotees of Taylorism took his teachings even further: management engineers Frank and Lillian Gilbreth, for example, used early cameras to watch workers. The field, dubbed motion study, reduced labor down to around seventeen distinct motions. The goal was "to eliminate waste motion."[8]

This supercharged form of management gave supervisors the tools to obsessively surveil and quantify their employees' every move. Within Taylorism, the more data you had, the more control you could exercise, the better. But it could not be maintained without a supply of competent, loyal workers and a rigid hierarchical order to keep them from resisting the dehumanizing, "scientific" methods of their superiors. Enter the middle manager. Taylor called this role "functional supervision." In practice, it meant a series of foremen, each with his own specialization: the gang boss, who operates as a foreman, surveying operations, or the disciplinarian, enforcing the rote, efficient rhythms of the workday. It's also worth noting that this intense focus on optimization spread outside work, as well as into the home. As Lepore noted in her 2009 piece, office efficiencies didn't contribute to more leisure time at home; they made domestic life more hectic. "Scientific management isn't the kind of thing you can leave at the office," she wrote.[9]

Taylorism would evolve over the years to come as management theory embraced the understanding that positive attention could **also** compel employees to work harder. In the 1930s, for example, business theorist Chester Barnard defined good managers as "value shapers concerned with the informal social properties of an organization."[10] In other words, creating culture. Instead of eagle-eyed foremen glaring down at hunched laborers, managers were newly conceived of as organizational stewards, charged with maintaining productivity but also the emotional well-being of their employees.

Today, the legacy of Taylorism is most visible in employee-monitoring computer software, which not only screenshots the websites an employee visits but calculates how much time is spent typing and moving the mouse—something we'll talk about at length later in the book. But it is also present in the managerial process of gathering and analyzing data and in the idea that perfect productivity is possible, if you just magically find a balance between pushing workers to their breaking point and not running them into the ground.

Maintaining that balance has proven treacherous if not impossible. Those at the top of an organization often lack proximity to the vast majority of their employees, which means they have only the vaguest understanding of what's happening in their day-to-day work lives. The task of maintenance thus falls to managers, who serve as the connective tissue between the top and the bottom of an organization. The product that managers transmit back and forth is, in some form, the company's culture. They're its primary conduit:

no one, not even the CEO, touches, shapes, or directs it more.

The Organization Man

As office work began to expand over the course of the twentieth century, workers were sold on promises of comfort and satisfaction. Instead of toiling on a factory room floor, welding the same joint over and over again, you could sit in an office, filing the same report over and over again. Your collar, as Upton Sinclair famously put it, would be white; your work, at least in the vast majority of cases, would be salaried and steady.

After the prolonged, destabilizing trauma of the Depression and World War II, you can see how those offerings would be immensely appealing. The corporation offered not just financial safety but a sense of belonging: both to a corporation and its mission and to the rapidly expanding middle class and its attendant cultural trappings. Just as millions of returned GIs flocked to civic organizations, from the Elks to the Rotary Club, hoping to duplicate the feeling of collective mission, many workers were equally eager to give themselves over to the larger, corporate effort with the promise of making their everyday lives feel **meaningful.**

A new sort of company culture, embodied by the so-called organization man, began to grow around this feeling. The journalist William Whyte coined the term in his 1956 best-selling book to describe a specific genre of competent, middle-class office worker. Employed in the offices of companies like GM, General Electric, and 3M, he was not destined for the corner office, but he was okay with that. He worked hard and had faith that the benefits of good work would trickle both up and down the corporate ladder. This, again, was a symptom of the age, when feelings of collectivism—so foreign to our current, highly individualized moment—were at an all-time historical high.[11]

The organization man was confident, Whyte noted, that "the goals of the individual and the goals of the organization will work out to be one and the same."[12] The company culture that sprang forth was one of loyalty and trust, in both one's leaders and one's peers. Which is part of why reading Whyte's book today feels like peering into some foreign, utopian land: the organization man is, well, **satisfied.** He's not ambitious, but he's not lazy, either. He's eager to maintain a semblance of a nonwork life and uninterested in distinguishing himself. "Trainees hope to rise high and hope just as much not to suffer the personal load of doing so," Whyte writes. "Frequently they talk of finding a sort of plateau—a position well enough up to be interesting but not so far up as to have one's neck outstretched for others to chop at."[13]

But the dark side of postwar office culture is right there in that sentence: make yourself known—by thinking differently, by challenging the status quo, by rising too quickly—and make yourself a target. Individuality wasn't just discouraged; it was tantamount to career suicide. The goal was to keep your head down, do what was expected of you (but nothing more!), and encourage others to do the same. Workers conformed, but they did so, according to Whyte, with a placid smile: they were undergirded by real support, whether in the form of their salary, their pension, or their enduring job security. "It is not the evils of organization life that puzzle him, **but its very beneficence,**" Whyte explained. "He is imprisoned in brotherhood."

And that imprisonment extended to the home, where the ethos of organization man culture was instrumental in shaping the structures of (white) middle-class life. Early suburbs were quite literally built to accommodate and incubate organization men, their families, and their social lives, which became appendages of the company. Social status was cemented through perks like local country-club memberships, while the organization man's family, especially his wife, became a form of corporate asset, valued for her ability to host and socialize. Employees were expected to leverage their family life to woo clients and executives alike. "Actually, it's hard to tell where the workday ends and the 'pleasure' begins," one manager told Whyte. "If you count all the time required for cocktails, dinners, conferences, and conventions, there is no end to work. I think any responsible executive these days works practically all the hours he is awake."[14]

It's no coincidence that during this period—

the twenty-five or so years following World War II—the idea of a "career" became a staple of the white-collar world. Unlike a job or a gig, a career is above all else **strategic** and demands not just work but appropriate assimilation into workplace culture. A career entails showing up every day and putting in concentrated hours **and** wholeheartedly leaning into a company's ethos; distinguishing yourself **and** disappearing. It calls for the concerted, eager sublimation of the self to the corporate good but also a deft charting of one's path through the organization. Be ambitious, but **appropriately** so.

This sort of contradictory messaging is a hallmark of toxic company culture, in part because it outlines a vanishingly small line for employees to tread. Which is why its primary legacy, still evident in thousands of workplaces, is a culture built on homogeneity and exclusion where pedigree, evidenced in the form of education, family name, dress, even manner of speaking, become crucial passports. Without them, there's no way up the career ladder. No matter if some, or all, are unavailable to wide swaths of the

population. It becomes, as one McKinsey
managing director wrote, "the way we do
things around here."[15]

For those inside this company culture, especially those who have given themselves
over to it, it starts to feel invisible, like some
inevitable creation. Which is convenient: it's
always far harder to resist what you can't see.
But nothing about this sort of company culture, or **any** company culture, is inevitable.
It's designed by people and almost always
oriented toward the financial interests of
the company. Still, some cultures are more
durable than others—better at convincing
all involved, from workers and customers to
leaders and shareholders, that a particular
mode of operating is in everyone's best interest.

The cliques, perks, and stability that flowed
from the organization man culture were very
real. But its endurance sprang from the fact
that it managed, however temporarily, to
convince clerical workers, middle management, and executives that their interests were
aligned. Like so many company cultures, it
was a bit of coercive storytelling: a half lie

repeated until it felt like truth. Going to work every day might feel stultifying, even suffocating, but what more could you ask? Your family was living the American dream and would continue to live it for the foreseeable future. For the white men who could find their way into the system in the first place, it all worked pretty well. Until it didn't.

We're Not All in This Together

Between the end of World War II and the early 1970s, the United States enjoyed a period of unprecedented economic growth and stability—what some economists refer to as "the golden age of American capitalism." That golden age, and the ideas about company growth that accompanied it, made organization man office culture possible. But starting in the early 1970s, a wave of recessions and economic stagnation shook even the strongest of those companies' foundations. Behemoths of respective industries entered the decade fat and happy and naive—characteristics that, under the unforgiving eye of a slumping economy, quickly morphed into bloated, occasionally lazy, and flat-footed in the race to compete globally.

Their solution, as we noted in the last chapter, was cuts. In the first eight years of the 1980s, Fortune 500 companies cut more than 300 million jobs, many of them the stable, middle-management positions that had not only helped expand the modern middle class but functioned as the organizational sentries of culture. DuPont, Xerox, General Electric—good companies with sterling reputations—started shaving away benefits, first with temporary cuts, then with permanent ones, and then, when that didn't work, layoffs. The results were devastating. Those who'd bought into the collectivist company culture and reoriented their lives around that loyalty realized they'd been sold out. What was good for the company was no longer good for the organization man.

The journalist Amanda Bennett chronicled the grisly fallout in her 1990 book, **The Death of the Organization Man,** which concluded that a generation of workers were lulled by paternalistic companies, only to be betrayed by them the moment times got tough. Before writing the book, Bennett worked for **The Wall Street Journal,** covering the auto industry from Detroit. She'd watched the home offices of blue-chip car manufacturers like GM and Ford delight in the stability of the postwar economy. At Ford's executive lunch room, for example, white-gloved men served up silver-platter lunches at $120 a plate, all subsidized by the company.

Workers on the assembly line were subject to periodic layoffs and rehirings, but at HQ jobs were plentiful. The company hired aggressively, building out labyrinthine org charts overflowing with managers. As Bennett explains, "a big part of a manager's job began to be relating to other managers" as "organizations got so big and so complex that some people were hired whose job was simply to help navigate the organization."[16] Company culture had become a hall of mirrors, a tautological story devoid of substance. We are because we are; we do because we do.

It didn't take much for that hall of mirrors to collapse in on itself. As companies began to cut, loyalty "often kept the Organization Man working against his personal interests and financial interests," Bennett writes.

"Dozens of managers stayed with their companies in the face of disastrous situations, working, and working hard. These were the loyal soldiers, staying at their posts no matter what."[17] These middle managers might have felt like loyal soldiers at the time, but they were blinded by loyalty and perks and a workplace "family" that didn't allow them to see that their battalion had been moved to the front lines in order to be sacrificed.

When you create a corporate ethos in which employees base their self-worth—and the very foundation of their identity—on their job, removing them from that job is **hard.** Bennett described the ramifications of downsizing as "the same as suffering a divorce or a death in the family."[18] For the downsized, losing a job wasn't just losing financial stability but expulsion from one's social life. Losing the physical space of the office meant disconnection from their daily rhythms and the hundreds of seemingly inconsequential actions that defined their lives. Many had been with their companies for decades and had no idea how to begin to search for new jobs. They'd built careers, and those careers had become their lives. Now that the career was gone, what, if anything, remained of their lives?

The result was a new brand of corporate cynicism, one that has become deeply embedded in contemporary workplace culture. The lesson that many corporations took from the cuts of the 1980s and 1990s was to never again find themselves in the position of having to drastically downsize. But instead of rethinking company culture from the ground up, they opted to methodically strip the elements of corporate life that had provided stability to workers. In this global brand of cutthroat capitalism, the futurist R. Morton Darrow explained, managers who were once perceived and treated as **assets** were transformed into **costs**.[19] The idea of working at one place for an entire career became quaint, because the specter of another round of layoffs loomed around every corner. Employees grew increasingly less loyal—with good reason. The new mantra was "it's not personal, it's business," which might have felt true if the results of business decisions weren't so personally destabilizing.

Even Terrence Deal and Allan Kennedy, the

same pair of consultants who, back in 1982, regaled readers with the story of NCR's "hard driving, sales-oriented culture" that survived an air raid, were chastened. "When times are tough," they had written in the final paragraph of **Corporate Cultures,** "these companies can reach deeply into their shared values and beliefs for the truth and courage to see them through."[20]

In 1999, looking back from the vantage point of nearly two decades of layoffs, mergers, and outsourcing, Deal and Kennedy realized they had been deeply wrong. They lamented the slavish dedication to "shareholder value and short-term results," which both eroded and poisoned corporate culture. They decried the "slide toward corporate anonymity" and "thoughtless management actions in pursuit of short-term goals." They could see a logic, however faulty, in the culture-demolishing cuts companies had made over the last two years. But now was the time to correct it.

In their new book, titled **The New Corporate Cultures,** Deal and Kennedy had all sorts of suggestions to remotivate an unmotivated workplace, reknit cohesive bonds, and even, as they put it, throw a little fun in the process. But their obsession with improving culture was hardly new. In fact, the pair had launched a culture "craze" upon the original publication of their book, which had been the first to truly articulate the "phantom force," as they put it, that "lay underneath the rational-technical veneer of business."[21] In the years that followed, the explicit cultivation of company culture had become a business school cure-all as companies attempted to follow advice to cut costs and "stay lean," but also somehow make their employees less dour and anxious about everything.

As workers devoured productivity books, executives and human resources departments became obsessed with culture: they flocked to management gurus, tried out combinations of quantification and obsessive optimization, wondered if "positive" organization might engender more productivity. Some believed that if companies released their iron grip on employees—and embraced a more democratic style of management—maybe employees would feel not just happy but cared for, like part of a family. Instead of providing employees with actual stability, the thinking went, they'd provide them with more freedom over their own work, which would theoretically revitalize company culture.

Leaders might not have been dedicated to the shifts that would actually change company culture. But they sure liked the **idea** of it. And they got their ideas from books. Books like the original **Corporate Cultures** and **In Search of Excellence,** which sold more than 4.5 million copies and became defining corporate texts of the 1980s and 1990s.

In **Excellence,** two consultants, Thomas Peters and Robert Waterman Jr., profiled dozens of companies, highlighting open-door policies and fluid organizational structures where "small bands of zealots operate outside the mainstream" to come up with new strategies and products. They saw not organization men but innovative obsessives.[22] To support those employees, they argued that companies needed visionary managers who gave employees autonomy while also still holding the reins. "As a leader you are authoritarian or you are democratic," they advised. "In reality, you are neither and both at the same time."[23]

This loose-tight management might sound

enlightened; its prime directive is, essentially, treating employees like adults. Yet in practice, managers' hold on the reins was often uncomfortably tight. The leaders Peters and Waterman venerated "believed in open doors" but were also "stern disciplinarians, every one"; "they gave plenty of rope, but they accepted the chance that some of their minions would hang themselves."[24] A family, then, but a fairly ruthless one.

Like **Corporate Cultures, In Search of Excellence** inspired a glut of knockoffs, spin-offs, and sequels in the business book section, all featuring case studies of successful corporations that appeared to have figured out the new global economy. These companies were more nimble, less stodgy, more willing to experiment. They threw parties and peculiar product launch pep rallies. Who cares about the cuts—many of which had been suggested, uncoincidentally, by consultants just like Peters and Waterman—when you have a "fun" atmosphere where people work and play hard.

These books were billed as providing new "management strategies," but they rarely touched on how to deal with your team through a leveraged buyout or manage cash flow. They weren't teaching leaders how to rebuild corporate culture so much as how to craft a cheap fix out of the wreckage that remained. These strategies rarely, if ever, offered true autonomy or equality to workers. Hierarchies were still rigid. Benefits were still a hollow echo of their previous selves. The new policies and team building and hoopla of the so-called New Management were mostly a distraction from the tightness of the rope around workers' necks.

Who Needs Middle Management When You've Got Venture Capital?

If you work in a corporate environment, the legacy of these ideas about culture and management, accumulated over more than a century of business theory, surround you. They're in your open office plan—something we'll talk more about in the following chapter—but they're also in the break room or the canteen or the catered lunches. They're in your happy hour outings that coexist with your company's refusal to match your 401(k). But they're most visible, and most noxious, in the start-up world.

In **The Search for Excellence,** the descriptions of loose-tight practitioners from the 1980s often sound like blueprints for the Silicon Valley companies of today. At 3M, there were management groups that not only tolerated but embraced and supported failure; Hewlett-Packard and Tupperware trumpeted "flex hours" and "hoopla" that included frequent employee "jubilees." At Caterpillar, they used to dress up new earthmovers in costumes and throw parties. Even the workplace "campus"—now a staple of Big Tech—is cited as promoting a successful loose-tight company, as was the case for 3M, Kodak, Dana, Dow, P&G, and Texas Instruments.

But modern start-up culture will always have a slightly different DNA from the corporate behemoths, which, no matter how much hoopla they add to employee jubilees, were still built on a foundation of loyal company men. Start-up company culture started from a premise of rejection: of old-school rules of decorum, dress code, and departmental organization, but also of traditional notions of innovation and growth. Instead of trying to paper over and cure the corporate cynicism of the 1970s and 1980s, start-ups consolidated it and used it to power "entrepreneurship."

No wonder business school interest in entrepreneurship boomed over the course of the 1980s: it was a new armor against the unpredictability of corporate life. "It's a lack of trust that underlines entrepreneurship," the Harvard business professor Howard Stevenson observed. "If they're going to foul it up, they'd rather do it themselves than rely on some idiot on Madison Avenue, or something beyond their control."

Success stories spurred would-be founders, even as tech bubbles swelled and burst. The scale and connectivity of the web helped nurture the belief that any person with the right idea, in the right place, at the right time could not just achieve staggering success and wealth but fundamentally upend or "disrupt" an entire industry, even with a bare-bones team, operating out of their garage. It was a new, alluring version of meritocracy. Sure, the American dream was broken. But you could hack it. If there had been any doubt that individualism had subsumed the collectivist ethos of yore, the tech boom put it wholly to rest.

Venture capitalists, a group often composed of the most successful disrupters, underwrote this fantasy. Along the way, they helped build what we now know as start-up culture: a hybrid of old, toxic corporate elements, the entrepreneurship ethos, and a celebration of new, iconoclastic ideas. The industry developed a founder worship that would look familiar to the vaguely cultish inner workings at, say, IBM, whose company songbook included a song dedicated to its chairman, Thomas Watson, with the lyrics "We know and we love you, and we know you have our welfare in your heart."[25]

But the core value was an all-consuming, obsessive devotion to the company. Not just its financial success, but its greater ideal or **mission,** which was frequently framed in utopian language. Given the near-infinite playground of the internet, and the millions if not billions of dollars of funding at stake, it wasn't enough to just build an app. You had to connect the world as never before, solve an intractable problem, reimagine an entrenched industry—"disrupt" the status quo. **That** was worth venture capital investment. Which meant it was also worth giving over one's life. Worshipping at the altar of the God of Scale requires making sacrifices on behalf of the business.

Squint at start-up culture and you can see vestiges of the organization man and his fealty to the greater corporate good. Tech entrepreneurs would throw their $12 IPA in your face if you called them that. Start-ups conceived of themselves in opposition to "big business": they're companies, but they're not **corporate.** To prove it, many embraced an irreverent work hard/play hard culture. Founders indulge in a sort of extended adolescence: days-long work benders capped off with real ones. For the most intense, this ethos served as the final destruction of any semblance of work-life balance. Complete devotion to the cause meant living in the office, and transporting all of the outside elements of one's life—partying, exercise, romance—into that space. Early Silicon Valley companies had recruited engineers for decades whose personalities lent themselves naturally toward workaholism.[26] But this was another level.

As these companies grew, they'd shed some of the juvenile elements but not the all-consuming devotion and obsession, which was valorized in the culture through early war stories of all-night code binges and epic company parties. As start-up culture became more visible and desirable, these stories consolidated into a genre, now infamously known as hustle porn. Meanwhile, a secondary hustle industry began to emerge, populated with "thought leaders" and conferences dedicated to providing instructions on how to win the disruption lottery. First you'd need an idea and the talent. After that, it was a relentless hustle and struggle. To call it work ethic doesn't do it justice; it was the complete sublimation of a person in pursuit of a hazy idea of success.

Rejecting the old-school corporate culture didn't just mean embracing small teams and Ping-Pong tables. It also meant doing away with hierarchies altogether. Corporate infrastructures like HR—or even something as simple as an organizational chart—were eschewed until absolutely necessary. They were building the plane as it flew, which meant that many of the load-bearing elements of a company were installed without much thought or care.

It would all prove culturally disastrous. But such structural weaknesses took time to reveal themselves, and whatever problems they did cause, at least for a time, were offset by dazzling growth and plastered over with a scrappy origin story, a founder myth, and an inflated sense of mission. Who has time to worry about middle management or org charts or HR complaints, after all, when you're disrupting the world?

But with time, growth, and exposure to the spotlight, start-ups like Google, Facebook, Amazon, Uber, and hundreds of others were forced to conceive of themselves as corporations. The quirks of their culture were codified: the treatment of management as an afterthought, the hollow perks in place of actual benefits, the inattention to HR, the fetishization of productivity, and the reliance on the "flexible" contract worker spread across corporate campuses with elaborate free sashimi bars and complimentary laundry services, and trickled into disparate corners of the non-start-up world. Today, start-up culture isn't a fad or a novelty. It's the new ideal for so many companies, regardless of their product or their history.

As the pandemic made abundantly clear, that culture is simply not sustainable. It's not sustainable for the individuals, in and out of the office, who power it; it's not sustainable for our families; and it's not sustainable for our communities or the world where we make our homes. Profits might be steady, even soaring, but the workforce, like the communities and our lived environments, is collapsing.

It's worth pausing here to explain what we mean when we talk about this collapse. We understand that an executive reading these words might see this as hyperbole. **My employees aren't miserable. They don't hate me.** This might be true. But the collapse we're talking about has to do with a relationship to work that's grown increasingly unsustainable.

First, there's the sheer number of hours we're working. According to the Organization for Economic Cooperation and Development, the average American works more hours than the average laborer in any peer nation. But unlike many Western nations, where increased productivity and wealth tend to lead to more leisure time, Americans continue to overwork themselves despite productivity gains. The OECD found that "the US works 269 more hours than its enormously wealthy economy would predict—making it by this measure the second-most overworked country in the world."[27]

Then there's how we work. "Long before Covid-19 hit," **Vox**'s Anna North writes, "Americans were expected to work like they didn't have families."[28] This expectation, however unspoken, was codified after World War II, when the office workforce in particular was dominated by men. In 1960, only 20 percent of mothers worked. By 2010, 70 percent of children lived in homes where all adults were employed in some capacity.[29] But workplace policy, particularly in the United States, has failed to evolve to fit this new reality—whether in the case of family leave policies or expectations for after-hours work. The "ideal" worker is still the worker with as few familial obligations as possible. For parents—and mothers in particular—attempting to contort themselves to fit that ideal, the result is stress, fatigue, burnout, and, in some cases, dropping out of the workforce entirely.[30]

Some of these expectations and failures are specific to the United States. But workers are struggling globally as well. Microsoft's 2021 Work Trend Index surveyed more than thirty thousand workers in thirty-one countries and found that 54 percent reported feeling overworked, 39 percent felt exhausted, and 20 percent said their employer didn't care about work-life balance.[31] Even with all of this time allocated to work, global GDP has remained stagnant since 2012.[32] According to the 2017 Gallup report **State of the Global Workplace,** 66 percent of adults say they're not engaged at work, and 18 percent say they're actively disengaged. The report argues that companies that orient performance "around basic human needs for psychological engagement" are most likely to "get the most out of their employees."[33] But few organizations seem to have figured this out. Instead, they stifle productivity and enthusiasm through haphazard management, a generalized lack of worker autonomy, and increasing hours and expectations that lead to worker burnout.

Granted, the global workforce has not actually collapsed. And perhaps it never will. But the trends listed above all seem to signal a rot at the center of the way we think about our jobs and the way we're asked to perform them. Our relationship to work is broken. Our attitudes are toxic, our demands on individuals too great, work's rewards are not commensurate with the time spent, and many of our policies—especially in the United States—do not provide the support needed to continue as we do our jobs.

These are the conditions that make collapse possible. And while it might not happen on a macro level, our reporting suggests that on an individual level it is happening all the time, every day. In one sense, this means that if you're a manager or executive, this isn't (necessarily) personal. These dynamics are systemic, and many workers will rightfully find that the only way to address them is through a union. But it also means that even if your employees appear satisfied with their roles and with you as their leader, they are still operating in this system. As their leader, any commitment to reevaluate and reshape our relationship to work ultimately runs through you. In this sense, it should feel deeply personal. It sounds hokey, but you have the power to significantly change people's lives. What are you going to do with it?

If we go back to the office and restart the rhythms of company life as if nothing has happened, there will be a halcyon month where everyone revels in the novelty of being somewhere, anywhere, that's not their home. But the wounds of the pandemic year are still open and raw. If companies keep their focus on short-term growth, leaning on the sort of flexibility that is just code for passing risk and precarity on to workers, distrust and exhaustion will continue to grow. Managers will collapse under the burden of communicating the company's ongoing demands to a burned-out workforce. The culture, no matter its character, will rot. If it wasn't breaking before the pandemic, it will soon.

But we can reject this scenario. We can understand that if companies actually want to cultivate that ever-alluring "good" company culture, they have to rethink not just the amenities and office space they're providing their employees but the entire style of work, the whole ethos of optimization and presentism. Doing so will demand authentically embracing flexibility, as we discussed in the last chapter. But it will also mean reconsidering core values beyond "growth" and "scale," and understanding that you cannot compel or surveil your way to sustained, quality productivity. Productivity is the byproduct of a workforce that has had its essential needs met.

This isn't a matter of grafting a new, flashy, prepackaged idea of culture onto your existing one. It's about rethinking what's made your culture the way it is, connecting that structure with the struggles that have followed, and thinking through how flexibility could change it. This is arduous, endlessly challenging work. But you have to till the ground before you can even begin to germinate the seeds of something new, vibrant, and capable of sustainable growth.

What Does Flexible Work Culture Look Like?

Paul Hershenson doesn't do Fridays. For the last eight years, when most people in the working world are getting itchy and starting to run out the clock on the week, Paul organizes a backpack and gets in the car. On the drive out to the wilderness from his home in San Diego, he'll maybe take a call or two— not always, but he reserves the option. "It's a good stretch of time, where I'm available to think," he told us when we got hold of him on one of those Friday mornings, already well on his way out of town.

Paul has not worked in an office in thirty years. And even that framing is a bit dishonest. In his career as a software developer, Paul has never really worked in what he calls "a normal job." But his company, Art+Logic, has never had a formalized work space and attributes that to their success with building a cohesive work culture. Still, Paul is wary of doling out business advice. He admits that what works for him might not work for **anyone** else, and that includes those inside the company he helps to run. Which is why he helped design Art+Logic to be truly flexible and for the work to be completely and totally asynchronous.

Paul's hikes are part of that design. For him, finding time at the end of the week to get out in nature clears his mind and reduces stress. With his kids at school, he's not off-loading the burden of care on his partner. Nor does he have to be at work; the time is truly his. A number of the other sixty-five employees at the company have similarly unique schedules. Two years ago, a graphic designer redesigned her schedule after the birth of her child. She works a stretch in the middle of the day and a stretch from roughly 7:00 to 10:00 in the evenings. "She built the day so she could continue earning a living and doing what she loves but also fulfill her desire to be the principal caregiver, which was equally important," he said.

Another developer at the firm is an avid golfer and plays a few times a week. "I don't even know when he does it or how often, really," Paul said. "But I'm 100 percent confident that he'll make that time up when he wants to."

It's entirely possible you're rolling your eyes while reading this. **Good for Paul and his sixty-five employees living in fantasyland!** It might even piss you off a little. **Friday hikes! Must be nice!** Before the pandemic, you likely thought that sort of flexibility was probably all but impossible in your job. But a few months into working from home, you might have asked yourself, Why did we ever think choosing one's hours—or finding time to build work around hobbies or caregiving— sounded like an extravagance?

In many ways, breaking this cynical, closed mindset is the goal of this book. But it's difficult to imagine it if you can't see it or why it works. Art+Logic is an example of a flexible culture that works in service of its employees, including those at the top. Company and employee goals are established up front and clearly communicated—part of the everyday work of what Paul describes as "establishing reasonable expectations." Those expectations are designed to provide an understanding of what work is flexible and what, if any, needs to remain rigid. For example, employees are expected to be largely available during regular business hours but can create schedules that work for them, provided they are up front about it and hold to them.

Art+Logic employees can work asynchronously because they are transparent about what needs to be done and who needs to do it, which, in turn, allows for more accountability.

Theirs is a culture built on trust: not the sort of empty phrase that shows up in mottoes and job ads, but actual trust that employees will meet expectations. And part of that trust is granting real freedom to make small and occasionally large decisions about when work should be done. But the company also has a long-term strategy to match and accentuate that trust. They're focused not on immediate growth but on long-term vision: retaining valuable employees in a competitive industry.

The culture at Art+Logic can't be ported over to any company, because there's no such thing as a magic formula. Culture naturally works differently at different scales: what works for a 60-person distributed software company might spell certain death for a 250,000-person global firm. But size doesn't ultimately matter when it comes to Art+Logic's cultural success. That's because they get the essential part of company culture right. What the company **says** it's asking of employees and what it's **actually** asking— they're the same thing.

So what makes for a healthy, flexible culture? Well, management. Not tacked-on management, throwaway management, old-school management, but management that meets the needs of the current moment. We have a few areas where you can begin to survey your existing management culture and ways to change it, but this isn't a checklist. It's a map. You can use it to find your own route. Just keep in mind, the changes your company needs are rarely the ones that jump out at you as the most straightforward. Find the section that makes you feel the most vulnerable, the most **seen,** the most broken and exhausted. That's where you need to start.

Who's the Manager?

Melissa Nightingale and her husband, Johnathan, were among the first wave of employees hired at Mozilla in the first decade of the twenty-first century. They were young and didn't have a lot of experience, but like a lot of talented people who get in on the ground floor of a start-up, they found themselves quickly rising through the company ranks. People just kept promoting them, giving them more managerial responsibility, even though they didn't understand what the hell they were supposed to be doing.

Since 2017, the Nightingales have been working as a new sort of management consultant, specializing in growing companies. Every day, they spend time listening to how bad companies are at communicating and managing their employees. A **lot** of time. And then they try to fix it.

"It's usually not malice," Melissa told us, referring to the way most companies are run. "It's ignorance. There **are** malicious actors out there—people acting out power fantasies. But a lot of that tactical stuff happens at the margins. The reason office work sucks is the same reason why remote work could also suck. It's because management sucks."

In their positions at Mozilla, the first teams the Nightingales managed were scattered all over the world. Melissa and Johnathan were tasked with trying to coordinate their team's work while **also** avoiding assigning any tasks that would take place outside daylight hours in each employee's respective time zone. Back then, Slack didn't exist. "Collaboration was really hard," Johnathan said. "We were just kind of making it up," Melissa added. "And we kept getting more and more mandates from our superiors. Finally, we hit this point where it was just like, is anyone going to tell us how to do this job?"

The answer, they realized, was essentially no. They were alone. They looked around at other managers and realized that more often than not new managers were plucked from nonmanagement jobs—usually because they were quite good at what they did—and asked, "Do you want to be a manager?" The move was always framed as a promotion and a big career advancement. The pay was better, too. Most employees would say yes and then immediately find themselves in the managerial deep end with little or no training.

"They'd end up as shitty managers and make life shittier for everyone around them," Johnathan said. "But again, it's not out of malice. It's out of ignorance. Nobody told them how to do it."

This practice isn't limited to any industry, but the Nightingales argue that it's especially pervasive at tech companies. For years, they'd read stories of dysfunctional start-ups and scandalous bad behavior coming from Silicon

Valley and sigh, knowing that the likely problem has an easy but elusive fix. They started their company, Raw Signal, based out of Toronto, to try to diagnose the problem in the wild.

But it was worse than they thought. For all the rhetoric around executive vision, the day-to-day experience of working at a company—the culture, the opportunities, the frustrations—was rarely dictated by those at the top. Instead, it was middle management, a person's **direct** manager, who set the tone for whether their job would feel like a daily experience of passive-aggressive warring or something collaborative, generative, and satisfying.

Take, for example, maintaining anything approaching work-life balance during the pandemic. A skilled manager will approach each remote employee differently. They'll attempt to understand their employee's individual needs: how they work best away from the office, what stresses and pressures they have in their lives, and how to work around them. They'll offer trust and space or attention and guidance, depending on the employee's needs. In short, they'll actively, dynamically manage.

But most managers haven't been trained on how to navigate even small disruptions, let alone massive pandemic-induced ones. And without training, they often manage on one of two extremes. Either they micromanage needlessly, because they know no other way to make their work visible or meaningful, or they treat managing the way **their** managers do: as an afterthought. Employees are left desperate for feedback, sending Slack messages into the wind.

All of this was true before the pandemic, when people were still largely working in the office. Remote work didn't create a new problem; it exacerbated an existing one. Which is why Melissa and Johnathan think the success of remote and flexible work will ultimately have little to do with the adoption of new technology, or strategic organizational planning, or even the preferences of the CEO or board of directors. It will live and die with middle management.

"When people talk about remote work, I hear, 'We can work less and still be productive,' and I'm like, 'Okay, true. I'm excited.' But if you're poorly managed, I can give you a four-hour workday, five days a week, and burn you straight out," Melissa said. "If I live in fear that if I don't have enough eye contact or enough Slack messages with my boss I might get fired, working fewer hours will not help. And guess what: you won't even work fewer hours. You will compensate for precarity by over-delivering and burning out."

And the problems go well beyond burn-out. A lack of training creates a learned helplessness among mid-level managers: instead of functioning as a sort of bulwark to protect employees, pushing back on bad decisions, they become passive vectors for what (often clueless) executives demand of them. Lack of (good) management allows inequities to grow and microaggressions to become macroaggressions. But how do you tell someone who's been doing a job for five years, maybe even ten, that they've missed the point of their job this whole time?

People may be bad managers out of ignorance, but that doesn't mean they're blameless. There are pernicious, long-lasting effects to bad management. "We've seen women who've had pay adjusted simply because a manager woke up," Johnathan said. "The reason she was underpaid on the team was not because her boss was cackling in the corner. It was because nobody told the boss it was their responsibility to look at the fucking spreadsheet."

As Melissa and Johnathan point out, "If you're cashing the paycheck, it's time to find the training. You can't just experiment and figure out as you go on actual human beings." So what does that look like? It doesn't look like a single-day off-site training session, or a two-hour webinar playing in the background while you scroll Twitter. Some of the work has to be simply realizing that in most modern organizations, "management" has become something to tack onto someone's existing job description, like a high school teacher getting extra money to coach high school volleyball. No matter that they've only played a few games in their lives; somebody's gotta do it, and who doesn't want a pay bump?

Alternately, management is used as a way to reward workers who distinguish themselves for their productivity, whether at sales, writing grants, data analysis, you name it.

But as a recent study by **Harvard Business Review** pointed out, the skills associated with high productivity—including knowledge and expertise, driving for results, taking initiative—are almost all indications of **individual**-oriented competencies. Management requires skills that are **other** oriented: being open to feedback, supporting colleagues' development, communicating well, having good interpersonal skills.[34]

Good managers are often productive. But productive people are not always good managers. They end up in those positions because most companies don't actually value good management enough to take the time to identify its qualities and then recruit and retain employees with them.

This tendency to treat management as an "add-on"—as opposed to an actual job, requiring a refined skill set—is, as the Nightingales found, rampant in start-ups, both new and long solidified. But it's also common in cash-strapped nonprofits, in academic departments (see department chairs), and in "legacy" companies that overcorrected the sprawling, management-heavy org charts of the 1960s and 1970s. Back then, people often dealt with bad management by expanding the org chart with even more badly trained managers. Now we deal with it by ignoring it.

Many of these companies view middle management as bloat, waste, what David Graeber would call a "bullshit job." But that's because bad managing **is** waste; you're paying someone **more money** to essentially annoy everyone around them. And the more people experience that sort of bad management, and think of it as "just the way it is," the less they're going to value management in general. The key, then, is to think of how to treat management as a discrete, valuable skill: a deliverable that contributes to the overall value and resiliency of your organization. Otherwise, managers will continue to feel like deadweight, no matter how flexible an attitude you embrace.

But before a company calls someone like the Nightingales—or signs up for any other sort of management training—it's worth thinking about who's currently in management positions. How many people with no real aptitude or investment have taken on the responsibility because there's no other way to distinguish oneself? How many hate it? How many feel they'd love to devote more time to managing their team, but find they have so little time and space to dedicate to it beside their other work obligations?

In other words, maybe some of your managers shouldn't be managers. Maybe **you** shouldn't be a manager. Maybe you're not a manager, have never thought of yourself as a manager, but actually have the aptitude for it. Managing has been pegged to promotion for so long it's eclipsed what's actually vital about the position. It's not about power. It's about figuring out how to actually create the conditions for your team to do their best work. That work is often invisible, but your company should be treating it as invaluable.

What Does Management Look Like Now?

People have felt adrift, anxious, and unmanaged in their work for years. So now it's time to reconsider what management's been missing and how to reintegrate it into the fully or flexibly remote future.

Corine Tan, Andrew Zhou, and Sid Pandiya stumbled upon this realization almost by

accident. All three spent their early careers
with different start-ups; Pandiya and Zhou
worked in engineering and product, and Tan
was in business development and marketing.
Even when in an office, they noticed that
their jobs were increasingly isolated, taking
place primarily on screens. Co-workers were
becoming abstractions—an email reply waiting to be answered instead of, well, a human
being. They all found themselves interested in
answering a fundamental question: If people
actually understood each other's work-style
preferences, could they work together better? So they formed a company, called Sike
Insights, to study remote work.

In October 2019, they started reaching out
to tech companies cold via LinkedIn with a
few basic questions: What do you love/hate
about remote work? They spoke with managers and low-level employees and C-suite
executives from companies like Uber Eats,
Glassdoor, Hubstaff, Evernote, and Mozilla.
They were in the early stages of data analysis.
And then the pandemic hit.

"It's crazy," Tan told us. "We have this whole
spectrum of data. At first it's like, 'Remote
work is great!' then, 'Whoa, global pandemic

has changed everything, this is pretty stressful,' and then, 'I onboarded at my company six months ago, and I've never met a single human I work with.'"

The data Sike Insights collected offered a bleak picture. Over ninety hours of Zoom calls with 110 different companies and their employees, they found that most workplaces were buckling under the pressure of forced work from home. People were Zoom fatigued, but more than that, they were struggling to connect emotionally with their teams. "Somebody we interviewed summed it up perfectly," Zhou said. "They told us they were 'talking more and saying less.'" The emotional disconnect was creating anxiety but also sucking all of the small, intangible joys out of the job. The cause was clear: management and a lack of emotional intelligence.

They found that remote managers they surveyed had an average of about 4.87 direct reports. That might not sound like much, but it was overwhelming most managers as they attempted to deal with 5 different emotionally complex human beings, all under stress and with their own needs and demands. Worse yet, 21.5 percent of the remote managers they spoke with had less than one year of management experience when mandatory working from home began. They'd stumbled on the same problem as the Nightingales had: managers were under-trained, under-experienced, overworked, and forced into a stressful new reality. As a result, everyone was suffering.

"To be a good manager, you need to be emotionally intelligent," Pandiya told us. "It's our whole company thesis: the emotional intelligence of the managers is what makes a company's culture miserable or excellent. And it's hard to be emotionally intelligent when you're not in the same room." As a result, the trio saw that middle managers were absorbing much of the stress of their employees while **also** feeling pressure from higher-ups to make sure their teams felt cared for.

Their attempt at a solution is Kona, a software platform that tries to measure the emotional health of employees working remotely and help managers establish "empathy-based communication." Every morning, Kona "checks in" with employees, asking them to evaluate their mood that day. Employees respond with a color (green means feeling good, yellow is ambivalent, red suggests they are struggling) and are presented the option to add more detail. The results are then shared with managers in order to synthesize what the Kona team described as "a general vibe as to how people are feeling."

Managers can also chart the emotional temperature of their team over time in order to arrive at a sense of how a project or a particular set of policies may affect the team. The platform also asks employees to answer questions about work style and then, if granted permission, uses artificial intelligence to analyze employee communication over platforms like public Slack channels. Kona then creates a personality profile of the employee that they can see and, if they want, make it public for other employees to use.

The hope, the team told us, is that with enough honest data, Kona can help workers, especially managers, communicate more effectively in real time. "Imagine you're typing out a message in Slack or writing an email and Kona pops in and says, 'I see you're talking to Andrew and using a data-driven argument full of numbers, but our research shows that Andrew responds best to emotionally driven arguments,'" Pandiya said. He described other plausible scenarios, including Kona pops in to tell you that the email you're "looping back" on is not urgent and, in fact, Rebecca is currently in six hours of meetings and feeling stressed today. How about sending tomorrow?

A platform that feeds off the emotional data of employees is **incredibly** fraught. It could be abused by manipulative co-workers; there are real privacy considerations related to scanning certain public communications across corporate channels like Slack or calendar apps. Some employees might not mind telling a bot what their mood is for the day and won't hesitate to let others know when they feel like crap. Many will find it unnaturally, annoyingly invasive. But that, the founders argue, is exactly the point. Opacity and lack of communication are at the very core of so many of today's management problems. Most people are flying blind, tiptoeing around their company trying not to get fired, left to divine the emotions of their colleagues and superiors from vague blocks of text. If flexible work means less in-person contact than before, how do you ensure that people are still expressing and processing the small tics, glances, postures, and belly laughs that function as the unofficial language of the in-person workplace?

"We talk about company culture all the time, but what we're talking about is so vague," Zhou said. "Imagine actually being able to **analyze** your culture. Imagine you could show managers team health reports and trends and tie that to specific decisions they've made." It's a tantalizing idea indeed: Say, an overzealous manager needlessly pushes up the due date of a project by a week, causing his employees to drop everything and crash it. The experience leads everyone to feel miserable and the end result suffers. A platform like Kona would theoretically allow that manager (and the manager's manager) to trace these decisions and learn from them.

"This might feel niche right now, but companies will adapt to this kind of management," Pandiya said. "And ten years from now those who didn't embrace this hybrid style will look like dinosaurs. It'll be like companies in the early 2000s who saw the internet and said, 'Pass.'"

But this "hybrid style," in which effective management becomes a mix of analytics and good old-fashioned human insight, is possible only if managers create an environment where, say, employees don't feel as if they just have to report their emotional state as "green" every day and the managers are actually receptive to the story the accumulated data tells them, even if it runs counter to their own self-perception.

Take the slightly less invasive example of Microsoft's "Leadership Insights," available to managers in companies that use Microsoft Teams. Once enabled, the Leadership page allows managers to track how much one-on-one time they've allocated with each member of their team, team meeting lengths and characteristics, and when your team's "quiet hours"— a.k.a. times when they're authentically not online and working—naturally fall. Managers can't see how many emails you're sending, or precisely what sort of work you're doing—just that you're logged on to Teams and using it.

The information can help managers be more honest with themselves about their own management behavior: you think that you run focused meetings, but the Leadership page shows that you're multitasking in 75 percent of them—an indication, according to a previous Microsoft study, that the rest of your team is as well.[35] You might think you're checking in regularly and equally with all of your employees; the analytics will report back whether that's the case.

One manager, who works as a librarian, told us that for her the analytics, particularly around quiet hours, have been "eye-opening." She used to reserve between 5:00 and 7:00 p.m. for attending to emails. But the analytics showed her that her emails were consistently interrupting her team's "quiet hours"—time when they had stepped away from work—and pulling them back in. Now she still sends her emails between 5:00 and 7:00 p.m. But she schedules them all for the morning, during her team's active hours. She had a choice: keep telling herself, as many managers do, that her team understood that they didn't have to immediately read and respond to emails sent after hours. Or look at the data, and see that they were still reading and responding during these times, and change her behavior accordingly.

The secret to good culture and even good management isn't some weekend off-site or even a fancy piece of technology. As Tan put it, "There's no way to Ping-Pong table or happy hour your way out of it." Analytics won't magically turn you into a better manager. You can use them to inform and transform your own behavior, but only if you actually have a vested interest in managing with more empathy and intentionality.

We're all figuring out what our jobs are going to look like in this new reality, and if we do it on our own, remote work will continue to look like the anxious, endless jumble of the pandemic year. The process is going to require a significant amount of experimentation and grace, communication and transparency. But the way we help each other do it, especially as managers, is to understand that everyone, up and down the org chart, is a full, messy, complex, vulnerable, and struggling human in need of support, affirmation, and boundaries. You can teach others that posture. But you also have to learn it for yourself.

Kill the Monoculture

In 2020, 92.6 percent of CEOs on the Fortune 500 were white.[36] A survey conducted that

same year of more than forty thousand workers at 317 companies found that while white
men make up just 35 percent of the entry-
level workforce, they compose 66 percent of
the C-suite.[37] For every one hundred men
who were promoted to manager, only fifty-
eight black women and seventy-one Latina
women were promoted. Only 38 percent of
respondents in entry-level management positions were women of any race.

You've heard these statistics, or something
approximating them, before. No matter how
many diversity, equity, and inclusion workshops your organization requires, if your
leaders and managers aren't truly diverse,
then the monoculture will prevail.

The word "monoculture" comes from the
agricultural world, where it is used to describe
growing or raising one specific type of crop or
animal. Businesses don't grow crops, but they
do yield workers; every organization know-
ingly and unknowingly creates conditions in
which a certain type of worker will thrive. In
most companies, the profile of that worker is
the same as the profile of the person set up to
thrive in most situations in America: white,
male, educated, middle-class, congenial,

sociable, and able to delegate obligations outside the office to others, whether in the form
of a partner, a parent, or paid labor.

Left to its own devices, monoculture will
self-sow and replicate itself endlessly. The
things that a white male, for example, might
understand as the hallmarks of "good leadership" and "good management" are the things
that feel like good leadership and management to **him**—characteristics that can manifest themselves in everything from standards
of professionalism to tone of voice. He will
naturally promote, elevate, or otherwise privilege workers with those attributes and mar-
ginalize or ignore those without them.

Frequently, those perpetuating the monoculture aren't even aware they're doing it. But
this is how monoculture persists: people endlessly promoting people like them for the rest
of time. In the ag world, years of monoculture eventually suck all the nutrients from the
soil. Farmers require more and more fertil-
izer and pesticide to keep harvest levels high.
The entire process wreaks havoc on the eco-
system. Why do they keep doing it? Usually
because it's cheaper and easier. They focus on
the short-term effects rather than the sort of

long-term devastation that will eventually put them and their families out of business.

It's not just that the soil is wrecked. The yields decline, too. Some businesses have slowly realized as much when it comes to their own version of monoculture. Maybe it's **good,** they start to think, even invigorating and generative, to have a company that's not filled with people with the same life experience. You can see the growing popularity of this idea all over consultant reports and business publications, which have filled with phrases like "diversity is profitable," "the relationship between diversity and business performance persists," and "the business case for diversity is overwhelming."

This "business case" for diversity developed alongside growing societal pressure to address social and racial justice within the workplace. Many companies responded by adopting some version of "diversity, equity, and inclusion" initiatives, corporate-speak for efforts to not only expand the diversity of hires and employees, in all senses of the word, but also make the workplace less toxic for those same employees. Some workplaces have a "head" of DEI; others outsource workshops and

trainings to the multibillion-dollar DEI industry. In 2020, Bain launched a DEI con-
sultancy with more than two dozen staff
available to beam down into companies willing to pay for their services. The head of the
department, Julie Coffman, called diversity
"the next digital."[38]

The success of these efforts has, perhaps
unsurprisingly, been mixed. Even companies
that manage to successfully recruit diverse
candidates are often horrible at retaining
them. What's more, consultancies like Bain
often frame success in terms of achievable
metrics—for example, percentage of "diverse"
candidates interviewed for a position—that
don't actually require any form of substantive
change to the way a company works, particularly when it comes to leadership. A pair of
studies from 2007 and 2016 found that firms
with some form of DEI training did not, in
fact, hire significantly more diverse managers
and actually **decreased** the number of black
female managers.[39]

When you conceptualize diversity as something you add onto an existing monoculture,
chances are high those employees will always
feel as if they were somehow on the outside

of it. And when you treat DEI as a module to complete, you can blind yourself to the way your company fails to integrate its ethos into basic, day-to-day operations.

One woman told us about attending a DEI workshop where the conference room scheduled for the event was not wheelchair accessible. A colleague in a wheelchair was asked to listen in from just outside the door. Another woman recalled a DEI-branded meeting during Black History Month where the only speakers were white. A professor described a DEI committee at her college with no funding and little support from the college's dean. Attendance at DEI faculty workshops was not mandatory and, as such, poorly attended— usually by the same small group of people. The women on the committee performed all of the work. It felt, in the words of one committee member, like "functional window dressing."

Stories in this vein are everywhere. They aren't just anecdotal blunders. They're evidence of a holistic misconceptualization of DEI, in which trainings and metrics ultimately function as a panacea for white guilt instead of a blueprint for enduring cultural change. So long as companies continue to approach diversity within this framework, they'll continue to waste time, money, and employee patience. The shift to remote and flexible work won't solve the problem entirely—not even close. But it can begin to disassemble structures that have long felt immovable and start to build new, unexpected, more inclusive ones in their place.

Before the pandemic year, Stephanie Nadi Olson would regularly encounter this sort of attitude in her meetings with huge companies—sprawling ad agencies, tech giants, retail conglomerates—that were attempting to grapple with their "DE&I problem."

"Right before lockdown, my last business trip was to meet with two tech companies," she said. "And I told them, 'You cannot look at me and say you care about having a diverse, world-class organization, and **also** say that everyone who works for you has to move to Seattle.'"

When Olson gave companies that advice pre-COVID, their eyes would glaze over or they'd nod politely and do nothing. But the combination of the pandemic and the renewed call for substantive corporate action when it comes to social justice and hiring has shifted their position. "COVID has given them permission," Olson told us. "They can see that remote work is possible, and a real way to address their DE&I problem."

Olson's solution almost feels like a cheat code. Her organization, We Are Rosie, works as a twenty-first-century version of a long- and short-term temp firm, connecting more than six thousand workers in the marketing field with companies and agencies across the world. Some of these "Rosies," as employees are called, work for a few weeks on a "pop-up" project at an organization. Some work on political campaigns. Others become long-term placements at legacy organizations, from Bloomberg to Procter & Gamble.

But We Are Rosie is not a traditional subcontractor. It takes the reality of the existing fissured workplace and attempts to stabilize it for its employees. Rosies can be remote and work from wherever they want. They can find actual part-time work that still pays well. They have a robust online support community. And if a company tries to cut corners on their contract, treat them poorly, or change the parameters of the project they've been hired to complete, they have an external advocate whose primary interest is retaining the Rosies, not the client.

The result: a workforce that's more than 90 percent remote, more than 40 percent Black, indigenous, and people of color, or BIPOC, with 99 percent gender pay equity. Some Rosies are moms who spent years struggling to find meaningful work that was legitimately part-time, instead of "twenty hours" that always turned into forty or more. Some are veterans with PTSD that made it difficult for them to commit to full-time work in places outside their own homes. Some live in rural areas they don't want to leave because of the community or their partner's job or the proximity to family. What they share is simple: they've been overlooked or underappreciated by the monocultures in various industries. But that didn't mean their work wasn't valuable.

We Are Rosie combines the positive attributes of "flex"—especially in regard to diversity and inclusion—while protecting against the exploitation and instability that so often accompany it. To do so, the leaders at We Are Rosie have fostered an environment in which their workers feel empowered and supported when they speak up. First, the diversity of the team mirrors the sort of diversity they want to attract among members. Their headquarters is in Atlanta, not on the coasts. The founder is the daughter of a Palestinian refugee; she grew up in a multilingual, multireligion home.

"We're activist oriented in our marketing, and our newsletter and communication is activist oriented," Olson told us. "It creates an environment for Rosies that makes them feel comfortable bringing something to us. It's not uncommon, for example, for someone to have an interview with a client and for them to come back to us and say, hey, because you're so loud about your values, I know that this client or this individual doesn't seem aligned with them."

In several cases, this has meant We Are Rosie passing on a client. "This business is a mechanism for the distribution of access and opportunities and wealth to people who have traditionally not had access to these things," Olson said. "We just always have to do the right thing. There are big companies where we have Rosies, and have to keep having the conversation about whether it's the right thing."

The problem, Olson says, is that a lot of the leaders at these companies are trying, as best they can, to "just ride this shit out." They're spectacularly eager to rubber band back to the way things were before: location-bound, obsessed with presentism, equating leadership material with "constant availability," still thinking of DEI as something that can be solved with a committee. They'd never admit it, but they want to preserve the monoculture. Olson knows she can't change the minds of these sixty-three-year-old white male CEOs. But she can make it very easy to connect their organizations with workers who would otherwise be shut out of them.

There's a dark scenario, of course, in which monoculture is allowed to persist in the office, among full-time employees who show up every day and continue to rise through the ranks, while "diversity" gets subcontracted out to people across the country, or, as has been the case in call centers, executive assistants, and more, across the globe, for far less money. Which means that an organization could hire some Rosies, but what they really need is to be more like We Are Rosie itself: hiring and retaining diverse workers up and down the org chart and engendering trust that they're not just shouting about their values for PR effect but attempting to live them.

We Are Rosie was founded in 2018 and built DEI into its DNA from the beginning. Most companies are battling years, if not an actual century or more, of monoculture. To shift that legacy, you have to survey its contours and crannies, do what For the Culture, an equity and culture shift firm founded by four women of color, calls "See": identify and articulate the current organizational climate so that you can start to think about what shifts are needed.

But a lot of organizations are resistant to actually seeing themselves clearly. "Folks have the best intentions, trying to figure out how to respond to chaos or tension or shifts in culture," Nia Martin-Robinson, one of the founders of For the Culture, told us. "And people think, if I can find this DEI consultant, if I can just get this training for my staff, then everything will be better. So they come to us, and they say, 'We just want the training.' And we say, we need to chat with your staff, we need to figure out the primary cohorts, we need to figure out what you actually **need.**"

"When DEI isn't seen as mission critical, it becomes a sort of mission add-on," Sabrina Lakhani, another For the Culture co-founder, explained. "Training will only get you so far. It doesn't change the inequities."

This type of accounting looks like the stats that opened this chapter: Who holds the leadership positions? What's the difference between the percentages that make up entry-level positions, management, and higher leadership? Ignore the longitudinal data for now: you might have increased "underrepresented" groups in management by 10 percent from last year, but that might have just meant going from zero BIPOC managers to **one.**

Once you've established a baseline, you need to get more granular and detailed in your conception of diversity. Too often executives take the wrong approach here and begin to try to "collect" an employee from every race. Instead, try the following questions: Is everyone in management able-bodied? Do

you have a mix of parents and nonparents?
Straight parents and LGBTQ+ parents? Is
the majority of your workforce from one
generation? What percentage graduated from
Ivy League schools? From HBCUs? Maybe
you've upped the number of women in the
C-suite. But are all of those women white?

The point isn't just upping your diversity
metrics for the annual report or to fulfill some
consultancy-approved metric. It's also not
trying to perfectly match every person with
a manager who has a similar background or
life experience. The point is continuing to
dilute the sort of monoculture that makes it
so difficult for hires to thrive. Which means,
in many cases, relinquishing ideas of what
the office should look like and how it should
operate. As Martin-Robinson points out,
companies are often eager to transform but
incredibly resistant to thinking of that transformation as **letting go**—of old hierarchies,
old pathways to power, old understandings
of what productivity should look like.

Getting rid of the monoculture isn't just
about hiring or promoting people. It's about
figuring out how to organizationally shift the
locus of power and control away from those

who've had it, without question, for so long. This is, in a sense, a radical change when it comes to power dynamics inside companies, and the process will likely create some sort of tension. But it's wrong to think of these changes one-dimensionally—as a power grab, or an overthrow of an old regime. That kind of thinking is zero-sum, destined to fail, and not how inclusion actually works.

Getting rid of the monoculture sounds like a deletion, but it's actually an addition. Inclusion means adding voices, which is precisely where the process derives its power and value. Diversity and inclusion aren't about ripping all status and privilege from one group and conferring it to another. They're about balance.

It's not just We Are Rosie, after all, that's able to recruit monoculture castoffs. It's "distributed" companies like Doist, which has employees in thirty countries across the world and a 97 percent retention rate, because the job descriptions are legitimately flexible and don't require workers to show up every day in an office. It's organizations like the 19th, which understood that the only way to recruit journalists who could make their coverage truly intersectional was to allow them to live in and cover the communities they called home. If you legitimately cast your net wider, you're going to get more fish eager to swim into it.

But to keep them around, you also have to keep illuminating—and dismantling—the monoculture. That means considering all the unspoken norms that ossified around the culture that was: expectations for work socialization, how to solicit advice, how to climb the organizational hierarchy. Many of these ideas have been so thoroughly normalized that unless you've struggled to fit within them, it's difficult to see just how exclusionary they can feel.

Offices, for example, are naturally social. And while that's not necessarily a negative quality, the social rhythms of many American workplaces—even the most progressive ones—tend to have vestigial elements of the predominantly white, predominantly male, and middle-class workforce of the organization man era. Socializing, especially after work, is often centered on alcohol and

caters to workers who don't have care obligations and are adept at or comfortable with
small talk.

Take the example of Helen, who told us,
eight months into the pandemic, that she'd
never been happier at work. As an employee
at a Bay Area tech start-up, she found that
her work didn't change very much once the
pandemic hit. The transition was more seam-
less than expected. What did change, though,
was her relationship to the company's culture.

"I'm a total introvert, and just much more
comfortable this way," Helen said. Before
the pandemic, she struggled with certain in-
person office tasks and interactions. Unlike
more gregarious co-workers, she worried that
she perhaps seemed aloof. Worse, there was
the nagging concern that she wouldn't be
recognized or come to mind. To prevent
being potentially left behind, she attended
after-work functions she hated, missing out
on precious time with her family in order to
have awkward conversations. And for what?

The company was using post-work functions to provide the connective tissue that
management should have provided. She was
continuously bending herself toward her

company's idea of culture, and the contortions were exhausting. But after the pandemic sent everyone home from the office, her company's culture started to bend toward **her.** Instead of attending an anxiety-inducing, stilted meeting, Helen was able to participate virtually in team discussions. She began to feel less guarded. Instead of second-guessing each proposal or question, she built up small reserves of confidence. She started leading more in nonwork conversations.

She became active in a Slack channel her office started for working moms, which was programmed to prompt participants every Thursday to respond with how they're doing by posting a GIF. "Sounds silly, right? Like it wouldn't work. But it's amazing," she said. "It's this wonderful thread of moms. And it's funny and it's emotional and it really has turned into something greater than what we thought. It's a genuine way for me to have a personal connection with people I didn't know that doesn't require live, face-to-face interaction."

In our early days at our previous employer, the social culture mainly revolved around full days staring at a computer screen followed by late evenings at the bar. The informal outings were mostly impromptu and by no means mandatory, but in a small company they were invaluable ways to bond with co-workers. As new employees, we learned that after-work gossip over drinks was the only way to figure out what was actually going on at the company, which managers were fickle, who was kind of a creep, and who was on thin ice. Just because it wasn't about work or didn't take place at work doesn't mean it was wholly separate from work.

Those who didn't show up at a crappy bar for overpriced gin and tonics weren't ostracized. But like Helen, they could feel at a disadvantage, or as if they were doing something **wrong,** simply because their personality didn't match the de facto culture. "I am not a fan of the happy hour," Helen's co-worker Sheela told us. "And it's been a really amazing development to find new ways to bring traditionally physical interactions into the virtual space."

Sheela thinks of herself as more extroverted, and she and her colleagues have ordered at-home meal kits and taken group cooking classes over Zoom. They use a Slack tool called Donut, which randomly matches willing participants and schedules a one-on-one meeting for them to talk about anything—work related or not. Some of these ideas can, at least at first, feel artificial or gimmicky, but they're no more or less so than the implicit expectation to meet in a bar after hours, and they're far more inclusive. They're also not a one-to-one replacement: the point isn't to **ban** happy hours; it's to stop making them the most valued mode of connection.

Sheela also appreciates how remote work has helped her juggle the different components of her identity: as a professional, as a mom of two, and as a woman of color. "I always felt so much pressure, wanting to be a mom and fully focused on work and figuring out how to turn those things on and off," she said. "But I found the load is so much lighter working from home. I see it less as work-life balance and more as work-life fluidity."

The monoculture at Helen and Sheela's company had privileged a certain type of in-person, after-work interaction. The pandemic broke that culture down and replaced it—at least partially—with one that helped highlight their strengths. But the shift to remote can also allow other standards, particularly the arbitrary and often very white and very cis-gendered ones of "professionalism," to recede as well.

When the journalist Chika Ekemezie first began interviewing women of color who had made the shift to working from home during the pandemic, she was interested in the ways that remote work liberated black women workers from (white) standards of professionalism in their offices. "I've long been a believer that professionalism is just a synonym for obedience," she wrote. "The less social capital you have, the more you are tethered to professionalism. It's why Mark Zuckerberg can wear the same T-shirt to work while Black women are punished for wearing braids."

Ekemezie echoes the work of the sociologist Cassi Pittman Claytor, who, pre-pandemic, found that black office workers—particularly those at companies with few black employees—often grappled with internalized pressure to groom and conduct themselves as exemplars. "For the sake of their careers, they try to be more 'put together' than their white counterparts and take far more care with their appearance," Claytor observed. "They describe wearing dress pants when their white colleagues are wearing khakis. While they are sure to wear clothing that is always clean and pressed, they describe white colleagues as wearing clothes that are wrinkled or have holes."[40]

But working from home, as Ekemezie put it, "has provided an opportunity for Black women to flourish outside of the expectations of professionalism, simply by nature of not being hypervisible and held to standards that weren't designed for us."[41] Some women told her they'd embraced a less formal wardrobe and less makeup; others felt freer to wear bonnets or wigs on days when they didn't want to spend time on their hair.

Surveys conducted during the first ten months of the pandemic illustrate the complex relationship that some BIPOC employees have to remote work. Data collected by Slack's Future Forum showed that black employees were working longer hours and experiencing higher stress around pressure to perform—a sign of a lack of mutual trust between the employees and the managers. But overall, black employees expressed a 29 percent increase in feelings of satisfaction and belonging working remotely, compared with being primarily in the office. One reason for this, respondents said, was that working from home meant less code switching or pressure to modulate their behavior for a boss or co-worker.

As workers' "offices" moved into their homes, though, some began to feel standards of professionalism extend to judgments about personal spaces.[42] What do my books, my art, my clutter communicate about my competence as a worker? Who's able to "professionalize" their home spaces for remote appearances, and who's trying to angle the camera so that colleagues can't tell they're Zooming from their bedroom? Which employees feel empowered to say, "Screw it, I don't care what my background is," and who is spending outsize time thinking about it?

The less privilege and power you have in an organization, the more these things matter. If you, personally, don't feel that they matter, chances are high you're observing from a place of stability or power—a place, as Ekemezie put it, with a lot of social capital. In a roundtable discussion six months into the pandemic, Tamara Mose, a professor of sociology at Brooklyn College and the director of DEI at the American Sociological Association, purposefully set up her work space so that her background was a blank white wall: she didn't want her home surroundings, and what they might have seemed to communicate about her, to become part of her interactions with students and colleagues.

But not everyone has access to a blank wall. One easy solution: standardize Zoom backgrounds, playful or serious, as the way you do remote work. Allow workers to turn their cameras off in scenarios in which face-to-face communication isn't necessary. And continue to rethink when face-to-face communication **is** necessary. Embracing remote work can help break down the monoculture, but only if you remain vigilant to the ways that it can also reproduce it. Until you can recognize that, efforts at creating a truly inclusive work culture will continue to fail.

Inclusivity cannot stop at happy hour alternatives. Understanding and attending to the needs of people with different abilities, different home lives, different work styles—all of it is part of the work of breaking the monoculture. The disabled community has been waiting for companies to wake up to this need for **years,** while its members have advocated for more truly flexible work options. But now that they've been thrust on the workforce at large, it's time to actually understand all the ways "accommodations" actually work.

Steven Aquino has been covering the technology industry from California for the last eight years. Before that, he was a preschool teacher, but his cerebral palsy made it difficult to meet the physical needs of his students, day in and day out. He looked for something he could do, ideally from home, that would be less physically taxing. He found it in writing and reporting.

That shift to working from home "really changed who I am," Aquino said. "I'm not always so tired anymore. Because I'm not so exhausted, and hurting, and thinking about it all the time, I've been able to concentrate on doing work I enjoy and take pride in." Working from home also helped with Aquino's social anxiety, which was exacerbated by his stutter. Still, the rhetoric of the current moment and the opportunities of flexible work have felt, in his words, disorienting. "We're in a society where diversity and inclusion is a big subject right now," he said. "And it's inspiring to see. But it isn't evenly distributed. We talk about inclusion, and then people like me are always off to the side, way over there."

"It's been hard to hear people saying, 'Oh my God, I've been trapped at home and I've had to change my entire life and I'm stuck with my kids and I've had to learn Zoom!'" Aquino told us. "I sit here and think, 'Yeah, it **is** hard. You're finally seeing what people like me have had to do.'" Members of the disabled community have spent years trying to force, plead, sue, or kindly request workplaces to become more accessible. And **now** people are complaining that remote tech is bad and no one knows how to manage boundaries?

The disability advocate and inclusion consultant Andraéa LaVant spends a lot of time trying to communicate a very basic message: having a disabled person on your team isn't a **cost** but a **benefit.** "It's going to benefit everyone, because we see life through a different lens," LaVant said. "And if we add other intersectional lenses, well, me as a black disabled woman, you're going to get a whole different perspective."

"Companies think that accommodations have to be expensive," LaVant continued, "even though the average accommodation, before the pandemic, was less than $500 a person. But they still think **extra.** They think physical accommodation. If you ask for something out of the norm, or out of the standard of what has already been supplied, they assume you're going to cost them a lot of money."

But what's happened with the pandemic has proven just how straightforward inclusivity can actually be. It often means expanding the standards for able-bodied people and adopting components of universal design. Take, for example, the conferences and networking events from the pandemic year, all of which were moved online, made **accessible,** in other words, to people who often could not attend them for whatever reason in the past, because of either mobility issues, care demands, location, or cost. Sure, they might not feel as intimate or exclusive. But that's the **point.** Actual accessibility means letting

go of bullshit arguments whose ultimate purpose is preserving the status quo. Is something
lost in our interactions when they move out
of the physical world and online? Likely, yes.
But that loss dominates the conversation at
the expense of what so many, especially those
previously unable to participate, gain.

Universal design—in physical offices, in remote tech, in the way we conceive of communication—is the anti-monoculture. It's not as
expensive as people fear; it's not as disruptive
as people imagine. But it requires everyone
involved believing that the more you expand
the number of people you can allow at the
table, the more you actually **value** those people, the better, as an organization, that you'll
be. Better at understanding the broad base
of people that your organization serves, in
whatever capacity, but also better at reducing
employee turnover, and better at fostering
creativity and collaboration.

"Who doesn't benefit from a captioned
meeting or a transcript?" LaVant asked. "It's
not just helpful for a deaf person, or someone
who has a neuro-cognitive disability. There
are **so many** benefits to universal design in
physical workplaces. I mean, why do you

think so many people want to use the disabled stall? It's **better.**"

Some companies have already figured out what it feels like, building a diverse, equitable, and inclusive culture—either from scratch or on the rubble of the industrial monoculture that preceded it. Their argument, like LaVant's, is pretty simple. It's just **better.**

You're Not a Family

Valerie is an Australian expat, currently living on the outskirts of London, who found her way to nonprofit work after a toxic experience in the corporate world. She currently works as a fundraiser for a nonprofit organization that does significant outreach work in the community. She enjoys her job, because, in her words, "I can see what is achieved through the money I raise." But Valerie's previous experience in the corporate world taught her the necessity of maintaining distance between her work and her identity, which requires pushing against the culture of her company.

"Like every arts and charity organization,

there's a real stated culture that we're a family and we're all working together to achieve something," she told us. "And like every other organization, what that means in real terms is that you're expected to push yourself and you end up overworked."

Chera, who's a professor in Virginia, has endured similar messaging from her university, which "describes itself as being like a family," which usually just means expecting them to do more with less, while "highly competent people are being consistently burdened with extra work and underperformers slide by." Shelby, who works at an architectural firm in Texas, said that her company likes to talk about how its people are its biggest asset and, of course, that they're "like family." "I think we're a somewhat dysfunctional family, if that," she said. "We're still learning how not to be an old boys' club."

The problem isn't that these companies are wrong in calling their employees "family." Many of these organizations are evoking, reproducing, and incentivizing relationships that feel **familial.** But family relationships can just as easily be manipulative, passive-aggressive, and endlessly confusing. Family members can be racist, exploitative, sexist, transphobic, and emotionally abusive, but because they're **family,** it's often considered impolite, or uncivil, to confront them about the very real injuries they do to others. As the comedian Kevin Farzad put it on Twitter, "If an employer ever says 'We're like family here' what they mean is they're going to ruin you psychologically."

Don't mistake us: families can be loving, compassionate, and endlessly supportive. So, too, can the companies that aspire to behave like them. But you already have a family, chosen or otherwise. And when a company uses that rhetoric, it is reframing a transactional relationship as an emotional one. It might feel enticing, but it is deeply manipulative and, more often than not, a means to narrativize paying people less to do more work. Family evokes not just a closeness but a devotion and a lasting bond, infused with sacrifice: **family comes first.**

Treating your organization as a family, no matter how altruistic its goals, is a means of breaking down boundaries between work and life, between paid labor and the personal. When you're assaulted by powerful feelings of familial obligations from all sides—your **actual** family, but also your manager and your colleagues—it's all the more difficult to prioritize. And in these situations, your actual family, which is often more forgiving, more malleable, and more attuned to your needs, will always suffer.

The rhetoric of "workplace family" has developed over the course of the last half century, but is often meant to evoke a bygone, romanticized notion of a simpler way to do business. Dr. Sarah Taber, a crop consultant who has worked in farming for more than twenty years, argues that the business of agriculture has helped perpetuate the false stereotype of the family business by portraying family farms as an agrarian, utopian ideal. "We're sold this idea that, sure, life may be screwed up, but if we can just get back to the old ways, we'd be saved and that, somehow, offices are responsible for the death of work-life balance," she told us. "That's just not true."

In reality, Taber argues, family farms are just as hierarchical, patriarchal, and exploitative of workers. She points to the historian Caitlin

Rosenthal's book, **Accounting for Slavery,** which traces how early slave plantation farms developed many of the management and accounting practices that still structure corporate life. The early agrarian economy was ruthless. It was also a family business, and the abolition of slavery didn't magically destroy the power imbalances present in agriculture, even on family farms. "Working on a family farm means working in somebody's home," she argues. "There are tremendous gaps in wealth and status and power."

Put differently, there is no work environment immune to abuse, even in industries that don't toil under fluorescent lights. The workplace family is billed as a way to engender cohesion and community. But often it works as a means to distract or compel workers to ignore their own exploitation. It's a subtle means of discouraging requests for raises and time off, dismissing complaints about coworker behavior, and deflecting managerial malfeasance. It dissolves the best attempts at boundaries. And it's used to excuse the inexcusable: sexual harassment, massive pay discrepancies, and the enduring whiteness of management. You can and should cultivate a workplace where people feel supported and valued. But you cannot be a family.

So how do you break that dynamic? Distance and boundaries. This is what the genuinely flexible work future can provide: a means to separate yourself from your workplace, and the space to cultivate and grow a personality, relationships, and community outside the labor you do for pay. Organizations of every size and shape are always trying to figure out the most desirable, most effective perks their budgets allow, when the easiest one is right there in front of them. They can give their employees the immeasurable gift of a schedule and flexibility that will permit them a world away from work and lift the psychological burden of that second family from their shoulders.

A healthy work culture creates the circumstances for all employees to do their very best work. But a sustainable, resilient one understands and eagerly invites them to have lives outside it.

3

Technologies of the Office

Back in the early 1990s, the Japanese steel company Nippon decided to get into the computing market. Instead of developing a desktop model to compete with the industry giants IBM and Apple, it opted to compete in the newly established laptop market. The dimensions of the Librex 386SX Notebook were about the same as a laptop today, but it was two inches thick. It weighed six and a half pounds. Like a lot of laptops during this time, its screen was a bit wonky: it boasted sixteen shades of gray, but you never quite knew what the screen was going to do when you opened it. Its list price: $3,299—just over $6,100 in 2021 dollars.

Who could spend that much on a personal computer? Most families were buying desktops to be shared by the household, so the laptop was marketed straight at the coveted business market. In one Librex ad, a forty-something-year-old sits in an Adirondack chair in Dockers, a T-shirt, and ball cap. The outline of a mountain hovers in the sun-setting distance. In his right hand, he holds a hulking cell phone. And then, balanced on the left of his chair, there's that cinder block of a Librex. It didn't matter that the battery lasted just ninety minutes or that it then took a full five hours to recharge. The Business Dad of the Future was ready to get to work.

At that point, working from home, then referred to as telecommuting, had been on the rise for more than a decade. In 1975, a full third of the 2.6 million people considered "working from home" were farmers.[1] By 1994, an estimated 7 million Americans were telecommuting, and companies like Hewlett-Packard employed an "alternative work options manager." **PC Magazine** reported that 50 percent of prospective telecommuters had already purchased their own PCs, or planned to buy modems and software to facilitate the transition.[2]

But the slow spread of the home computer began to change things, at least for those with the funds to sit in the first-class cabin of an airplane, which is where a 1990s ad for the Kodak Diconix envisioned the user of its mobile printer. "The sight of a passenger hunched over in an airplane seat, pecking away at a computer, no longer draws stares," the editor of **PC Magazine** wrote in the introduction of an issue dedicated to laptops, which included a foldout "Road Warrior's Guide," complete with the phone numbers in major cities to dial to connect to CompuServe (a.k.a. the internet) and basic instructions for logging on to a bulletin board system and email services.[3]

These workers could transition from the office to home, from home to the hotel on a business meeting. But as we discussed in the previous chapters, this sort of "flex" has a dark side: the ability to take your work anywhere means the ability for work to infiltrate all corners of your life, including those, like the wilderness, that previously repelled it. The Librex ad with the Adirondack chair looks quite a bit different when you look at it through this lens: Business Dad isn't liberated from the office; he's trapped by it. He just happens to be out in nature.

This is what happened to us when we moved to Montana, when the time we used to spend commuting into Manhattan—which we thought we'd allocate to hikes and kayaking and cross-country skiing—was simply absorbed by **more work.** And if you are reading this book, chances are you are living in the paradox of Business Dad: stuck in a technological purgatory, caught between its utopian promises and its dystopian perils. Every one of us now keeps a tiny supercomputer in our pockets that would make the Librex's hard drive melt with jealousy. We can pull the internet down from out of the sky in even the most remote location. Work can find us in every moment: on the subway. On the chairlift. On the running trail. In the bathroom. It is a golden era of connectivity and, by extension, **efficiency.**

By constructing elegant solutions to enduring annoyances—say, an app that monitors traffic patterns to get you the quickest route home, or a program that finally tames the jungle of your in-box—our devices purport to chip away at the messy inefficiencies of everyday life. Increased efficiency means more of the most precious commodity: time. But time for what, exactly? Usually, to do **more work.**

Despite the miraculous technological affordances in our life, few of them have liberated us as advertised. And nowhere is that truer than our working lives, where today's office tech has absorbed all of the formalities, anxieties, and oppressive mundanity of corporate life and ported them into every corner of our lives. The magical ability to see your co-workers face-to-face from anywhere in the world morphs into Zoom fatigue. The lively, collaborative instant messaging app gives way to an always-on surveillance tool that lives on company servers forever. A shared digital calendar evolves into a way for others to demand our time and attention until there's none left for ourselves. The more efficient we become, the more overwhelmed we feel.

This paradox is not new. For as long as people have been laboring, new technologies have promised to streamline how and where work gets done. Some are implemented with best intentions; others have been cruelly or cynically applied. But almost all have un-intended consequences, even when they're not digital. From the open office plan to the Aeron chair, new ideas about the physical de-sign of the office have reshaped not only our work environment but also our relationship to work. Innovations that were supposed to make the office more **humane** get co-opted, put through cost-efficiency calculators, and end up making the workplace feel even more like an overdesigned cage.

Part of the problem is the obsession with thrift: the best, most inclusive design **costs money and time,** resources that many com-panies are hesitant to part with. But even the sprawling, no-expenses-spared campuses of Silicon Valley share a fundamental flaw with the mundane fluorescent-lit cubicle. With a few utopian exceptions, all of these designs have been oriented toward efficiency and productivity. Not in the service of less work, but in the hopes of fostering a life enveloped by it.

In truth, office technology—and the cult of efficiency in which it is breathlessly adopted—have never been about getting all of our work done in less time. At least not since the dreaming days of the early twentieth century, when economic theorists and labor advocates saw technology as a way to finally achieve the thirty-hour, twenty-hour, even ten-hour workweek.[4] That dream was devoured long ago. Instead, the ever-accelerating goal of office tech and design has been to clear space in someone's life, then immediately seed it with the potential for more productivity.

This is why our current moment feels so full of possibility and so incredibly treacherous. We're in efficiency purgatory, caught between all the liberating and oppressive effects of office tech and design. Even from the stifling gloom of the pandemic, we could see the faint outline of a future that makes good on office technology's grand promise: to actually free us not only from the commute or the tyranny of the open office plan but from the creep of work into every inch of our personal lives.

It's an alluring vision: What if our tools could actually, legitimately, make us work **less**? And what if the time we regained from stamping out inefficiencies was truly ours?

Office technology and design are not

essentially evil. But we have to commit to using those tools to add dimensionality to our lives, instead of further flattening them for the ease of our jobs. In order to realize that vision, we need to understand all the ways that tech and design have successfully beguiled us in the past. We have to know how to spot when a flashy technology, a gorgeous office setup, or a new way of communicating is actually just an invitation for **more work** in new camouflage. We must begin to see productivity and efficiency as a means to an actual end, not a means to **more work.**

The stakes of this moment are high. If we aren't vigilant, we risk squandering this opportunity for a genuine shift in the way we orient ourselves to work, and the tools that facilitate remote work will become even more robust apparatuses of surveillance and control. As with the tech and design shifts of the past, the degradation of these tools won't be readily apparent. There will be no cackling executive rubbing their hands together greedily behind closed doors. It'll just feel like our brightest hopes fading to the slow grind of one long endless Wednesday.

We aren't doomed to repeat the mistakes

of the past. But if we do, we may very well be unable to reverse them. The final, flimsy barrier between our personal lives and our work lives, already buckling under the pressure, will come crashing down. All the worst, mind-numbing parts of working from home during the pandemic will be our everyday reality. If that sounds like hell, it's time to arm yourself against it: with the knowledge of how we corrupted the tech and design of the past, and an actual plan for how to avoid them moving forward.

In 1981, while working on a book about the future of work, a young Harvard business professor named Shoshana Zuboff visited an old pulp mill. The mill's bleach plant had recently been redesigned and outfitted with state-of-the-art technology, including digital sensors and monitors that fed signals to a shiny, new centralized control room, stocked with computers whirring away on brand-new microprocessors. To an outsider, it was all very impressive. But, as Zuboff quickly learned, the workers despised it.

Their primary object of scorn were the

doors. In order to keep the considerable heat and potentially noxious fumes of the bleaching room from entering the control room, the factory had installed an air-locking system: push a button, step in, and the sliding glass door closes behind you. The next set of doors won't open until the other is shut.

The new doors offered an added layer of safety. But for the workers, the extra steps were tedious and frustrating. For years, they'd been able to move from room to room as they pleased. So they took matters into their own hands: every day, they plowed through the corridor and wedged their hands through a rubber seal that ran down the center of the door. With the mighty heft of their shoulders, they brute forced the door open. The door eventually just stopped sealing.

For Zuboff, the workers' reaction was "a living metaphor" of worker ambivalence toward automation. "They want to be protected from toxic fumes," she wrote in her 1988 book, **In the Age of the Smart Machine,** "but they simultaneously feel a stubborn rebellion against a structure that no longer requires either the strength or the know-how lodged in their bodies."[5]

What Zuboff observed wasn't just the casual frustration of a few blue-collar workers but a defining anxiety amid an age of massive technological change. The nature of work was undergoing a fundamental reorganization. Suddenly things that had been resistant or impossible to measure became quantifiable, analyzable, transformed into streams of data and reports. Armed with that data, businesses could see, often for the first time, what they were wasting, opportunities for more efficiency, and how employees were actually allocating their time.

In theory, all this new data might have made a worker's job better. Hands-on activities like mixing chemicals or manually cranking valves in a pulp plant are physically taxing; doing them from the safety of a control room would be easier for everyone. But automation had the unforeseen consequence of turning their jobs from something tangible—with rhythms of touch and feel—into an abstraction. Or, as Zuboff put it, it "felt like being yanked away from a world that could be known because it could be sensed."[6]

Technology robbed workers of what had been highly valued physical knowledge about a job: they knew the precise way to unstick a gear, how a finicky gauge always reads five degrees higher than it is, or the sound a machine makes when something's about to break. That knowledge, accumulated over years on the job, had served as leverage over management: if the company refused to come to an agreement with their union, it would take the company weeks, if not years, to find workers with the skills to replace them. The threat of a strike had real power, because workers' knowledge was precious.

Sensors and computers took the craft behind that work, quantified it, and automated it—a process often referred to as de-skilling. The worker's knowledge was made obsolete. At the same time, managers were newly vested with quantitative authority over their employees' work lives. They held the data and the ability to wield it in accordance with their desires, which meant they also held the power. In this way, technological innovation wrested the most valuable elements of workers' lives away from them and handed them straight to management. No wonder they resented it.

Of course, executives and big businesses

framed the story quite differently. These tools were not just ways to juice productivity and profits; they were also good for the worker. Less manual labor meant less strenuous and often less dangerous labor. For some workers, doing backbreaking work in mills or smelting plants, it was a genuine reprieve. But it also introduced new problems: a skilled machinist, talking to the MIT researcher Harley Shaiken in 1985, said the experience of operating a computerized machine tool made him feel like a "rat in a cage." Another worker, tasked with operating a robotic welding system, said, "You don't have time to light a cigarette. I'd take my old job hand welding any day."[7] A third employee, forced to monitor a numerical control, or NC, system, said, "I'm a worker, not a sitter. I like to be kept busy. My day goes by faster, my mind is more active. You get a little weak-minded on the NC."

Automated work, Shaiken found, was not always more efficient, nor was it necessarily more reliable. But it was sold to workers as the only route forward. When General Electric began modernizing a dishwasher factory in the early 1980s, adding an "electronic nervous system" that oversaw a complex maze of robots and "24 computer lieutenants at critical points on the factory floor," they met with union reps, foremen, and other workers to communicate the same argument: modernize or we'll all be out of a job. "Companies are not going to survive in the marketplace without this kind of equipment," a senior VP at GE told **The New York Times.** "The future demands it."[8]

Across the manufacturing industry, automation was treated as a sort of magic bullet: a means of gaining back the ground American companies had lost to the global market in general and Japan in particular. Automation would increase productivity, and productivity would provide the solution to all American woes. That idea extended to the office, which over the course of the twentieth century had come to be understood as its own form of factory—just one that produces paper and moves it around from desk to desk.

Back in 1925, William Henry Leffingwell, a disciple of the Frederick Taylor school of optimization, had drafted plans for the "straight-line flow of work." He redesigned the office into a sort of paper assembly line so workers could move documents "without the necessity of the clerk even rising from his seat."[9] The overarching principle was this: every time a clerk left his seat, he lost precious seconds of productivity. But these Taylorist reforms of the office were met with the same resistance as in the factory: workers hated them. Other efficiency efforts were easier to sell, especially those cloaked in the language of technological advancement: elevators, fluorescent lighting, movable walls, and air-conditioning, popularized over the course of the twentieth century, were all means of upping productivity. Same for the open office, which was first proposed by a pair of German brothers, Eberhard and Wolfgang Schnelle, in 1958. In place of rows of desks and corner offices, the Schnelles saw dynamic clusters and movable partitions: an office landscape, or **Bürolandschaft.**

When the idea for **Bürolandschaft** was first introduced, it felt scandalous: the same way, say, working from home would later feel in the early 1980s. When the renowned interior designer John F. Pile first encountered the plans in the pages of an esteemed architectural journal, he described finding them "so shocking in character as to make me assume that I was in the presence of some British joke."[10] But **Bürolandschaft** was designed to deal with an organization problem endemic to German offices: staff were arranged in totally illogical ways, crammed into rooms with people in different departments, all doing different types of tasks. Employees would distract each other, compete with each other for no reason, and when they needed to meet with the other people on their team, they'd be forced to go to another floor or even another building. "In such a setting," Pile wrote, "needed communication becomes slow and cumbersome, competition and rivalry thrive, and all the kinds of wastefulness and stupidity one associates with bureaucracy become commonplace."[11]

The setup of the **Bürolandschaft** was designed to follow the natural lines of communication, decrease inefficiencies, and, as an added bonus, cost less: no real hierarchies meant no expensively furnished offices for management. One huge room was far easier to heat, cool, light, and electrify. Yet the design, however well-meaning in theory, was a disaster in practice. Many companies embraced the cost-shaving elements for the "gang" employee spaces—which were loud and antagonistic to anything approximating concentration or privacy—but balked at actually eliminating offices for higher-ups. They were desperate to decrease costs, but they were also fiercely protective of the status quo.

In Germany, Scandinavia, and the Netherlands, the experience of working in an open office design was so miserable that in the 1970s local worker councils effectively mandated their removal. But not in the United States, where, as the architecture critic James S. Russell notes, Americans "characteristically reworked" the plan into "something cheaper and more ordered." The "curvilinear informality" of the Schnelles' design was formalized into workstations with shelves, cabinets, and dividing panels—what would eventually devolve into the cubicle.[12] (The development, like so many in American history, was facilitated by the tax code: The Revenue Act, passed in 1962, allowed for a seven percent tax credit on property with a "useful life" of eight years. You couldn't deduct the cost of a fixed wall. But a partition? Go for it.)

· · ·

A cubicle offered the **illusion** of privacy but with little of the reality. You can still hear the conversations of your neighbors; managers still have access to a full view of your current work; you were still hundreds of feet from the nearest window or source of natural light. But these offices weren't built to make employees' experience of work **better** or more bearable. They were meant to match the demands of the "flexible" organization, poised to expand and contract to meet market demands, shedding and accumulating employees as needed.

For Frank Duffy, the author of one of the first books to introduce "office landscaping" to the United Kingdom, the felted gray cubicle represented "the equal distribution of misery within which anyone and everyone can be replaced in any order and at any time."[13] The cubicle costs so little, bears so few traces of its occupant, and is so easy to dismantle: the perfect structure for an economic mindset and an attitude toward labor in which the workforce was increasingly figured as disposable.

The open office was celebrated and implemented with a mind toward worker efficiency: a means of facilitating communication and undamming the flows of information, decreasing conflict and competition in the office. And as Nikil Saval points out in **Cubed,** even the bastardized American version did make some forms of communication easier; you could still talk, after all, even with the sounds of the office in the background. But in so doing, it made concentration and contemplation nearly impossible. "In the rush to open-plan the world" in the 1970s and '80s, Saval writes, "some crucial values for the performance of work were lost."[14] Including, somewhat ironically, the very efficiency and productivity that these designs were intended to create: a 1985 study of offices found that levels of privacy were a primary predictor of job satisfaction **and** job performance.[15] Designing with a mind toward efficiency, in other words, produced increasingly inefficient workers.

When you implement a new office design with an eye only to what it **facilitates** and not to what is **lost,** you will simply create a new set of problems. Same for short-term strategies to cut tax burdens or real estate footprints: if a technology promises to cut costs quickly and significantly, chances are high that there will be perhaps as-yet-imperceptible effects of those cuts, and they will be absorbed by your already overburdened workforce. New office technologies, including the spaces where we expect employees to work and that determine how they interact with people while doing that work, are never simply "good" or "bad." But their effects have never been, and will never be, neutral.

When it came to the ideals of productivity, office design could promise to do only so much. The most skilled typists, even in the most scientifically arranged office, could type only so many words per minute. As the day went on, precision levels went down, and it took longer and longer to type an error-free document. But the word processor—coupled with the Xerox machine, the Dictaphone, and the office printer—promised to liberate efficiency goals from human limitations.

Across the office world, workers were promised that these new technologies would make their lives easier. And yes, it was great not to have to type the same letter in triplicate. But many of the machines were situated in spaces that simply weren't designed for them: mimeographs in rooms without ventilation, word processors in spaces without proper lighting. Thousands of workers reported migraines, severe eyestrain, cataracts, bronchitis, and allergies.[16] Automation was literally making office workers sick.

But they were also mentally miserable. Shoshana Zuboff spent hours interviewing workers in industrial settings for **In the Age of the Smart Machine,** but she also spent significant time with clerical workers. Like their blue-collar counterparts, the people she interviewed were adrift as the result of the fast technological changes of their jobs. Dentist office employees and insurance claims workers both saw their jobs, which were once social in nature, turn into glorified data entry positions. Cubicles visually walled them off from their colleagues, turning co-workers into an annoying buzz of wafting voices and telephone rings and keyboard clacks. As the job increasingly tethered them to their desks, they became more estranged from their managers, who in turn began to view them as drones.

"We used to be able to see each other and

talk," one insurance claims representative told Zuboff. "Sure, sometimes we just talked about what we were going to make for dinner, but we always worked while we talked." Another representative described the feeling of losing touch with the outside world: "The only reality we have left is when we get to talk to a customer." Indeed, the most striking part of her reporting comes when Zuboff asks the workers to draw themselves in their new jobs. Their illustrations were grim and childlike: "chained to desks, surrounded by bottles of aspirin, dressed in prison stripes, outfitted with blinders, closely observed by their supervisors, surrounded by walls, enclosed without sunlight or food, bleary-eyed with fatigue, solitary, frowning."[17]

But as was the case on the factory floor, few people listened to the people tasked with actually using the technology. Leaders often attributed worker reticence to initial fears of losing their jobs: there would be a breaking-in period, but then employees would get to know the technology and see how great it was, and everyone would gradually embrace the new normal. Executives brandished stats showing that automation didn't lead to layoffs—just higher productivity. America would be competitive again; why should anyone be afraid?

Workers might have been initially scared that they would be made obsolete. But the animating anxiety concerned the experience of the work itself and how effectively the gospel of productivity blinded leaders to all other concerns. In a 1980 episode of **The MacNeil/Lehrer Report**, the journalist Lewis Silverman questioned a lawyer who'd recently implemented automating technologies at his firm if he ever worried about how it had "depersonalized" the experience of work.

"I don't think that's in any way a factor in this type of automation," the lawyer replied. "I think what we will see is that as the ability to produce documents more quickly increases and frees us to do other things, we will find that rather than doing as many documents in half the time—and then have half the time to do nothing—we will be producing twice as many documents as we did in the past, and working on twice as many transactions." Productivity, in other words, increases output, and potential profits, but it doesn't make the clerks' jobs easier. It doesn't give them more time to rest, or increase their pay. It just sets new standards for the sheer amount of work they should be accomplishing in a given day. The benefits flow in one direction: away from the worker.

For a counterargument, Silverman turned to Karen Nussbaum, the head of the National Association of Working Women, the organization of office workers previously known as 9to5. She quickly listed off the arguments that automation had made workers feel as if they had less control over their work, less connection with their co-workers, and that the technology was affecting their health. Part of the problem was the machines themselves, she said, but an even bigger issue was the productivity they required: when you're operating at peak efficiency, there's no space for any of the human parts of the job. What's more, automation was normalizing doing more work for less pay.

But again, leadership didn't see it that way. Jack Walsh, then director of telecommunications and office services at Avon, explained that some secretaries had felt empowered by the new tech, and even gained additional skills. The company conducted a study that found that 10 percent of a manager's work could be delegated to a secretary and that the secretary's role was thus "enhanced."

Nussbaum's reply was cutting. "Technology can enhance the work, but that's not what's happening for the large majority of office workers," she said. "I'd be interested to know whether Mr. Walsh increased the pay of any of those secretaries who are now doing the work of some of those managers." This was, and remains, the dystopian reality underlying the redesign and automation of the office. Its mandate is never "You figured out how to do your tasks more efficiently, so you get to spend less time working." It is always "You figured out how to do your tasks more efficiently, so you must now do more tasks, for the same pay."

As workers, we've always been assisted by technologies in some form. Those tools have become more sophisticated with time, but as their users we remain stubbornly human, and there are limits to the productivity that any body or mind can sustain. In the early 1980s, workers began to brush up against those limits but were driven into survival mode by the continued volatility of the American economy. It didn't matter if the office sucked, if it made you feel ill, if it made you resent your co-workers. Attempts to organize, like those led by Nussbaum and Working Women, ran headfirst into a massive wave of antilabor sentiment and legislation. It felt as if there were no recourse, no way to push back. And so a whole generation of employees internalized their employers' quest for productivity as their own, settled for less pay and less stability, and got back to work.

In 1983, three employees at Chiat/Day advertising dreamed up an idea that would become one of the most famous Super Bowl ads of all time. A runner, dressed in a tank top bearing a drawing of an Apple Macintosh computer, destroys Big Brother and saves humankind from a future of surveillance and conformity. The ad was hailed as a masterpiece and cemented Chiat's place as one of the most influential ad agencies of the late twentieth century, crafting campaigns that somehow transformed brands as banal as Energizer batteries and the NYNEX White

Pages into ad campaigns that took up occupancy in your brain and refused to leave.

A decade later, the co-founder Jay Chiat had a creative revelation, supposedly while skiing at Telluride, that had nothing to do with an ad campaign. It was time, he decided, for an office revolution. He wanted to get rid of not just cubicles but personal space altogether, in the hopes of creating a space of "creative unrest."[18] In one of the new offices, built in Venice, California, and designed by Frank Gehry, there would be no cubicles, no filing cabinets, no fixed desks. Every employee would check out a PowerBook and portable phone upon arrival and find a place to work for the day. They could even work at home, or at the beach, if they chose: your office could be wherever your mind was.

None of this will sound wild to anyone who's visited a start-up in the last ten years, but at the time Chiat's vision of the first "virtual" office was just as titillating as those original plans for the open office. The receptionist's desk was framed by the outline of bright red lips. A picture of a man peeing led the way to the men's bathroom. The floor was covered in a rainbow of hieroglyphs. For meetings, there was a club room, a student union, a romper room, and a series of conference rooms filled with cars rescued from old Tilt-a-Whirl rides.

At first, the Chiat/Day offices were celebrated as the work of a creative visionary: the Manhattan office, designed by the Italian architect Gaetano Pesce, was hailed by **The New York Times** as "a remarkable work of art."[19] But as with the original open office plan, workers hated it almost immediately. Employees from the time recalled feeling at once rootless and constantly surveilled; desperate for a space to call their own, many began setting up shop in the conference rooms. In response, Chiat would roam the halls, demanding to know if an individual had worked in the same spot the day before. The company had under-anticipated the plan for everyday demands of PowerBooks, and the lines to check them out were interminable. With no place to call their own, employees resorted to using the trunks of their cars as file cabinets.[20] "People panicked because they thought they couldn't function," Chiat later admitted. "Most of it, I felt, was an overreaction. But we should've been more prepared for it."

Chiat sold the company in 1995, and the new owners almost immediately began to soften the most outlandish and unsustainable components of the design. In December 1998, they moved the West Coast offices into a new, equally ballyhooed space in Playa del Rey. The desks were back, and so were the phones, placed in "nests" and "cliff dwellings" divided into "neighborhoods" lined with indoor plants. The message of the office, as **Wired** put it, was "Stay a while. Stay all night. Hell, you can live here. Which makes obvious sense in a business that is fueled by twentysomethings pulling late-nighters."

In hindsight, the Chiat/Day offices anticipated the "hot desk" gang offices of the pre-pandemic present. But Chiat had misunderstood how to actually unroot his workers from their desks and incentivize productivity and creativity. It wasn't through art, or Tilt-a-Whirl cars, or flashy graphic design. You just needed to make them want to be there all the time.

· · ·

Chiat/Day was far from the only company eager to construct an office design that aimed to reflect its iconoclastic mission. If your company was creating truly innovative products, it should follow that it was working out of a truly innovative space. Like the Chiat/Day Venice campus, these environments were designed as competitive advantages: they'd look cool and attract talent, sure, but the spaces, too, would be generative—a perfect mix of socializing, collaboration, and deep focus.

Of course, none of these companies were any less ruthless about productivity demands on the work, and the nature of work was no less transactional. If anything, organizations actually baked more precarity into workers' lives in pursuit of growth and shareholder value. But there was a highly cost-efficient, low-friction way to distract employees from this fact: just group them in inviting environments that fit the company's projected cultural values of "dynamism" and "community." The office, in other words, as city—or, even better yet, as campus.

Back in the 1970s, midwestern corporate

giants like 3M and Caterpillar had designed sprawling, bucolic office parks for their thousands of employees, and early Silicon Valley companies like Xerox famously embraced the campus layout in the 1970s. These early campus environments made economic sense: they allowed companies to abandon costly urban real estate, and their location was easier to sell to prospective employees who planned to make their homes in the suburbs.

But as William Whyte, author of **The Organization Man,** explained, there was a deeper, more subliminal intent to the design, particularly for recent graduates: "The locale shifts; the training continues, for at the same time that the colleges have been changing their curriculum to suit the corporation, the corporation has responded by setting up its own campuses and classrooms," he wrote. "By now the two have been so well molded that it's difficult to tell where one leaves off and the other begins."[21]

Corporate campuses were not quite fortresses, but they were private, guarded, and intended to be as self-sufficient as possible. And like a small liberal arts college campus, their cultures were insular, loyal, and generally easy to control. Their skill at innovation stemmed, at least in part, from the not-so-subtle blurring of work and home life: the corporate campus shaped the organization man, and then the suburbs became, in Whyte's words, "communities made in [the organization man's] image." These workers might not have slept on campus, but office norms extended far beyond the corporate walls, in social structures built to accommodate and reinforce the rhythms of the devoted worker.

The office complexes and campuses of the last thirty years extended this notion even further. They're even more gorgeous and eminently photographable, but they are also expertly designed by cutting-edge architects to be "cohesive communities." The goal is not just productivity but, as the architect Clive Wilkinson put it in his 2019 book, **The Theatre of Work,** something far more aspirational and dignified: in these spaces, "human work may finally be liberated from drudgery, and become inspiring and invigorating."[22]

Wilkinson, who designed Google's 500,000-square-foot Googleplex campus in Mountain View, California, says he had his first epiphany about the office in 1995. While reviewing old studies and surveys about worker habits, he came upon a study that measured how office workers spent their time between 9:00 a.m. and 5:00 p.m. He was immediately struck by just how much "unaccounted" time workers were spending away from their desks—that is, not in meetings or any other explicit work function. But Wilkinson found it hard to believe that all of these workers were taking multi-hour bathroom breaks, or simply leaving the office together. They were still in the office; they were just hanging out in hallways, chatting in foyers, clustering around someone else's desk as the occupant tells a story.

"It blew my mind," he told us. "And it made our team realize that the planning of the office was fundamentally flawed." His realization was straightforward: office design had long revolved around the placement of desks and offices, with the spaces in between those areas treated as corridors and aisles. But that "overemphasis on the desk," as Wilkinson recalled, "had worked to the detriment of working life, trapping us in this rigid formality."

And so he set out to liberate it, shifting the focus of his designs to work that took place **away** from the desk. In practice, this meant designing bleachers and nooks in places that were once poorly lit corridors, and spacing out desk clusters to incentivize more movement among teams. A kinetic office environment, the idea went, could increase spontaneous encounters, which would then spark creativity. The design also allowed for private areas—many with comfy couches and push ottomans to replicate a family room feel—to do deep work, away from the noisy bullpen of desks.

Google's founders, Larry Page and Sergey Brin, were especially fascinated with this new brand of office. In early meetings, Wilkinson recalls that the pair's ideas for design were heavily influenced by their time at Stanford, where engineers tended to gather in small groups and often flocked to far-flung enclaves of the campus for coding binges and study groups. They wanted to merge the traditional office with the university environment, creating a space that would incentivize both collaborative and self-directed work.

Wilkinson thus developed a design whose

unifying goal—like that of a college campus—was self-sufficiency. That meant flexible work spaces, designed to accommodate constantly shifting teams and new projects, but it also meant abundant green spaces, mini-libraries, social hubs, and "tech talk zones," which Wilkinson later described as "areas along public routes . . . where almost continuous seminars and knowledge sharing events would take place."[23]

In service of this continuous knowledge sharing, the Googleplex was outfitted with a staggering array of amenities. Volleyball courts, valets, organic gardens, tennis courts, and soccer fields dot the campus, which also includes a private park for exclusive Google use. Inside the Googleplex, workers have access to multiple fitness centers and massage rooms, as well as multiple cafés, cafeterias, and self-service kitchens. Unlike traditional company cafeterias, where food items are often gently subsidized, everything at Google is free. In 2011, when the company had around thirty-two thousand employees, the food service budget was estimated at around $72 million per year.[24] Since then, Google's workforce has more than quadrupled.[25]

In Wilkinson's recounting, the Googleplex design was meant to allow for "all of your basic work-life needs" to be met within a contained space. As he saw it then, supporting workers with generative, social environments— plus significant perks, like meals and wellness services—was a means to foster true community and sustained creativity. More important, it was a humane, considerate way for companies to treat employees who were working long hours and building products designed to change the world.

Reflecting today, Wilkinson's less sure of that vision. Over the last two decades, his brilliant, innovative designs have rippled through the architecture world, as large-scale tech companies and smaller start-ups alike have cribbed elements of his team's dynamic workplaces for their spaces. And Wilkinson's increasingly aware of the insidious nature of those same perks. "Making the work environment more residential and domestic is, I think, dangerous," he told us in late 2020. "It's clever, seductive, **and** dangerous. It's pandering to employees by saying we'll give you everything you like, as if this was your home, and the danger is that it blurs the difference between home and office."

The danger Wilkinson is describing is, of course, exactly what happened. The new campus design had a profound impact on company culture. Some of that impact was undeniably positive: he created work spaces where people genuinely want to be. But that desire becomes a gravitational pull, tethering the worker to the office for longer and longer, and warping previous perceptions of social norms.

Imagine this scenario: You're an ambitious engineer, a few years out of school. It's easy to get to the office extra early and stay late into the night because you can always get a gourmet dinner, absolutely free, with little effort on your part. During these meals, you often meet with co-workers. You talk about a lot of things, but you mostly talk about work. To blow off steam, you show up at one of the many company gyms for a game of three on three, or you play Frisbee in the company park. When the company brings in an interesting speaker, you attend the lecture; when you're on a code binge, you camp out together in the comfy free-use spaces. When you're done for the day, you grab a beer on campus before riding the company shuttle back home to your apartment in San Francisco, chatting with your friends as you catch up on back emails using the shuttle's WiFi connection.

With time, your colleagues become your closest friends and, with even more time, your **only** friends. It's easier to hang out and have a social life at work, because everyone's just already there. Life feels streamlined, more efficient. Even fun! Sometimes you're just goofing off, killing time, kinda like back in the dorm room in college. Other times you're working together, like those endless nights back in the library. Sometimes it's a hazy hybrid of both, but it's generative nonetheless. It's the new organization-man-style company devotion, only the country club's moved on campus.

While we didn't work for a Big Tech company in Silicon Valley, we both experienced shades of this trajectory while working for a media start-up in New York City in the middle of the second decade of the twenty-first century. As earlyish employees, we quickly fell into the perks that drew us to the office longer. A weekly Thursday afternoon "brews" all hands was capped off by free pizza and then a collective call out to the bars. Quickly, our colleagues became our closest friends (it's not lost on us, of course, that these events are how the two of us eventually met).

The company culture's gravitational pull meant we started dedicating less time to other friends and fledgling nonwork relationships. It was always far easier to transition from the office straight to socializing than somehow planning a meetup halfway across town. We knew all the same people and had all the same conversational shorthand. During happy hours with co-workers, bullshitting could quickly turn into discussions about a work issue. Were we working? Sure. But none of us would have thought to call it that.

We love our old work friends. We've been to their weddings; we're watching their kids grow up; we continue to share our lives with them. Those actual friendships aren't what we regret, and never will be. When we moved away from New York, however, we came to realize how work friendships had functioned as Trojan horses for work to infiltrate and then engulf our lives. These relationships didn't make work-life balance more difficult. Instead, they eclipsed the idea of balance altogether, because work and life had become so thoroughly intertwined that spending most of our waking moments with some extension of our corporation didn't seem remotely odd or problematic. It was just . . . life.

Most white-collar workers don't have the privilege of catered daily meals or sun-drenched atriums arrayed with ergonomic seating for impromptu brainstorming sessions. But just because they can't head to the quad for pickup volleyball doesn't mean they're not similarly trapped by the design and tech of the office. Consider, for a moment, the long history of your in-box.

Email's road to ruin is, like most technologies, paved with good intentions. In 1971, the ARPANET engineer Ray Tomlinson used the now famous @ symbol to direct a message to a very small number of superexpensive networked computers. At the time, it was just a small coding workaround: this was in the early days of answering machines, and there was just no good way to leave a message for someone, especially if they didn't have a secretary or answering service. But leaving a message for a unique user on a computer— maybe that could work.

By the time Tomlinson realized the gravity of what he'd done, just over two decades later, email was in the process of being adopted broadly in the workforce.[26] The pitch for workplace adoption was simple: instead of drowning in a sea of paper, office work could shift to the computer. No more printing or mimeographing by hand or faxing, no more hand delivering. Just push a button and send a message. But instead of dismantling the culture of interoffice memos and correspondence, email simply soaked up all of their formalities, anxieties, and oppressive mundanity, and then made them readily accessible at every moment of the day.

The spread of email led to, well, a whole lot more email. So much that it generated a cottage industry of how-to guides and books with titles like **The Executive Guide to E-mail Correspondence** and **E-mail: A Write It Well Guide.** The authors of these books spend hundreds of pages painstakingly outlining templates for every situation,

like how to send a "request for cooperation" email. In one book there's a chapter
titled "Delicate Situations," which includes
templates for emails on "reassigning fault,"
"request for special treatment," "misplaced
document," and "refusal to participate."[27]
Blueprints for bad habits abound, like this
section from **The Executive Guide to E-mail
Correspondence:** "The message, 'I'll be on
vacation next week . . .' communicates unfa-
vorable news. You're on vacation? Does this
mean you're NOT working? . . . Even when
you're taking the well-deserved break, it's
a good idea not to brag about it. (Or even
mention it.)"[28]

The problem should be familiar by now:
adopt a technology or design for its efficiency
or cost savings—and without thinking
about its holistic effects on the office and its
culture—and you'll end up with an entirely
new set of problems. Email might have been
direct and fast, but it failed, almost immediately, to make good on its promise to "kill"
paper in the workplace. In one study from the
mid-1990s, researchers found that the introduction of email within an organization led

to a 40 percent average increase in paper consumption.[29] As the cognitive and computer
scientists Abigail J. Sellen and Richard H. R.
Harper found in **The Myth of the Paperless
Office,** published in 2001, "It seems much
of the information on the Web needs to be
printed in order for us to read it and make
sense of it."[30]

There was still a glut of paper, in other
words, **and** an increasing glut of email. By the
early twenty-first century, it had become such
a problem that an engineer at Google named
Paul Buchheit attempted to hack together a
fix to save the technology from itself. If you
could effectively **search** your in-box, the
idea went, you could create an entirely new
way of using email: instead of stressing out
over deleting or saving messages, you could
save them forever, creating a massive, readily searchable archive of past correspondence.
Google called the service, which it debuted
in 2004, Gmail and offered each user a free
gigabyte of archive space—a massive amount
of storage at the time. Of course, each user
"paid" for the service by allowing Google
backdoor access to their data, but as with so

many privacy exchanges the cost to the individual user seemed, at least at the moment, negligible.

Nearly twenty years later, there are roughly 1.5 billion Gmail accounts in the world. Universities and organizations across the globe have adopted the service as their official email application, while its closest competitors— Yahoo and Hotmail—gradually adapted their services to fit the Gmail style. Email has become far less formal, but also more ubiquitous; because in-box space was essentially limitless, we stopped attempting to control it. Filtering tabs decluttered the in-box but pushed many emails out of view and lowered open rates for email marketers, resulting in more promotional emails.

Google had attempted to "fix" email but couldn't save it from being corrupted by our worst impulses and insecurities. In 2014, when the **Time** journalist Harry McCracken tried to send a message to Buchheit, he got an away message: Buchheit was on email hiatus. When McCracken finally got hold of him, Buchheit was unsparing in his critique of what Gmail had facilitated. "There's a 24/7 culture, where people expect a response. It doesn't matter that it's Saturday at 2 a.m.— people think you're responding to email," he said. "People have become slaves to email. It's not a technical problem. It can't be solved with a computer algorithm. It's more of a social problem."

Instead of confronting the social problem that allowed email to eat the whole of our lives, we sought out ways to wrangle it, control it, zero it, put it in handcuffs. We created productivity tools to manage a productivity tool, and found ourselves deeper and deeper in a hole, desperate for the solution that promises to finally allow us to dig ourselves out.

In 2012, McKinsey was on the hunt for just such a solution: something, anything, that could decrease the email burden on workers and boost productivity among its clients. In a report from that year, its analysts found that the average knowledge worker spent 28 percent of their workweek managing email, and nearly 20 percent looking for internal information, or simply tracking down colleagues who could help with specific tasks. They believed some sort of collaborative chat—or "social technology"—had the potential to raise the productivity of knowledge workers by between 20 and 25 percent.[31]

Nearly a decade later, the "social technologies" the McKinsey report envisioned have integrated themselves, in some capacity, into all manner of workplaces. There's Microsoft Teams ("a hub for collaboration"), Facebook Workplace ("connect employees with familiar video communication and collaboration tools"), Google Hangouts ("bring conversations to life"), and Slack ("a new way to communicate with your team"), plus dozens of videoconferencing tools, many with chat functions, whose use has skyrocketed since the beginning of the pandemic (Zoom, Webex, BlueJeans, Chime, Skype, and so on).

Most offices use some combination of "social technologies" in their office, but Slack is the paradigm shifter. Back in 2013, it was the first to beguile Silicon Valley, with the promise to "kill email."[32] The idea was just as simple and elegant as Gmail's had been: instead of hundreds of employees sorting through their in-boxes, hunting down attachments and first drafts and old Google Chats, why not connect everyone in one place and allow them to make little play and collaboration areas for themselves?

Slack worked. Brainstorming threads that once circulated wildly in in-boxes moved into Slack rooms; same for back-and-forths about ideas and execution. The platform was easy to use and, with custom emojis and integration with GIPHY, even intermittently fun. Usage spread organically, often through word of mouth: employees who'd heard about Slack from friends at other companies hounded HR to adopt the technology. Holdouts eventually became converts as the bulk of communication shifted from email chains to chat rooms. One analytics company reported that employees at large companies that had adopted Slack were sending an average of more than two hundred Slack messages per week, while "power users" sent out more than one thousand messages a day.[33]

According to one analysis by RescueTime—an app that tracks which apps you use and for how long—Slack and other social "chat" apps did decrease email use. Between 2013 and 2019, the percentage of screen time workers allocated to email went from just under 14 percent to 10.4 percent.

In reality, they just moved that time to chat apps, whose usage increased from 1 percent to 5 percent.

RescueTime data isn't exactly precise; if you have it installed on your computer, for example, it doesn't measure the time you spend emailing or Slacking from your phone. But this study demonstrates something annoyingly straightforward: technologies like Slack don't **decrease** the amount of time users spend communicating online; they just add another, even more demanding and distracting way to do so.[34] Exhaustion and frustration gradually begin to accumulate. "I felt increasingly unproductive, highly reactive, and simply overwhelmed by Slack," the programmer Alicia Liu wrote in a 2018 Medium blog post. "And the problem got worse the more time I spent using Slack. I kept being constantly pulled in by Slack notifications."

These sorts of interruptions come at significant cost: researchers have found that even short interruptions of twenty minutes or less increase stress among workers.[35] But because the interruptions feel urgent—and missing out on them feels negligent—workers often

struggle to ignore them, at least for long. Instead, we weave them into the workday, creating an ever-expanding tapestry of work, then
interruption, interruption, then work. At
some point, it begins to feel normal. But that
normal feels like crap.

If you listen closely, all of the criticisms of
Slack start to sound like the latest verse in
a decades-long lamentation over new design,
new tools, new apps. We're trapped in a de-
termined cycle to find an exact technological
fix, neglecting the evidence that as the cost
and difficulty of communication decrease, the
number of interactions—and time required
to process them—increase.[36] We ignore the
warnings of those who've watched their best-
intentioned ideas degrade before their eyes.
Recall the words of Gmail's creator: "It's not a
technical problem. It can't be solved with
a computer algorithm. It's more of a social
problem."

Social problems are **hard.** They can't be
waved away with an idea and a few years of
dedicated coding. They require collective action across many fronts, significant stores of
insight and patience, and, most important,

will—a potent mix of dissatisfaction with the way things are coupled with a vision of how they could, in fact, be different.

Back in the early 1980s, Karen Nussbaum saw just such a moment for office workers across the United States. After years of mistreatment, discrimination, and dropping wages, many workers were pushed over the edge by automation. Their offices were making them sick, they were worn out, and now their bosses were asking them to do more work for less pay.

"We understood that we had about a five- to ten-year period to deal with the impact of automation," Nussbaum told us. "It was a major disruption in the structure of work, and there was an opportunity to reach workers during this period when their individual jobs were dramatically changing." But Nussbaum knew they had to act fast: "Once workers had cycled into a new job, with the new norms, that same moment of questioning what standards there should be—it would be gone."

Nussbaum and the National Association of Working Women had the will and the vision to help organize clerical and office workers. But they ran up against a cultural wall: of anti-union sentiment, antifeminist sentiment, and an overwhelming American boosterism amid the Cold War. The wall is of a slightly different character today, but no less formidable: in countries all over the world, people will say the focus should be on rebuilding the post-COVID economy, on beating out the global competition, on innovating and hacking our way to a new office future. But as the last several thousand words have made clear, there is no one office design, no single technical innovation, that can actually fix the **social problem** of the way we've arranged office work.

We'll address some of the ways that you can begin to address that problem in the chapter to come. But for now, here's our best advice on how to peel back the layers of misguided utopianism, misdirection, and distraction that have accumulated around technology and design in your office and how, in this brief and wild moment of flux, we can begin to imagine and embrace a different way forward.

Stop Dreaming of the
Office of the Future

It's possible that the secret to breaking our productivity doom loop was discovered in an office somewhere in Copenhagen in the early 1990s. Exactly which office? We don't know. In fact, we don't even know the company's actual name; the researchers who conducted the case study refer to it only as DanTech, short for "Danish Tech company." But DanTech's story, chronicled by Abigail J. Sellen and Richard H. R. Harper in **The Myth of the Paperless Office,** is unique. Not because of what they make, or the size of their profits, or whom they employ, but because they managed to modernize an office without simply perpetuating all the mistakes and problems of the past.

DanTech's story begins in the 1980s. The company was falling behind in its industry and facing an uncertain future, and leadership decided to try something drastic: they would completely change their organizational structure and then start again from scratch. Employees were trained to do two or more jobs so that teams could be broken apart and reconfigured at will. To facilitate the internal reorganization, they moved buildings and physically reorganized the office space, filling it with generic desk clusters so teams could collaborate when necessary, then work separately with ease. They put a strict cap on how much paper any one employee could use or keep in their work space, instead encouraging workers to rely on electronic filing stations and early PCs.

These changes don't sound revolutionary today, but at the time it was the equivalent of, say, giving all your employees an Oculus headset and telling them to conduct all business henceforth in virtual reality. And not all of them worked out. One of their electronic filing databases was so complicated that employees had no real idea how to use it, which meant important documents ended up lost in a digital maze. With time, however, employees found a system that worked for them: they put a handful of workers, already proficient with the system, in charge. It was probably less efficient than training everyone at the company but more feasible. After roughly eighteen months, the company had managed to pull off what most workplaces then believed was unthinkable: they'd gone primarily paperless, becoming one of the early digital offices of the age.

For Sellen and Harper, who'd been painstakingly studying paper as the primary office technology of the twentieth century, DanTech was a rare example of real change. Since the mid-1970s, futurists and business pundits had been predicting the imminent rise of the paperless office. But, try as they might, the IBMs and Xeroxes of the world were still using plenty of paper by the 1990s. In the disastrous Chiat redesign in 1993, the sight of a piece of paper would trigger emails chiding workers that they worked in a "paperless office," even though much of the creative ad work was still done on storyboards and contracts with outside companies still needed to be printed out and signed.[37] The office of the future was still very much tethered to the printer.

And yet this team of Danes seemed to have stumbled into a paperless future, almost by accident. They did it by thinking about change in terms of **sustainability.** As Sellen and Harper explain, DanTech never set a goal to abolish paper use altogether. Instead, the company focused on ways to teach and incentivize employees to think about using paper **differently**. And, with time, they began to use less and less. "Promise a paperless office, and you set yourself up for disappointment and failure," Sellen and Harper wrote. "Promise incremental, realistic changes, and goals are more likely to be met, people more likely to be satisfied."[38]

This story and its lesson, though, are not really about paper or whether a paperless office is necessarily better than an office that does things the old-fashioned way. The Danish office in question is a lesson in how to create change in an organization that might stick. DanTech was playing the long game. The company managed its employees' expectations. It pushed for bold and potentially painful changes, but when they resulted in confusion or negative outcomes—as with the filing system—they were willing to revise and reassess. Last, as Sellen and Harper note, DanTech's overhaul was focused on the "real, underlying problems." Paper was never actually the problem. But they understood that modernization could be a means to fix the very real structural issues that had left them lagging behind their competitors. "Organizations need to look at the combination of people, artifacts, and processes to assess where problems may lie and how solutions can be implemented," Sellen and Harper explained. "They need to look both broadly and deeply at what exists already."

In practice, it probably felt pretty boring—or at least far less daring and invigorating than throwing out paper altogether, or issuing a bunch of bold proclamations. But that had been the fatal flaw in the plans of so many designers and innovation specialists: they imagined a future, then designed it entirely from scratch, with no eye to the ways it would exacerbate existing tensions or fail to address fundamental needs. That's precisely what Chiat/Day did, and they ended with a splatter-painted quagmire and people furtively hiding printouts, files, and contracts in their cars.

But some companies, like DanTech, conceived of the office of the future by attempting to fully understand the office of the present. In those cases, Sellen and Harper found that the plans rarely looked like implementing conventional digital technologies. The most lasting forms of innovation don't look great on a press release, because they're incremental, periodically involve pausing or reversing plans, and, at least to outsiders, seem tedious. They're honest about an organization's failings, unprecious about tradition, yet compassionate and empathetic in their solutions.

We've become so obsessed with our own techno-utopian visions—the open office, the paperless office, the remote office—but have so rarely taken the time to find the right, winding road that will actually make them a reality. That's why the history of the office is essentially one long game of tech and design whack-a-mole: you can deal with one problem, but then a set of new, equally stubborn problems pop up in its place. Solve for the real, underlying problems, though—the ones that don't sound exciting and innovative—and, like DanTech, you might notice truly innovative fringe benefits.

The pandemic has proven that flexible, remote office work is indeed possible at scale. But tech alone cannot make that future sustainable. More efficient tools and greater productivity—the end goal of most of our work tech—is not the solution, because productivity is not the problem. Look around any pre-pandemic office or drop into any post-pandemic Slack room, and you'll find that people are not miserable or demoralized because they lack ways to be productive. The problems are deeper, messier, and far more human. If we want an "office of the future" (and, more important, if we actually want it to **succeed**), we need to stop drafting blueprints for some color-corrected, Facetuned, sci-fi fantasy. Instead, we need to confront the unflattering, unsexy, foundational problems of the present and start building, sustainably, from there.

Level the Office Playing Field

The truth about post-pandemic work is that most of us are going back to the office, at some point, in some form. Maybe that sentence sparks a bit of joy inside you; maybe it fills you with dread. But if we are to look at the future from the present, it seems clear that—at least in the short term—many of us will head back to a familiar desk under the hum of fluorescent lights for anywhere between one and five days a week.

Many companies own or lease their office space on long-term contracts. And when the space is there, sitting on the company's expenses, it's likely that management is going to incentivize employees to use it. And after we've been trapped in our homes hiding from a deadly virus for well over a year, we're starved for social interaction. Many of our former commuting and workplace annoyances now sound like tiny luxuries. Some of us miss our colleagues. Others are just sick of their homes and apartments and, yes, even their partners and kids. The only question is, how?

It's a problem that has filled Jennifer Christie's days for more than a year now. As Twitter's chief human resources officer, she is one of the architects of the company's work strategy, which has meant divining a way forward for more than six thousand employees post-COVID. In May 2020, Twitter announced plans to make full-time remote work permanent for any employees who wanted it. The news prompted a flood of opinion pieces, all suggesting, in various formats, that this might be the moment the work-from-home revolution begins in earnest. Which explains why a lot of people are watching Christie and the company's plan closely: Twitter, along with a handful of other organizations, feel like bellwethers. The pressure to succeed—or quickly fail, and tell everyone to go back to the way things were—is high.

When we spoke with Christie in early 2021, she told us what every manager and consultant we've spoken with knows to be true. Remote work isn't the hard part. Neither, ultimately, is in-person work. It's the hybrid, flexible schedule that's tricky. And again, the fundamental problem with a hybrid schedule is inadvertently creating a new hierarchy based around physical face time. Of course, proximity issues inside offices are not new: pre-COVID, everything from desk layout to who gets invited to meetings with the boss can determine who is seen as a valued, hard worker, and who gets overlooked or has their contributions taken for granted.

Hybrid work threatens to deepen those divides. Single parents, workers with elderly family members, disabled employees, and those who simply don't want to live in

proximity to the office risk being over-
shadowed by those who come in every day.
And even if a manager is careful, a recency
and proximity bias might emerge. Ambitious,
competitive employees will sacrifice remote
flexibility and work relentlessly in person,
while remote employees, motivated by the
anxiety of not seeming productive, will live in
fear of managers and compensate with overwork. Both sides end up driving the other to
misery.

This is the nightmare scenario for Christie
and the focus of much of Twitter's early hybrid work planning. The solution? Destroy
the FOMO and level the playing field by
making the office **less** appealing. "You need
to eliminate the idea that you'll miss out if
you're not in the office," she told us. Which
is why they're attempting to figure out ways
to actively disincentivize people from coming
back to the office full-time. "For a long time
we've rallied around office perks and keeping
people around and in the building," she said.
"Tech companies have celebrated and mas-
tered it: come to the office, and you get fed,
you get cared for."

That whole well-fed, well-cared-for campus

philosophy has to change, Christie says. And it starts with the way the office is arranged and the expectations for people within those spaces. At Twitter, everyone inside the conference room will be asked to have an open laptop and dial into the meeting to make sure that remote participants can see all faces clearly and hear those who, in a different configuration, might have traditionally been far away from the conference microphone. The company plans to get rid of team spaces in offices, will transition fully to "hot desking"—a.k.a. unassigned desks—with some spaces reserved for deep work and others for busier, more social areas.

One of the main goals is ensuring that absences aren't felt: if desks were assigned and team based, the privileges of proximity would naturally flow down to those able or willing to come into the office on a more regular basis. Which isn't to say that in-person group work won't happen: Twitter is simply incentivizing teams to coordinate when they come in, aiming to create "episodic" moments of collaborative work.

"We don't want to be remote first or office first," Christie continued. "We want to level the field. And that means we have to stop doing some things in the office that we do well, like the current way we do food service. We're trying to disincentivize some parts of that experience that lull you into the office; we're trying to take away some of that ease."

For many managers and executives, the idea of introducing friction into a functional workplace might sound counterintuitive, or even straight-up foolish. But, at least in its earliest stages, Twitter seems to understand that merely layering remote work atop the current workforce is paving a path to dysfunction. "You have to commit your entire culture to this change," Christie said. "You cannot do it half-assed."

Achieving an equitable balance between in-office and remote employees is going to be fraught—even for the most thoughtful companies. You can easily imagine those who spend more time in the office resenting a workplace that privileges remote workers, and employees working from home will resent co-workers with easier access to superiors. That tension is the reason that Dropbox, a cloud computing company based in San Francisco, decided back in October 2020 to transform itself into a virtual-first organization.

Early in the pandemic, Melanie Collins, Dropbox's chief people officer, helped gather internal data on the company's productivity patterns. Like many software companies, Dropbox's product life cycle was undisturbed by the remote shift. Engineers were exceeding performance goals, and internal metrics and surveys showed that workers wanted the changes to stick; the vast majority of employees even expressed a desire for **more** flexible work schedules and locations. But instead of offering remote work as a permanent option, Dropbox chose a more drastic route: the company would shift all individual work to remote, with options for teams to come together and collaborate episodically as necessary. To that end, the company would redesign and build a new style of office, dubbed "studios," in four cities where the company previously had an official office. In other cities with clusters of Dropbox employees, the company would provide passes to co-working spaces.

When we spoke in April 2021, Collins told us that Dropbox was designing the spaces with meetings and other team-building activities in mind. Employees wouldn't have desks assigned to them, or any other spaces that would encourage them to camp out and establish unofficial office space. They're meant to facilitate collaboration, not function as shadow offices. But all of that is subject to change.

"The only way to design a collaborative space is to do tons of surveying," Collins told us. "We have a hypothesis informing the design, but we'll learn a lot more when people get into them. We already know that sales and engineering have different needs, but we'll need to ask, 'How are people using the space? What's the utilization look like? Are ten-person rooms fully booked or is just one person hanging out in it? Are rooms for team bonding used that way, or are they taking on a different role?' And we'll make changes accordingly."

Collins stressed that no company, Dropbox included, knows what these plans will look like in two or three years. As the company moves forward, it wants to be iterative, flexible, and willing to say "this isn't working" until they figure out the right configuration.

Within that flexibility, there's one certainty: they're not going back to a traditional 9:00 to 5:00 workday. For many workers, that will mean a set of "on" hours that overlap with all U.S. time zones, with the freedom to set their own schedules outside those times.

Not all employees are going to work well with that sort of transformation, and Dropbox realizes as much. "Our shift to virtual first is a deliberate shift away from office perks and entitlements to work-and-life balance," Collins told us. "And we know some employees didn't choose this when they joined. We know and expect there'll be some turnover while we build for the future." And even though some employees may opt to leave, Dropbox envisions long-term gains in the expansion of their potential hiring pool and their ability to attract employees who want flexible work patterns. As Collins put it, "We're taking some of the pain that comes with transformation in stride."

Both Dropbox and Twitter seem to understand that they're not going to get everything right immediately—not even close. In our conversation, Christie outlined the numerous, unsexy issues that a global company like

Twitter is anticipating: dealing with work authorization forms, immigration, visas, corporate tax structures, security and IT issues, business licenses, payroll setups, tax assessments, and more. "If you think you can just auto flip a switch and all of this just happens, it's not going to work," she said. "You can't re-create the office remotely, or you're just going to suffocate your employees." In other words, everything has to be intentional.

That intentionality especially applies to groups that are usually left out of the design process. For leaders in the disability community, the remote work shift can feel fraught. Flexible work—an accommodation people with disabilities have been asking for, and denied, for decades—is more available than ever before. But there's also a very real concern that the ability to work from home could end up making actual office spaces less inclusive.

"What I don't want to see is all employees who have disabilities relegated to working from home because newly designed spaces are even less accessible than they are now," Maria Town, the president and CEO of the American Association of People with Disabilities, told us. It's far too easy to imagine companies offering hybrid work but treating their disabled workers as fixed remote employees, thereby reinforcing the segregation of disabled people in the workforce.

"If we get into this world where we have fewer centralized offices, it literally means that employees are exposed to fewer people that are different than them," Town said. "There's a lot of cultural value in having people show up at work and be visibly disabled." She used herself as an example. Town says her cerebral palsy is most visible when she's moving around in a space. "During the pandemic, my disability has been completely erased. All you see is my head in a little Zoom box."

Town stressed to us that creating opportunities for visibility and community engagement among disabled employees is crucial and will require delicately balancing those concerns with the necessity to make more jobs available for telework for those who need it. In other words, accessibility needs to be embedded into every technology and space designed for the remote-first or hybrid work environments. To do so, organizations will need to involve different types of workers in the process of drafting their remote and flexible strategies, not just those in HR and the C-suite.

That's because physical offices, at least in the short term, aren't going anywhere. Dror Poleg is the co-chair of the Urban Land Institute's Tech and Innovation Council, and years before the pandemic hit, he was collecting data about the changing needs of employees and employers for his 2019 book, **Rethinking Real Estate.** Poleg believes there have been indications that the office market was "headed for a crisis" for some time: the benefits of the office had ceased to outweigh the negatives; office costs were skyrocketing; and offices did little to assist perceived or actual productivity.

Which means that even before the pandemic companies were looking for solutions to the problem of their real estate holdings. The sudden onset of work from home simply accelerated that desire. Still, Poleg is bullish that office spaces will continue to exist in some form but their location and utility will shift dramatically. "Most office activity will not move to homes or to the cloud," he wrote in **The New York Times.** "Instead, it is likely to be redistributed within and between cities, with a variety of new employment areas popping up and saving many people the trouble of simultaneous commuting to a central business district."[39]

What will that look like in practice? Coworking spaces, but also smaller, satellite offices, oriented around what office workers actually need from the office, depending on their field: large-scale printing and shipping capabilities, collaborative space, private yet public space to meet with clients, or a recording studio for podcasts or YouTube videos.

There's no easy fix—just the hard, continuous work of stripping out what's broken and designing the future based on the present. But if you shy from that work, you will likely find yourself outmatched by those who don't. "We didn't go down this path because of COVID," Christie, Twitter's head HR officer, says. "We went down it because the world was already shifting, pre-COVID, and we thought, 'We have to get on the bandwagon, or we won't attract and retain talent.' Companies that think 'this too shall pass, and we'll go back to being an office company' are sorely mistaken. If you miss this window, you won't be a great company for long."

What Do You Actually Miss?

As of this writing, the last time one of us was in a physical office space was December 20, 2019. As many of you have likely found, this sort of distance has afforded some perspective.

When you show up someplace each day, you think about it logistically. An office isn't an idea; it's a space to be navigated in the moment. But with time, maybe you've been asking yourself deeper questions about the place where you spent your days: **What is the point of being present in the office forty hours a week? Why did we all sit in cubes? Why were we crammed into an open pen? Did the office make me more productive or less?**

All those questions are subsets of a larger interrogation: **What is an office, really?** That might sound like a Philosophy 101 bong rip sort of question, but the answer matters. Is it the people? The space itself? The proximity? All of the above? None of it?

We've dedicated a lot of time here to warning against techno-utopian thinking. But at this moment, it's also worth asking if the office—or some meaningful experience of it—can be reproduced without the commute and the whole act of being in a physical space. And, if so, should we seek it out?

The virtual office is hard to love. What makes an office feel alive—the murmur of voices, the movement, the myriad social interactions, large and very small—that's what so many of us miss. The virtual office, manifested in some sort of chat platform, is usually a woefully inadequate replacement, no matter how many breakout and special interest rooms you create. But attempts to push the idea further, usually through some sort of **Sims**-style video game approach, complete with customizable avatars, feel immediately corny, uncanny, or just straight-up dystopian. It feels as if we should give up on trying to re-create an actual approximation of the office and let remote work be remote. At least that's what we thought until we spoke to Dayton Mills.

We first met Mills at his office. Shortly before, we bumped into each other just outside, on a recently mowed lawn with appropriately manicured shrubbery. We exchanged pleasantries, and then he welcomed us inside a modern, wood-floored room. As start-up offices go, Mills's was spartanly outfitted but still had the usual start-up design suspects: there were a smattering of succulents on the table, a mess of beanbag chairs, and even an unused pool table in the corner. He motioned for us to sit down on a gray couch with a flashlight that shot out a purple beam of light. We did as we were told.

In the office, Mills is no normal founder; he's a floating purple blob with a wry smile. Or at least that's what he looks like according to his avatar. In reality, Mills is a nineteen-year-old with big rectangular glasses and a mop of curly brown hair and kind, human eyes, a fact we learned when he turned his webcam on a few minutes into the chat. His "office" wasn't real, or rather it wasn't **physically** real. But it's still the full-time workplace of his company, Branch.

Branch markets itself as a platform for "spatial conversations" and combines the team chat elements of a platform like Slack with video and a 2-D Super Nintendo aesthetic. When you log in to an office, you become a colorful, smiley face blob. You have a bird's-eye view of the entire office and can guide your avatar around the different rooms, all of which are customizable. There are conference rooms, cafeterias, private offices, breakout rooms, game rooms, and even the dreaded copier/mail room makes an appearance. You can toggle your webcam on or off as you please. Once it's on, your face will appear in a little circular frame at the top of the screen, along with anyone who is within earshot. It feels a bit like corporate **Pokémon** or an early version of **Zelda,** if the purpose of the game were to survive a conference call.

The idea for Branch dates back to 2019, when Mills was working for his father-in-law's company. Because he was good with computers, he was tasked with modernizing the organization's sales team, which was made up of dozens of remote workers across the country. Their process was arcane, still heavily reliant on written invoices, fax machines, and printouts. When Mills introduced them to Slack, the team was stunned. Many of the employees hadn't seen or spoken to each other in half a decade. Quickly, they realized they'd been doubling up on work, chasing the same leads, and talking past each other for years. Many confessed that they'd spent years feeling isolated and deeply disconnected. Slack helped, but the feeling of proximity was still missing.

Mills knew exactly what they meant and how to give it to them. Growing up in a small, rural town in Missouri, he always felt far more comfortable in **Minecraft** than he did in school. In middle school, he found himself spending more of his life online than off it. He'd wake up, get on Skype, scroll through his list of friends, and chat all day. "Half the time, we weren't even playing the game," he told us. "We were just running around and talking and sharing our lives with each other. The connection was real. Some of my closest, longest friends I've never even met in person." He'd been spontaneously cultivating social relationships in digital spaces his entire life. Why not try to replicate that in the workplace?

Sitting in Mills's office, staring at his fake blob as his real voice told us this story, we were skeptical. Then he took us on a tour of the office. Branch's most interesting feature is proximity-based audio, something he cribbed from popular online environments like the survival game **Rust.** When one avatar gets within a certain radius of another, you begin to hear their voice as a soft whisper. As you get closer, the volume gets louder— much like, well, real life.

It's easy to dismiss this effect as a gimmick, but the effect is curiously disarming, maybe even a bit profound. Following Mills toward the cafeteria, we heard a faint murmur of voices that, as we entered the room, grew louder. We had stumbled upon a group of Branch employees chatting after a lunch meeting. This wasn't a demo for our amusement; it was actual Branch employees doing what they do: hanging out in the platform all day while working, meeting, and shooting the shit. When Mills led us past them, one blob said hello, while the rest kept talking. As we walked away, their voices grew quieter. It was the closest thing to an authentic, mundane office interaction we'd had in twelve months.

Branch has the potential to replicate some of the spontaneity of the office—especially the casual, quick pop-in that's been replaced with an endless parade of Zoom calls and calendar invites. It's not that the Zoom meeting needs to be an email; it's that it really needs to be a quick knock and a friendly "Hey! Do you have like five seconds?" It's the kind of distinctly human interaction that physical offices facilitate and that not even the glowing red dot of a Slack or Teams message can replicate.

Dysfunctional management can't be gamed away using some cute blob avatars. And a toxic culture of overwork might only be exacerbated by an app that incentivizes people to be present, even in the background. If abused, a tool like Branch could transfer the oppressive, consuming nature of the office and the pressure to always be "performing" engagement with your job—something we already find ourselves doing on Slack. But it's also easy to see the ways in which a virtual world could foster a more inclusive culture. For a self-described introvert like Mills, virtual workplaces allow him to be a company leader without the performance anxiety.

"Nobody cares what I look like; nobody is staring at me," Mills said. "You're more in control of how you present to the world. You can be who you want to be." And then there's the logging out. Many Branch employees spend long hours on the platform, but when they leave it, they've clearly signaled that their day is over. You can reach them when they log back on. Guardrails, ready made.

Maybe you're rolling your eyes at this. A virtual office could be a cute, quirky experiment, but gamifying your work life might feel like a bridge too far. Besides, the last thing you want is even more time with your face glued to a screen. All of those objections make sense. But there's plenty of evidence to suggest that time in the physical office is dominated by sedentary time, at one's desk, looking at . . . screens. Emails don't magically stop when everyone congregates in an office. Neither do Slack messages.

In fact, a great deal of our human presence in the office has been disrupted by the convenience of messaging tools that are text based. Branch, which is mostly voice based, offers something arguably more intimate and closer to the feeling of human presence than a vibration, a pinging noise, and a string of text. Branch probably won't drastically decrease the workplace interruptions and frenetic task switching that plague our days. But it might change the **tenor.**

Would co-workers butt in less if they had to speak their request? Would co-workers be less anxious if their digital interactions were received through a friendly voice- and video-based medium? We don't yet have definitive answers to these questions, but tools like Branch encourage us to ask them.

To be clear, there's no quick technological fix to what ails our workplace. What works best for Mills and his team of young, extremely online employees likely won't work for Linda or Mark in accounting at a regional auto parts company. What Branch does best, however, is clarify what the office actually means to you. Because what a lot of us actually miss about the office—apart from not being in our claustrophobic homes—isn't anything that practical. You might miss what tech executive and essayist Paul Ford calls its "secret, essential geography": knowing the best place to cry, or find privacy, or use the bathroom.[40] But what you really miss is a feeling. In some offices, that feeling is playfulness. In others, it's siloed concentration. For Mills, it's an empathic, ambient presence. "You can create connection just by being present, even if you're not saying anything," he told us. "People know if they do talk, somebody is there to listen."

Whether or not it's a long-term fit, the insights from experimenting with something like Branch may be worth the price of the software license. What feeling do you want to build on as you build a hybrid future? And what traditions and practices can be left behind?

Office tech works best when it illuminates and streamlines what's essential. It works worst, and feels most exhausting, when it layers another app, another password, and an endless number of notifications onto that essential element. You lose sight of your coworkers and your organizational goals, but you also lose sight of your own habits and what makes work feel good or comfortable or generative. As we rebuild the workforce toward a hybrid future, we have to keep asking ourselves not just what we need to jettison about the way we used to work but also what's worth saving and what these spaces meant to us. Maybe you, too, need some quality time as a blob to figure it out.

Stop LARPing

Do you ever find yourself sending an email at an ungodly hour that could easily wait until morning? Do you reply to a group thread on your company chat client with a bland observation or question that you already know the answer to? Have you ever written the words "just checking in" while on vacation?

If you haven't, you're more disciplined than we are. But most of you will recognize the slightly desperate act of performative work. You hate that you do it, but you don't know how to stop it. It's a form of LARPing—Live Action Role Playing—your job, and it increases in direct proportion to the amount of anxiety you feel about your performance, your place in the organization, and your relationship with your manager. It's also a massive, **massive** time suck.

The writer John Herrman first coined the term "LARPing your job" in 2015, in the wake of wide-scale Slack adoption across tech and media. "Slack is where people make jokes and register their presence," he wrote. "It is where stories and editing and administrating are discussed as much for self-justification as for the completion of **actual goals.**"[41] Of course, before office communications went online, people registered their presence through **actual** presence, but Slack, like email before it, accelerated both the perceived demand and the ability to do so.

The less tangible the work you do, the more need there is to LARP it. The more sudden a shift in your work situation, the more you LARP. Mass LARPing is a symptom of an organizational culture in disarray, where expectations are opaque, productivity is paramount, and guardrails are nonexistent. Naturally, it exploded during the pandemic and has the potential to metastasize even more as we move forward into a flexible work future.

LARPing is a virulent pathogen, but there is an antidote. It's just trust: cultivating it, communicating it, propagating more of it. When you don't feel as though your manager trusts you—or, more specifically, how you make use of your time—you feel the need to underline just how much of it you're dedicating to work. You update, you check in, you sneak in casual mentions of how late you worked on something. Maybe your manager actually does trust you but is incredibly bad at communicating it. Maybe they've never told you to update this way but have never told you to stop, either. What matters is that the distrust hangs in the virtual air, goading you to spend more time evidencing your work than actually working.

The wild thing about LARPing is that it doesn't just waste your own time. It somehow also wastes everyone's. A flare sent into the air to show you're working incites others to send up their flares, too. One email becomes five responses; one Slack update becomes a half-hour conversation; one project submitted on a Saturday afternoon creates the compulsion for others to spend their time similarly. Microsoft found that between February 2020 and February 2021 the average Teams user was sending 45 percent more chats after hours and 50 percent of Teams users responded to chats within five minutes or less.[42] More and more, we find ourselves in a fun-house mirror of performance anxiety that distorts our understanding of what work even **is.**

It's difficult to engender the sort of robust, enduring trust that can keep these sorts of anxieties at bay. But one of the companies that has managed to do so has a lesson for the aspirationally flexible office. That company is GitLab, a software platform that helps web developers build and share open-source code. If you've read about remote work before, chances are you've seen it mentioned as an example. That's because, even pre-pandemic, it had built its company on the premise of truly reimagining work. It doesn't have any offices and its employees live everywhere, across many time zones. It's fully distributed, fully remote, and fully asynchronous and it embraces a radical form of transparency.

Truly asynchronous work can look intense. But resist the urge to dismiss it entirely: it looks different because it **works differently.**

Because employees are working at different hours in all parts of the world, the company relies on meticulous documentation. Employees take extensive notes on calls, meetings, memos, brainstorming sessions, you name it. Almost all of it, including many of the company's internal deliberations and operations, is posted publicly. In practice, that means someone outside the company can get an idea of how its employees are building the product they might ultimately buy. Internally, it means that an employee in the marketing department can go into GitLab's system and follow what the legal, comms, finance, and engineering teams are doing. They can read the team's notes, monitor their objectives and reports, and follow along with colleagues as they work.

Employees are also encouraged to create detailed "README" pages, which include a full description of what their job is and how they do it and a personal "About Me" section. From there, the README can get very granular. Darren Murph, GitLab's head of remote, has README sections like "how you can help me," "my working style," "what I assume about others," "what I want to earn," "communicating with me," and "work from home office setup." The responses are thoughtful and friendly. They aren't demands or even instructions, but they offer a guide to collaboration.

GitLab's approach to documentation might sound exhausting—and many employees might never engage with most notes from a meeting or a given colleague's README. It would probably take a full day to read the entirety of GitLab's CEO Sid Sijbrandij's page, follow the links, and watch all the videos. Some of the language feels stilted, like Sijbrandij's README section titled "Please chat me the subject line of emails." There's not a ton of room for improvisation. But that's purposeful: GitLab's process isn't jazz; it's a meticulously composed symphony.

What does that mean in practice? Accountability. Ability to work whenever. The removal of all pressure to sit in on a meeting in which you have a tangential role, because the meeting is always recorded.

"Transparency enhances belonging," Murph told us when we spoke. "And it is vital in an officeless company. Even if people don't use the documentation or follow what other colleagues are doing, just seeing it creates an innate sense of belonging. There's a trust that's forged because you can see what everyone is doing. Most companies work exactly opposite of that intentionally: they want it fully siloed because they're afraid of too much feedback. But it's not the feedback you should be afraid of; it's alienating teams."

Murph is arguably the most visible remote work advocate in the country. He's also, at least as far as he knows, the first person to hold the title head of remote work for a larger company, and he's quick to tell you that a remote work revolution will change the world. But he's also a realist. Yes, READMEs and documentation are a more inclusive, more respectful way to organize a workplace. They're also, he argues, better business. "If somebody is telling you when they'll be most receptive to your offer or idea, what they're doing is giving you advice that makes **you** better at your job," he told us. "So many of us don't communicate, and we end up ultimately failing because of it. We waste so much of our own time talking to people when they can't hear us. Even if you don't have an altruistic bone in your body, it's a better, more efficient way to do business."

The officeless, totally asynchronous model of GitLab will likely seem too intense for most employers. But Murph thinks that even those who adapt to a hybrid system, with some office time, should adopt the remote-first ideology that guides GitLab's processes. In practice, that means designing all policies to benefit employees outside the office, with a **secondary** focus on co-located workers. His reasoning: most remote-first policies actually work great in the office. But it doesn't work the same way in the other direction. Office-first policies tend to alienate and exclude and decrease communication when applied to remote workers. "Remote first functions great during crises, the pandemic being just one example," Murph explained. "Remote first is building a business around being flexible, versus building a business around a rigid space that's locked in place."

At Ultranauts, an engineering firm that has been fully remote since its founding in 2013, all meetings, including those among the leadership team, are recorded, transcribed, and made available to the entire company. Resulting decisions are announced on Slack, along with the reasoning behind them; there are no unwritten rules.[43] All of this transparency and accessibility is with a purpose: the company's co-founders worked to craft a transparent, accessible workplace where "cognitively diverse" teams could flourish, and 75 percent of their employees are on the autism spectrum. It's yet another example of the benefits of universal design: if you create an environment where clarity and explicitness are paramount, everyone benefits.

At Slack, employees use a "one-pager" system, which includes the times of day they are most likely to be responsive, plus additional information about how they work best. Like GitLab's READMEs, a colleague can scan someone's one-pager before an interaction and quickly ascertain the best way to deliver a piece of information or the most optimal time to reach them. All of this might seem like a bunch of extra work just to have a conversation, but multiple Slack employees told us that reading a colleague's one-pager is considered an act of respect—with the added bonus of saving everyone's time. If you take a moment to recognize a fellow employee as a complex person, and not just the other end of an email transaction, your communication will just be **better**.

Transparency and trust mean less bullshit posturing and LARPing, which mean less overall anxiety and situational stress. This was true before the shift to a more flexible work environment, but it'll be even more true moving forward. You can liberate employees to spend their time doing better work. Or you can implicitly encourage them to spend their days playacting at busyness. Which sounds better for business?

Resist the Urge to Screw It All Up with Surveillance

There's a theme that runs through many of the efforts to redesign remote work: it takes time, effort, and money. And not just time, effort, and money directed at consultants to tell you what to do. Whether it involves reconceptualizing a physical space, interrogating unspoken norms in the office, or establishing actual guardrails around digital technologies, evangelists for flexible work all stress that the way forward requires approaching our jobs with more humanity and trust. And there's little about that process that's quick or efficient.

Many employers will attempt to ignore these best practices. The most shortsighted will resist change completely, forcing employees back into the office full-time. But many others, perhaps feeling the competitive pressure, will begrudgingly allow for some remote or hybrid work. They will likely frame flexibility much as they have before: as a benevolent corporate perk or, worse yet, as an opportunity only available to those who've earned the privilege, suggesting that it could be revoked at any time.

These organizations will not reexamine their offices or their management practices. They won't interrogate who benefits from existing structures, because they're pleased with who benefits from existing structures. They will view hybrid work as an annoyance to be tolerated or an incentive to be lorded over workers to keep them productive. And to ensure that their newly liberated employees are on their best behavior, they will take the easiest, laziest way out.

Surveillance technology runs through the history of work. Blue-collar workers have long had their movements meticulously cataloged with time cards and overseeing floor managers, and the spread of the personal work computers offered employers a direct yet largely invisible conduit to access and analyze employee behavior. More recently, large tech and logistics companies have introduced extensive tracking systems to surveil employees: cross-country truckers, fast-food workers, data-entry specialists, call-center employees—everyone gets their own, noxious brand of surveillance.

In the fulfillment centers where Amazon's orders are processed, packed, and shipped, warehouse workers' every move is recorded and cataloged to "track the rates of each individual associate's productivity."[44] The constant pressure has led workers to file complaints with the National Labor Relations Board, alleging strenuous and dangerous working conditions. The monitoring, the workers argue, has led to ruthless terminations where automated systems calculate worker scores like "time off task" and trigger firings without human input for offenses with robotic titles like "productivity" and "productivity_trend."

There's often a sense among white-collar workers that these sorts of blunt surveillance tools can't, or won't, be used on them. Surveillance is for workers in Amazon's warehouses, in other words, not the engineers making more than $150,000 a year. But surveillance has been creeping into offices for years, starting with clerical and secretarial workers, the vast majority of whom were women. Because their work was easier to quantify, it was easier to review, grade, and, if found lacking, use as grounds for dismissal. These office jobs became more unstable, then, not because the work was any less essential but because it was easier to surveil. As workplaces' business went more fully online over the course of the 1990s and first decade of the twenty-first century, surveillance began to expand outside the traditional clerical realm. By 2008, Forrester found that more than one-third of companies with over a thousand employees had staff reading employees' email, and more than twenty-seven million employees were monitored online.[45]

Today, surveillance is even more widespread among knowledge workers and far more granular. Companies like Humanyze, a workplace analytics organization, use employee ID badges to categorize what workers are doing in the office. According to a 2014 report by Data & Society, the company's insights track "who is talking to whom, for how long, with what tone of voice, how quickly they speak or when they interrupt, etc. to try to identify what makes for a good team."[46] Another product called SureView, made by the defense contractor Raytheon, relentlessly tracks employee movements across company devices: browsing histories, every keystroke, the content of emails, and scans the contents of any file uploaded and downloaded to a USB stick on company computers.[47] SureView's purpose is to protect companies against corporate espionage or outside security threats, but the software is readily exploitable by vindictive or imperious managers. The more you know about an employee's actions, the more control you have over those actions, and the easier it is to make a case for dismissal.

Some employee monitoring software—dubbed "tattleware" and "bossware" by privacy advocates—is actually marketed with an eye toward worker welfare. Sure, the software may be invasive, but as the companies behind these programs argue, the insights might actually make work **better.** An MIT study of Bank of America call center employees found that productivity actually **rose** when workers were given more time for social interaction—which led to the bank implementing a fifteen-minute coffee break.[48] Other companies argue that monitoring tools make it easier to identify and elevate productive workers who might have otherwise flown under the radar, and that other forms of surveillance can be used to assist human resources complaints or workplace harassment allegations. All of this sounds okay, or at least potentially helpful, in theory.

But the dark side of this form of surveillance consistently outweighs the benefits. In the spring of 2020, as lockdowns forced knowledge workers to labor at home, the **New York Times** reporter Adam Satariano downloaded a software program called Hubstaff. The program, currently used by more than thirteen thousand remote businesses, markets itself as "the all-in-one work time tracker for managing field or remote teams." Its website is bathed in cheery blues and whites, paired with photos of a diverse set of happily tracked employees. It looks like a productivity app, not a surveillance device.

"It's simple psychology," the site declares. "When your team tracks time with Hubstaff, everyone is more aware of how they're spending each minute of their day." After Satariano put Hubstaff on his computer, it began taking hundreds of screenshots: of the websites he visited, the emails he wrote, plus any other activities, personal or private. It then tallied up his time in a detailed report, with each ten-minute segment of work categorized down to the percentage of time spent typing or moving the mouse. Each day, it churned out a productivity score, ranking him on a scale of 0 to 100, and sent it to his manager.

But Hubstaff's dashboard didn't really understand the kind of work that Satariano did. Phone calls—a crucial part of a reporter's job—were not logged as "time working" by the platform, neither was reading online, yet another vital component of the job. Hubstaff's monitoring was focused on a small and rigid set of tasks and skills that were hardly an accurate judge of productivity. And so Satariano's score was almost always perilously low; one day he worked close to fourteen hours, only to register a score of 22.[49] And even though Satariano knew the software was inaccurate, he found himself working more to try to appease it. A lot of this work was of the performative variety, leaving work documents open on the screen so Hubstaff would screenshot them. Instead of increasing his productivity, it made him LARP his job more than he ever had before.

Companies like Hubstaff argue that workplace tracking actually gives employees peace of mind, even freedom. "This is a two-way street," the company's support web page for managers reads. "If your employees run Hubstaff's time-tracking software while they work, it means you can relax a little more. You won't need to worry about finding out exactly when they are working, or where they are working from."[50] Here, Hubstaff frames data harvesting as a way to establish better communication; after all, the "problem," according to the support page, is that "managing employees, invoicing clients, and paying employees are wasting too much of your time."

But effective communication cannot be made "effortless," no matter the promises of the company's marketing materials. Good management doesn't scale easily, because good communication isn't always efficient. It's often emotional and vulnerable, and it certainly isn't driven by algorithms and big data. Good management is ultimately built on trust—the very kind that surveillance undermines at every turn.

We get why a product like Hubstaff is

attractive: it promises managerial peace of mind **and** increased productivity. But most workers don't actually need productivity boosts. In September 2020, Mercer, an HR consulting firm, performed a study of eight hundred employers across the United States. Ninety-four percent reported that productivity levels were the same or higher than before the pandemic.[51] What companies need is trust and reimagined management skills, which are far more amorphous, difficult to cultivate, and even more difficult to measure. No wonder they're grasping for a technological shortcut.

If companies are worried about sustained productivity, not just the "I'm worried about my job and we're in the middle of a pandemic" variety, then trust is essential. The behavioral psychologist David De Cremer argues that companies fail to see the role or value of trust precisely because its effects are often indirect: trust means "information is communicated more openly, people are more willing to help one another and willing to test ideas even if these may ultimately fail."[52] With time, trust leads to more experimentation, more

creativity, and higher worker satisfaction—
the building blocks of quality work.

Monitoring software seeks to eliminate risk
and uncertainty in the workplace, but fostering a culture of trust actually **requires** a mod-
icum of risk and uncertainty. Ideally, both
are distributed across the workplace: managers trust the people they manage, and those
people in turn trust that their managers have
their best interests at heart. Each party has to
have faith in the other, which means all parties have to feel comfortable with a baseline
of vulnerability. But products like Hubstaff
disrupt that balance: they render one party
vulnerable and the other omniscient. That
may produce short-term gains in productivity, but the imbalance of trust will chip away
at morale and the very foundation of whatever company culture you're trying to build.

If we're not vigilant and proactive, these
tools will define the new, flexible era of work.
When the office was forced into individuals'
homes at the onset of the pandemic, companies instinctively reached for the crutch of
monitoring software. During 2020, one analyst estimated that an additional 20 percent

of U.S. companies purchased monitoring software for their employees during the pandemic, meaning that roughly 30 percent of companies are evaluating remote work via some kind of productivity monitoring tool.[53]

With this very real fear in mind, we got in touch with Shoshana Zuboff. Since watching the pulp mill workers struggle with that automated door thirty-three years ago, Zuboff has dedicated her research to thinking about the ways in which our use of technology constantly undermines our best intentions, most famously in her 2019 book, **The Age of Surveillance Capitalism.** And she's pessimistic about the way companies are already approaching remote work.

"I see these cycles repeated over and over," Zuboff told us. "I've been confronting the same issue, saying the same thing, for forty-two years, and it's crazy how much the underlying power dynamics remain intact." She believes workers and students will continue to be treated as "captive" populations on which new technologies of control can be tested, with little consequence, before migrating to the population at large. And she fears remote work will be the death knell for personal privacy, destroying the final flimsy barriers keeping corporate surveillance out of our homes. "As invasive as limitless worker surveillance has been historically," she said, "there's still a moment when you get up and leave the damn office."

The fight Zuboff has spent the last four decades describing—between humans and encroaching surveillance—is not, and has never been, a fair one. "You see this with work, but also with all technology," she said. "We're so emptied out. We become easy targets for this marketing of liberation, and companies exploit that to the max." Crucially, the costs of these tools aren't shared with the employers. They fall on the employees, especially the ones without labor power.

As we spoke, Zuboff sketched the contours of a grim potential future, one that hovers uncomfortably over the very premise of this book: many of the choices and privileges of a remote flexible future of work will be enjoyed—as they are now—by a select few with the labor power to negotiate and bargain for them. An elite group will get to reimagine workdays, workplaces, and company commitment to an equitable, flexible, more humane company culture; the rest get twelve-hour days at home and some pre-installed surveillance software that times your bathroom breaks.

Near the end of our conversation, Zuboff gestured to the same feeling of guarded hope that undergirds this book. Despite the deep imbalances of power and the exhaustion many of us feel fighting for dignity in our jobs, in our politics, and in our communities, our moment feels unusually plastic, alive with the potential for change. That is, in part, because many people are deeply angry and more aware of the inequities all around them. But also because the vast technological shifts of the twenty-first century have culminated in a pandemic that has forced us to reimagine the parts of our lives that felt the least flexible. In this moment, we are more motivated to agitate for change than at any time in recent memory.

We write this book in the hope that we might make use of this unanticipated window, but we also share Zuboff's ambivalence. Once you're familiar with the history of these tools, and the consequences of their implementation, it's all too easy to imagine a future where our best intentions and ideas only reproduce the inequalities of the past. But without imagining and articulating the future we want—and the sustainable ways we can try to get there—we are certain to remain stuck in the patterns of the present.

Zuboff sees a potential way forward, for technology and for our working lives, through politics. Not just new labor contracts, and laws that actually account for the ways that work has shifted in the digital age, but new social contracts, too—forged through collective actions large and small. Of course, collective action, even just basic civic engagement, requires time and energy. It demands space and attention that is so often devoted to our friends, our families, and especially our jobs. But what if we had more of that time?

At the beginning of this chapter, we argued that it's time to see our productivity and efficiency as a means to an actual end, not just a means to more work. Now it's time to think about what those ends might look like.

4

Community

If your grandparents or great-grandparents lived in the United States, they almost certainly belonged to some sort of social organization. Regardless of where they lived, what they did for a living, their race, their religion, or how recently they'd arrived in the United States, they were "joiners": members of the "long, civic generation" born somewhere in the decades surrounding 1930. They belonged to churches and choirs, quilting guilds and farm boards. They were Elks, Black Elks, Moose, Eagles, Odd Fellows, Sons of Norway, Sons of Italy, Mardi Gras Krewe members, Daughters of the American Revolution, Daughters of Utah Pioneers, Toastmasters, and Job's Daughters. They joined the VFW, the Knights of Columbus, the Grange, the PEO, the American Association of University Women, B'nai B'rith, the Junior League, the Luther League, and the Petroleum Club and had long-standing appointments to play bridge, and mah-jongg, and euchre.

And that's just a small smattering of the organizations that generation joined. The actual list feels as if it doesn't end, in part because the hunger for these sorts of groups felt limitless. They were secular and religious, ritualistic and informal, often delimited by age or race or gender or religion, and they composed the rhythms of your week. They were the way you met people, including love interests, especially when you moved to a new town. They were often a mix of social and philanthropic: opportunities to play cards, play dress up, shoot the shit, get drunk, and/or do good.

Some of these organizations were incredibly exclusionary; others propagated arcane ideas about race, class, gender, imperialism, and colonialism, you name it. The KKK, after all, was a social club with a racist agenda. Others provided a means of passing down language and ethnic traditions, or a space of refuge from the demands of living in white or male-dominated spaces. For W. E. B. Du Bois, for example, black societies provided a "pastime from the monotony of work, a field for ambition and intrigue, a chance for parade, and insurance against misfortune."[1]

Whatever their purpose, these groups provided the literal and figurative infrastructure of the community. People joined them because it's what people did: they paid their literal and figurative dues, and then they were repaid with a structure where they could gather, a full social calendar, and peers to fill it with. They formed networks of "loose ties," filled with people who aren't necessarily your best friends, but feel connected, and thus attentive to your well-being, in some way. In many cases, these groups also functioned as official and unofficial mutual aid societies, with monthly dues that ensured that in case of death, illness, or disability your family would be provided for.

No matter their ostensible purpose, these groups held yearly, monthly, and weekly fundraisers, parades, dances, and picnics; many had educational and self-betterment programming, specific philanthropic arms, and offshoots specifically for children and young adults. They spiked in popularity early in the second decade of the twentieth century, declined briefly over the course of the Depression, then ballooned back to life in the 1950s and 1960s. In urban neighborhoods, in the suburbs, in the smallest rural towns, some version of these social organizations existed, binding residents and their needs to one another.

In 2000, the political scientist Robert Putnam published **Bowling Alone,** the first book to take a broad look at the rise of these groups and the results of their widespread decline over the course of the late twentieth century. At that point, many of these organizations had spent the last two decades in denial, clinging to the belief that if they just sold their building downtown and built in the suburbs, if they just figured out how to recruit thirty-year-olds, if they elected a new social chair, if they built a gym next to the church, the drop-off in membership could be reversed. But their surreptitious decline had little to do with the amenities or offerings of a particular organization. It was a symptom of an ongoing shift as the ideals of individualism began to eclipse the collectivism that had structured the postwar period.

Collectivism is an overarching ethos of "we're in this together"—manifested in the tax code, the way we think of the social safety net, even the way we conceive of our responsibility to people we don't know. In **The Upswing,** his follow-up to **Bowling Alone,** Putnam frames the rise in collectivism, particularly in the early twentieth century, as a means of seeking social solidarity amid a time of profound technological and societal change. These groups provided "asylum from the disordered and uncertain world"—a sort of second, comforting home—while their mutual aid components provided reassurance that catastrophe would not pull an individual family asunder.[2]

In the second decade of the twentieth century, the collectivist ethos began to manifest itself in progressive policy making, which would continue, in various waves, through the 1960s and, at least for white people, transfer the mutual aid component of these organizations onto the state. The most famous of these reforms fell under the umbrella of Franklin Delano Roosevelt's New Deal, but they also included programs that worked to universalize and extend education at all levels, to decrease infant mortality rates and increase life expectancy, to fortify labor protections, and, via the tax code, to equalize the distribution of wealth. The Tennessee Valley Authority, a public utility program that worked to electrify and modernize one of the most impoverished areas of the United States, is a collectivist-minded initiative; so is Head Start, which was founded in 1965 to provide early childhood education and health services to low-income families.

The overarching mission of these programs was not just "we have a moral duty to help the poor." It was, again, that we are only as strong and resilient as our weakest member. The problem, of course, was that these programs were compromised by endemic racism. We're all in this together, but black and brown people are in it together over there, and women are expected to reconcile themselves to secondary citizenship. The civil rights movement, the women's movement, and the United Farm Workers' movement were all, in some way, attempts to create laws and labor protections that would spread the benefits of collectivism—and American citizenship—more equally.

Yet these movements' incremental successes coincided with pauses, cuts, and reversals to many collectivist gains. As Putnam points out, educational gains began to "pause" right around 1965. The membership in unions, which helped buoy the incomes of millions of Americans above a living wage, had already started its long decline in 1958. Tax cuts in the mid-1960s made it easier for the rich to stay and get richer, and waves of deregulation began to turn the purpose of previously public-oriented institutions over to the whims of the "free market."[3] Some of these shifts were responses to growing panic over the threat of global competition, but they were also implicit and explicit responses to the expansion of who was now benefiting from the collectivist ethos. The message: we'll let everyone into our "we're all in this together" party, but then we're going to turn the lights off, and it's every person for themselves.

That individualist approach—the overwhelming focus on me and mine—started

to take root in the 1970s and gradually became the dominant political and ideological
posture of the last forty years. Individualism
cloaks itself in the rhetoric of self-reliance and
stoicism and is often a response to economic
instability, the loss of professional identity,
and the overwhelming desire to create a better life for your children. It can manifest
skepticism toward government spending or a
deep resentment of any tax dollar not spent
to your family's direct benefit. It's a core tenet
of both libertarianism and neoliberalism, and
the corresponding inclination, in the economist Noreena Hertz's words, to "see ourselves
as competitors not collaborators, consumers
not citizens, hoarders not sharers, takers not
givers, hustlers not helpers, people who are
not only too busy to be there for our neighbors but don't even know our neighbors'
names."[4]
People who've adopted an individualist
attitude aren't necessarily sociopaths or ass-
holes: they'll still donate to a GoFundMe to
help a local kid with cancer, or even stop
to help someone on the side of the road if
they look "safe." They chip into the gift fund
for a co-worker's fiftieth birthday, tithe to

their church, and fundraise for their children's school. They do want to help others, but they want it to be on their own terms and arbitrate who's worthy of receiving it. They are often obsessed with the idea of "fairness": that one can benefit from something only insomuch as they've contributed to it themselves. Crucially, people who might politically embrace a collectivist ethos, like nationalized health care or mandatory parental leave, can still make deeply individualist decisions, especially when it comes to their perceived ideas of "safety," "good schools," and "doing what's right for our family."

Individualism creates and deepens inequities, it mires us in endless arguments about worth and "deserving," and it creates so much unnecessary suffering, alienation, and resentment. It forces us to obsess over the need to prove our value; instead of wondering why the perch where we find ourselves is so precarious, we obsess with how to best keep ourselves steadied upon it. It's a root cause of so many of our worst tendencies and afflictions, in and outside the office: the cult of productivity, widespread burnout and anxiety, sustained exhaustion, obsession with cultivating our children as mini-résumés for future success, lack of personal or community identity, and profound loneliness and alienation.

People say that we, as a society, worship consumerism, that we have made false idols out of **things.** But that pronouncement increasingly rings false, particularly for office and knowledge workers. We worship work. We remain faithful to it because we want to support ourselves and our families, but it's become more than a simple means of providing needs. Work has taken on such a place of primacy in our lives that it has subsumed our identities, diluted our friendships, and disconnected us from our communities.

Individualism induces work obsession, and that work obsession in turn keeps us mired in individualism. We have turned inward, toward our immediate families and our jobs, at the expense of all else—a process that has been facilitated by the digital technologies that allow us to not only work more but simulate the experience of actual connection with others. We have forgotten how to care for each other outside the bounds of family, or gather with each other outside the compulsion of our jobs or our children's activity schedules. We have lost or are barely clinging to our support systems. Our reliance on individualism has left us where it was always going to leave us: incredibly alone.

This devolution has been happening for years. We've just distracted ourselves from it with a quick vacation to convince yourself you were living a balanced life. But the pandemic has clarified just how untenable the situation had become: we need each other, we crave connection, and, as we've poured ourselves into work and productivity, its returns, particularly on the deep, soul-nurturing level, only continue to diminish. There has to be something more.

So what's the answer? Do we all just start going to religious services again? Find a nearby Toastmasters chapter? Pick a hobby, any hobby, buy some gear, and go for it? Our best selves can aim to do so, but if work maintains the same place in our identities and worlds, it's simply not going to happen. You'll google info on a group and forget about it, donate some money and step away, make plans to attend a meeting and cancel.

Most people will look at the list of organizations at the beginning of this chapter and think, "Who has the time?" But that's the thing: you could. Not by jam-packing your schedule to the point of breaking, or forcing all household duties onto your partner. By using the time freed up by a flexible, guardrail-enforced schedule and filling it with things that nourish you and working toward the sort of collectivist change we crave and need. Because this detailed, diligent labor to liberate ourselves from our addiction to work will be meaningless if its benefits extend only to people who work and live and look like us.

You might feel powerless or nihilistic about our potential as a society, convinced we will never be able to actually embrace collectivism again. But, as Putnam argues, there is convincing evidence that we are at the beginning of an "upswing" in collectivist sentiment, because the promises of individualism have proven so thoroughly unsavory for all but the most rarefied elite. Now, after a year of massive societal turmoil, is the time to embrace new and difficult solutions—ones that more equitably distribute risk and stability, that refuse to neglect the race- and gender-based inequalities that undercut the last collectivist swing, and that continue to underline our need and strength in each other—before we simply reconcile ourselves to the status quo.

There is such tremendous promise to a potential shift to hybrid, remote work. But there are great risks, too, particularly when it comes to the health of institutions that form the ever-fragile foundation of our communities. Because no significant societal change—especially one with the potential to alter the daily movements and habits of up to 40 percent of a nation's workers—happens in a vacuum.

What follows aren't intended to be detailed policy solutions. You could literally write a book on each of these areas, and there are people who are in the process of doing that work right now. But as we move forward in our thinking about the future of work and its place in a more collectivist society, there are so many areas that will demand attention, assistance, and protection. Here are some initial, but by no means exhaustive, ideas for where to focus.

The Post-Pandemic City

In May 2020, the CDC made a recommendation to employers: if you can, encourage your employees to stay away from public transportation. Instead, they should attempt to take personal cars or rely on cabs or ride shares. For Sara Jensen Carr, an assistant professor of architecture at Northeastern University and author of the forthcoming book **The Topography of Wellness: How Health and Disease Shaped the American Landscape,** that guidance was part of a host of pandemic-induced decisions, many made with the very best intentions, whose ramifications cities will have to grapple with for years to come.

"There have been very few documented cases of disease transmission on public transit," Carr told us in December 2020. "But the actual epidemiology doesn't matter. It's the narrative: what's embedded in people's minds. So when you have the CDC telling people that they should take their own vehicles to work, it rolls back so many of the positive transit developments that have happened over the last twenty years."

New car sales actually plummeted during the pandemic, reaching their lowest point since 2012. But they've rebounded in 2021, and used-car sales have skyrocketed. This is particularly true of people in urban areas who'd eschewed cars for years: suddenly a car felt like the only safe way to get anywhere outside walking distance, or actually out of town to visit parents or grandparents. For those who could afford it, a car felt like a solution to a problem of pandemic-enforced immobility. But those cars haven't disappeared, and neither have the newfound habits around them.

Whether because of increased remote work, increased reliance on personal vehicles, general reluctance to be in proximity to other people, or moves out of the city, the overall demand for public transit has gone down. But that does not change the necessity for that transit: even if ridership decreases 25 percent, there are still, depending on the size of your city, thousands, tens of thousands, even **millions** of residents who rely on it. Public transit is the circulatory system of a city; when it languishes, so, too, does quality of life within the areas it serves. If we want healthy cities, we have to figure out ways to treat it not as a perk, or a convenience, but as a necessity— regardless of our personal usage.

What does that take? Funding, for one. Otherwise "the financial situation that nearly every transit agency in America is in will certainly lead to significant service cuts, which inevitably lead to terrible spirals," Sarah Feinberg, the interim president of the New York City Transit Authority, said. "Service reductions are bad for commuters, devastating for essential workers, and detrimental to the economy."[5] If people leave New York— and newcomers don't immediately take their place—that will reduce the city's subway and bus revenue, which will lead to service cuts; that will make New York a harder place to live, so more people will leave the city; transit revenue will be reduced further, and on we go.

A change in how and where we work will likely change what we want out of our cities and their transportation infrastructure. According to Ben Welle and Sergio Avelleda, who study public transit and urban mobility at the World Resources Institute, the solution involves rethinking revenue models: reducing reliance on fares, just to start, and increasing taxpayer funding. But it will also require fixing and expanding the infrastructure that's already in place, even if ridership has gone down.[6]

Just because we're not commuting five days a week doesn't mean we don't still need mobility. "People working from home will still have to travel and go to meetings and live in their cities," Welle told us. But he argues the traditional "hub and spoke" model of transit systems—one that, in many American cities, was designed using old streetcar lines—may need to be reimagined and supplemented by crosstown and connector bus routes and space allocation like dedicated bus and bike lanes.

A change in working patterns—and, by extension, commutes—complicates this process. For many transit systems ridership is the success metric for the health of the system and often tied to funding. But if ridership is down, it could lead to more funding cuts and create a vicious downward spiral. To combat that, Welle said that the transit community is starting to look at different metrics besides ridership to gauge success. "People are starting to ask, 'How well does the transit system provide access to opportunities like access to health-care services or industry? How can it provide accessibility? Our current mobility system doesn't do a very good job of providing adequate access to this in most cities, but the pandemic may be a moment to reimagine what we want from these services," he said.

A major theme running through this chapter is that taking bits of our concentration away from work and reapplying it elsewhere will better our communities. But there's a secondary reason to support a robust mobility infrastructure in a remote or hybrid working world: combating isolation. There's a common misperception that a world where we spend less time in offices means a world spent isolated in our homes. That's certainly a risk, but it's all but guaranteed if we don't adapt our cities to our way of life. And that means creating more opportunities in our cities to have amenities within close reach of people by way of walking, bicycling, or a short bus or subway ride. "I imagine there's going to be a real acceleration in people wanting to have access to walkable urban neighborhoods," Welle told us. "If work is more flexible, our cities will need to be too; people will demand having quick access to parks or to private-public spaces like lunch spots or coffee shops to do work and meet people and form community."

We have to internalize that the more we fund these services, the more attractive and accessible we make them for all users, the healthier we and our cities will be. The same principle applies to public parks and green spaces, pools, community centers, public art projects: if the tax base declines because people have left the city, and you begin to neglect the very things that made the city special, even more people will leave, either by choice or by necessity, as the jobs that kept them otherwise tethered to a location disappear or go remote. It's a very slippery, very steep downward slope.

That scenario has occupied Cali Williams Yost, CEO of the Flex+Strategy Group, for the last year as she's advised dozens of companies on their plans for a new, flexible workforce. Sure, you can do all this work to make your office feel safe and figure out guidelines for remote work, she says. But it's all going to go to hell if we take our eyes off how this overall shift could affect our cities.

"Instead of jamming this way of working on everyone, we should be stepping back and meeting with city planning officials," she said. "Meeting with transportation people, meeting with politicians and public government organizations that address tax policy. We have to be working together to create a dynamic new vision of what the city is going to look like."

Yost lives in one of the long string of towns on the New Jersey transit line that, before the pandemic, funneled hundreds of thousands of workers elsewhere in the New York metro area every day.[7] In December 2020, the transit line sent out a survey, asking workers about their current and projected transit usage. "They're going to cut trains," Yost said. "And then train service will be even more horrible than it was before. And New York is going to try to claw back its own lost tax revenue by taxing us more on the way in, so it'll be even more expensive."

If you have the option to go in one day a

week or three—and the commute is a drag,
and all the restaurants around your office
building have closed up with no assistance
to restart them, and the movie theaters are
closed, and none of your friends are commuting in either—what's left to tether you to
the city?

"It becomes this reinforcing downturn,"
Yost said. "And no one's committed to figuring it out. There's just a total lack of imagination. If you own a corporate office, you need
to be calling up the transit people and saying,
we see the data, we are seeing the research,
this is going to be a new reality. So we need to
partner with you: How can we build a compelling vision of what's coming?"

Part of that vision will include workplaces;
they just won't necessarily look like what we
had before. "There's so clearly still a need,"
Leslie Kern, a geographer who studies urban
design and gender, told us. "The pandemic
showed us that. Cities and apartments aren't
built to be everything to everyone, both spa-
tially and socially." In the past, downtown
business corridors didn't have many services
nearby, in part because they've long been
built to accommodate the point-to-point

journeys of men in the workplace. But women's journeys, going back as far as the 1960s and 1970s, have always been much less linear: they're far more likely to drop off kids, do errands, and do eldercare along the way. What would new city planning look like that actually accommodates a more varied understanding of the tasks and needs of all over the course of a day? "Skyscrapers, for example, have been very single use," Kern told us. "So how could we reimagine the skyscraper as a multiuse space?"

Clive Wilkinson, who designed Google's corporate campus and spends his days thinking about the future of office design, is energized by the sheer number of opportunities. He thinks companies and corporate real estate developers will likely reimagine their holdings as fluid spaces, with much more flexibility for hot desking and short-term rentals of collaborative space. He sees hotels adding adaptable, actually attractive co-working spaces in order to accommodate influxes of remote and asynchronous workers or companies actually straight up purchasing hotels for collaborative work gatherings and retreats. Wilkinson has spent his career reinventing office use, using big-city planning as a primary inspiration. And while the "office as city" has been his long-running template, he foresees a reversal in coming years as metropolitan areas are redesigned around the idea of mobile, flexible work. Instead of the office as city, the **city** as office.

But Wilkinson told us that businesses are especially flat-footed in the moment. "Most of the clients we have, reps from and heads of real estate and facilities, are very confused," he said. "It will take a few big companies to create a new paradigm and reframe the office as a highly communal social place that supports episodic work. There's so much potential, but I get the sense there's a fear and a certain laziness about it."

Some of these big reimaginings are exciting. There's the 15-Minute City Project, a movement that advocates that everything a city dweller needs in life ought to be available within fifteen minutes, without the use of a car or mass transit. But even small overhauls in other metropolitan areas show a viable path to a healthier city. During the pandemic, the mayor of Paris pushed the city to add fifty kilometers of bike lanes; according to some estimates, the amount of cyclists in the city has increased by more than 65 percent since the spring of 2020, and close to 15 percent of all transit trips in Paris are now made by bike.[8] In Manhattan, the city government restricted traffic across town on Fourteenth Street to buses and local deliveries. The results were immediate: less congestion, more access for pedestrians, and bus travel times down between 15 and 25 percent.[9]

These kinds of small gains have urbanists imagining and designing a future where city streets are no longer dominated by tens of thousands of noisy, slow-moving individual cars. What might that look like? Well, according to Vishaan Chakrabarti, a former New York City urban-planning official and the founder of Practice for Architecture and Urbanism, it means more community spaces, luxurious sidewalks and opportunities for vendors and commercial space, streetside dining, quicker commute times, lower pollution, and a transit system that is more accessible for underserved communities.[10]

It's a big ask. But if these sorts of collaborations and intentional designs fail to materialize, Yost's predictions for the future of cities, like those of many others we spoke to, are bleak—especially if suburbs do the imaginative, collaborative work instead. In Westfield, New Jersey, a commuter suburb about an hour's train ride from Manhattan, the pandemic put the nail in the coffin of a sprawling Lord & Taylor department store that had been struggling for years. A nearly century-old picture palace, the Rialto Theater, had suddenly closed the year before. Over the course of the second decade of the twenty-first century, the downtown had clawed its way back from the recession and the competition of online commerce. Who knows how long it would take to revive this time?

But the city council saw an opportunity to transform the empty department stores and parking lots into a space that would actually keep commuters local. It voted 8–1 to approve a redevelopment plan of eleven different downtown properties, plus the Rialto, and seven parking lots. In their place: mixed-use development, including a 15 percent set-aside for affordable housing, and the hope to attract businesses and foot traffic that might have otherwise gone into the city.[11] The lesson: if urban centers don't make a concentrated effort to retain the qualities that made them magnetic, the more affluent tax base will be magnetized elsewhere.

And elsewhere, as it turns out, is booming. As we write this—with the pandemic's end in sight but still uncertain—one short-term trend seems clear: the pandemic's reorganization of people and resources has effectively supercharged midsize cities. According to data from LinkedIn, over the course of 2020 cities like Madison, Wisconsin; Richmond, Virginia; and Sacramento, California, saw the largest influx of tech workers.[12] Some of these metropolitan areas and their suburban sprawls share similar characteristics. Many are college towns with lively downtowns populated with locally owned small businesses and restaurants. They have burgeoning or robust arts scenes already in place.

Real estate is cheap, at least compared with the country's biggest cities, but not too cheap, which generally means that these towns were often in the throes of an affordable housing crisis pre-pandemic. They're walkable, livable, still culturally rich areas near reliable airports, and they're eminently attractive to active, upwardly mobile early or mid-career knowledge workers looking, at last, to put down some roots. Less than a year into the pandemic, the phenomenon had already earned these places a name: Zoom towns.

Many Zoom towns, particularly those that function as gateway communities to outdoor areas in the West, have found themselves in a precarious position as the very attitude, vibe, and community that attract people to the area in droves are threatened by the influx of coastal salaries. Danya Rumore, an assistant professor at the University of Utah who studies urban planning challenges in these communities, argues that the influx of workers is creating "small towns with big-city problems."[13] The gap between median wages and median housing costs just keeps getting wider and wider: in Bozeman, Montana, for example, the cost of living has soared to 20 percent higher than the national average, even though the median income for those employed in town is 20 percent lower; in February 2021, the average rent for a two-bedroom apartment was $2,050 a month—58 percent more than a year before.[14] As Heather Grenier, head of Bozeman's Human Resource Development Council, put it, "We have such low vacancy rates that if they lose a rental, there's literally no other place to go."

According to Rumore, this type of "natural amenity migration" to places in proximity to nature and recreation is a "probletunity." It's important to highlight the downsides, but there are upsides, too. Right now, Rumore says, the elected officials and leaders in many of these small communities are relying on anecdotal evidence and observations, which don't tell the entire story. That's why Rumore's team at the Gateway and Natural Amenity Region Initiative are trying to collect hard data on migration patterns and their effects—the sort that can help communities craft long-term plans for the future.

Though it's still in its early days, the Gateway and Natural Amenity Region Initiative is trying to connect smaller western towns—many of which have seen amenity migration expedited by fifteen years because of COVID—with leaders in places like Jackson, Wyoming; Vail, Colorado; and Moab, Utah; all of which have spent decades dealing with their own influx of tourism, second-home purchases, and permanent migration. Leaders in, say, Sandpoint, Idaho, don't have to go through these growing pains without guidance, the wisdom of experience, and which arguments will never really be settled.

"We hear communities endlessly debating whether this is good or bad for their community, and the hard truth is that when you're one of these towns, you don't get to make that decision," Rumore told us. "This change will happen whether they like it or not, so instead the conversation needs to be 'How do you protect the things you hold dear?'"

A big hurdle, Rumore admits, is that many of these desirable rural western communities are politically polarized: liberal enclaves in a sea of deep conservatism. The ideological split can make something as seemingly straightforward as a community meeting incredibly fraught.

But residents of smaller gateway communities tend to share a love of place—its natural beauty, or its seclusion, or its history. When you frame discussions around what's worth preserving, it can bring people together, even if they disagree on the way to actually go about protecting the places and spaces they love.

"The questions towns need to be asking are 'What tools and techniques and resources do we need?' and 'Who do we want to be when we grow up?' We have people who say we don't want to grow up. But you have to. You can't close the door behind you," Rumore said. "If you adopt that mindset, you end up doing nothing and it leads to uncontrolled growth."

As with so many aspects of this book, the pandemic did not create the problems associated with mass natural amenity migration. But those problems had been neglected for so long that pandemic-induced acceleration pushed them to crisis level. And it's not that these cities, as governmental entities, don't want remote workers per se: many of them have struggled to cultivate industries outside the extractive economy or tourism for years and crave the spending capacity and tax dollars that higher-income residents bring to town. Some midsize cities have been grappling with the constant drain of talent for years, coupled with the dawning reality that there is no new company that's coming to town, building a skyscraper, and throwing a thousand jobs into the mix.

Yet there is very little accounting for the ways that an influx of remote workers disrupts the quality and texture of other residents' lives. They can create a more fractured and volatile cultural, political, and economic environment, particularly when there's little guidance, funding, or past experience to draw on in order to handle new stresses. What's needed, then, is a system to assist, monitor, and mediate the transition—one that can protect the existing community while fostering sustainable growth.

Tulsa, Oklahoma, offers one template. Back in 2018, the city, with extensive support from the George Kaiser Family Foundation, embarked on a new experiment, offering remote workers a $10,000 incentive to move to Tulsa and take part in an intentional effort to build community. They can use the $10,000 toward a down payment on a house or for choice rates at apartment buildings in the new revitalized downtown, with prices between $650 and $1,250 a month, and access to downtown co-working space. While the $10,000 figure put Tulsa Remote into the headlines, the most compelling part of the project is the infrastructure. The initiative has a full-time staff that not only selects the recipients of the stipend but also helps integrate new residents into the community.

Ben Stewart, the executive director of Tulsa Remote, told us that they struggle with cultivating the necessary balance. "We take each applicant so seriously," he said, noting that the goal is to build what he referred to as an intentionally curated community. The program has had more than 50,000 applicants since its inception; in 2020, they welcomed 375 of them to the city. They try to select applicants who are dynamic and motivated and want to be members of the community; an ideal candidate is someone with a history of community service who is interested in new experiences. "We are looking for people who want to add something," he said. "Just coming here with a six-figure job working for Microsoft isn't really what we'd call a community alignment."

Tulsa Remote says its goal is for its "cohort to look like the rest of the United States," which means an intentional focus on geographic, ethnic, sexual orientation, and gender diversity. But they also understand that in order for the program to work, it needs continued nurturing. Each remote grant recipient becomes part of a mentor system, designed to both answer questions about the community and ease transition, but also address potential problems or conflicts—sort of like the neighbor who can tell you the best place to get tacos, or what a Sooner is, or just what is the George Kaiser Family Foundation and why is its name on so many projects in town.

There's potential for a program like Tulsa Remote, which has been duplicated in northwest Arkansas, Vermont, and northwest Alabama, to help bridge the gap between a new set of residents and the more rooted community, especially as new citizens begin to get active in local politics. "There's so much more access to power and decision makers in any smaller community, and you have the ability to impact and make change right away," Stewart told us. "But you want to help foster the natural collaborations, which means finding those people who are the glue in one community and bringing them together with those who are the glue in another."

In Obum Ukabam's case, moving to Tulsa was a chance to make up for lost time. In

2015, Ukabam nearly died from complications related to diabetes. Lying in a hospital bed in Los Angeles, battling sepsis and unsure if he'd survive, he remembered thinking that not only was he not ready to die but his life had been far more one-dimensional than he'd hoped. He'd been so focused on grinding through a grueling job that he had been unable to put down roots anywhere. He'd stopped volunteering, which had brought him great joy and purpose, years ago. He spent large chunks of his day stuck in soul-crushing traffic and often came home too tired to enjoy anything besides staying in. "I look back at those days and see that, really, I was just trying to survive," he told us. "And that wasn't just hurting me; it was taking away from others. How can you help people when you just need to help yourself?"

Then Ukabam came across the Tulsa Remote program. His friends—especially his wife's friends—were wary. "It was all, 'How are you going to make friends?!' and 'Be careful as a black man in Oklahoma,'" he recalled. But he was chosen in 2018 to be a member of Tulsa Remote's inaugural class, in part because of his desire to be an active member of the community and rediscover his passion for volunteering.

Ukabam looks back on his arrival in Tulsa and sees the emergence of a different version of himself. He immediately got in touch with the local community theater, where he produced and co-authored ten one-act plays centered on the massacre that decimated Tulsa's Black Wall Street in 1921. His wife rediscovered her love of cooking, launched a pop-up food truck, and now runs a permanent stall at the local food hall. Ukabam joined CAP Tulsa, an early education community action program to fight poverty. He volunteered with organizations like Teach Not Punish, 100 Black Men, and Show Me Shoes, a young women's mentorship organization he helped launch in town. He joined Leadership Tulsa, began volunteering with the Tulsa Debate League, and secured a $40,000 investment for social and emotional learning programs in the city. After less than two years, he was named one of three finalists for the Boomtown Award, honoring Tulsa's citizen of the year.

Ukabam moved to Tulsa for the remote

program, but he ended up leaving his remote job to work with the Holberton School, a software development boot camp with a local campus. He's acutely aware that his story sounds like a fairy tale, and he remains a realist when it comes to the potential of the program. Moving to Tulsa wasn't necessarily easy, he says, even with the program's helpful infrastructure. He could sense people were initially apprehensive about outsiders, especially given the highly publicized $10,000 stipend program. He felt he had to prove himself and earn the trust of longtime residents. Even now, having been honored by the city, he understands the boundaries of his still-new residency: he works hard to respect the city's history, including its tragedies and successes, and refuses to speak on behalf of the town's descendants, regardless of race.

It was still hard work, in other words, to put down roots. But Ukabam says that a program like Tulsa Remote can provide an on-ramp, and the sort of early support that felt essential. As he sees it, the $10,000 stipend gets all the headlines, but the intentionality and infrastructure of a municipal remote worker program is the real investment. More small and midsize towns should have similar networks in place—stipend or not.

"It sort of reminds me of the gold rush," Ukabam said. "There's a gold rush happening right now—except it's for quality of life. Places like Tulsa, and all over the beautiful Mountain West, they're going to have a lot of people coming in search of a better quality of life. And it just makes sense to give people a way to acclimate to the city. To give them the resources and help guide and shape the change. Because they're coming. Like it or not, they're coming."

We've thought about this a lot in our own role, moving to Missoula, Montana, back in 2017 to work remotely. As the participants in Tulsa Remote have shown, there's no simple checklist to become a conscientious member of the community and no carbon-neutralizing payment you can make and forget about. Buying local and tipping well, that's great. So is taking the bus a few times a week. But when it comes to larger solutions, they're kind of like personal recycling: individual choices that make us feel good but can also let us off the hook for the much larger task of grappling with collective problems.

Even if you can now afford your dream house, a city where housing is unaffordable for most is a broken city. Even if you can afford to buy and use your own car, a city where transportation is difficult for many is a broken city. Even if you have a backyard, a city where green space is unsafe, underfunded, and inaccessible is a broken city. The effects of a broken or breaking city are most immediately felt by those who are most vulnerable. But they ripple into the lives of everyone who lives there and in the surrounding area.

So many of the institutions that make up our cities were breaking or long broken pre-COVID. But the decisions we make moving forward have the potential to aggravate preexisting problems or, if we think expansively and collectively, can begin to begin to fix them. That work requires the political, financial, and on-the-ground support of people with the social capital to effect change. If you are reading this book because you're confident a remote future can work, then this means you.

Whether you're in the city, in the suburbs, or in a rural area, whether you've recently moved or have pledged yourself to the long haul where you are, there are ways for you to support the infrastructure of your immediate and extended area. First and foremost, that means getting on board with paying for civilization, better known as taxes. But it also means articulating support, and helping to sway public opinion, about the need for infrastructure, even if, **especially** if, you are not its primary beneficiary.

Look at your community and ask yourself, what do you, as a relatively privileged knowledge worker, like about living there? Maybe it's the schools, the ease of getting from one place to another, the public bathrooms at the playground, or the great local library. Now how can you work to extend those benefits to people who don't work in the same sort of job as you do? The answer is pretty simple: pay for the robust maintenance of public institutions.

For example, maybe you or your company can afford dues at a local co-working space. So how do you support the creation of more public, affordable, or subsidized work areas for others? Maybe you live in a neighborhood within walking distance of a park or trail. How can you work to elect local leaders and support initiatives that make that sort of access a priority in every zip code? Maybe you're making an income that makes it easy to pay your rent or mortgage where you live, but the people who make up the beating heart of your community can't find anything in their price range. How can you demand affordable housing, **even** if that housing will be in your neighborhood?

You can fine-tune your at-home workstation, and your company can figure out the most inviting setup for collaborative work in the office. But the whole point of all of this flexible work is to cultivate a life outside our offices, untethered from our laptops. Unless we continue to invest in the world outside those spaces, what is any of all this ultimately for?

Reimagine Childcare

Long before the pandemic, the problem with childcare in the United States has fundamentally been a problem of individualism. There was a brief opportunity, back in 1971, to head off this fate: the Comprehensive Child

Development Act of 1971 had made its way through Congress with overwhelming bipartisan support. Building on the success of Head Start, which had launched in 1965, the Child Development Act would've made high-quality childcare available on an affordable, sliding-scale basis for all. But Nixon vetoed the bill—a move that, as Anna K. Danziger Halperin, a historian of the childcare movement, explains, "surprised even officials within his own administration."[15]

The reasoning, according to Danziger Halperin, was fear from the right wing of the Republican Party that the CDA would encourage women to join the workforce, thereby destroying the "integrity" of the middle-class family unit, while also providing solutions that felt dangerously close to communistic, "un-American" care. There was also conservative concern that the bill was an "overreach" into the lives of the poor and that its primary beneficiaries were families of color. As Professor Elizabeth Palley, who also studies the history of childcare, explained it, "White people don't want to pay for Black people's children to be cared for."[16]

Nixon's veto—and the accompanying legacy of childcare as the responsibility of individual families, subject to the whims of the free market—have stuck. The coalition behind the bill dispersed, and feminists' focus, particularly over the course of the late 1970s and the 1980s, was more on getting women into jobs in the first place and protecting them from discrimination once there. "They stopped fighting for childcare, and other sorts of collective issues, and really focused on individual professional success," Danziger Halperin told us. "But when you think of childcare as a personal choice, it creates all of these new inequalities. Women of color, black and immigrant women—they end up caring for the children of professional women. And those professional women, in turn, don't want their whole paycheck going to childcare, so it gets undervalued and underpaid."

That's how you get our current hodgepodge of a system, filled with wait lists for care centers, nanny shares, "kith and kin" (a.k.a. close friends and family) care, unpredictable subsidies tied to working hours, low wages for caregivers, and astronomical cost burdens for parents. Middle-class workers may have more access to quality care, but that care comes at great, destabilizing cost, which will only rise in the post-pandemic landscape.

This has been a problem for **years,** but the pandemic has underlined just how unsustainable the system has become. Part of the problem is that childcare crosses so many different policy areas: Should it be considered, first and foremost, an antipoverty program? An educational program? A program for mothers, for workers, for families, or for children? Solutions have been fragmented and, as evidenced by the current difficulty in finding affordable, high-quality care, completely insufficient.

So here are your options. As your work schedule becomes more flexible, you can use it as an opportunity to bend yourself around your children's care schedule and keep paying as much as, if not more than, before. You can keep dreaming of a scenario like the one available to workers at Patagonia's headquarters and distribution center, where childcare is on-site, multilingual, and subsidized, while you keep trying to cobble together nanny shares and stay awake at night thinking about how long you can rely on your mother-in-law to cover Fridays. Or you can use this opportunity to advocate for a real paradigm shift in the way we think of care.

Utah senator Mitt Romney's 2021 proposal to offer significant subsidies to families with children—$4,200 a year per child under six, and $3,000 per child aged six to seventeen—acknowledges the extent of the problem. But it's still an individualistic solution that does little to actually address the dearth of affordable quality care options. As Elliot Haspel, author of **Crawling Behind: America's Childcare Crisis and How to Fix It,** put it to us, "I don't think a childcare subsidy of even $10,000 a year is enough to bring us out of this nosedive."

What we need are solutions like what nearly happened back in 1971 and what's successfully taken hold in the United Kingdom and so many other countries. We have to start thinking of early childcare and education the same way we think about public parks, or sanitation, or libraries, or public schools: as foundational to a functioning society whether or not you directly benefit from its existence.

"We've been so stuck on this idea that there should be sliding scales, eligibility qualifications, or tied to work," Haspel explained. "It's been so, so destructive. We have to move away from seeing childcare as an entitlement, and toward seeing it as a **public good.**"

This scenario is only possible, of course, when and if early childhood care is robustly funded, just as public schools are, with tax dollars. That sounds like a straightforward solution, and in some ways it is. In other ways, it's endlessly complicated. The conversations that most people have about childcare usually start with the astronomical cost, touch on the difficulty of waiting lists, glance toward the difficulty of finding a "good fit" (often code for perceived quality), and then stop. Families somehow figure out a way to make it work, even if that means someone dropping out of the workforce, relying on informal "kith and kin" care, or emptying out savings, and then everyone breathes a deep sigh of relief when the youngest kid hits kindergarten. The struggle to pay for care is acute, but ultimately too short-lived to accumulate political might.

That can change. Regardless of whether you have children, whether you have three in care or yours have already left the home, we can identify the burden—and the way it exacerbates racial inequities, sustains the gender pay gap, discourages parenthood, and just generally makes life really, really hard for millions of people—and agree that it doesn't have to be this way.

The easiest way for that to happen? Some people think it has to happen on the federal level, others on the level of the state. Biden has put forth a plan that envisions free pre-K for three- and four-year-olds. But as Nicole Rodgers, founder of Family Story, explains, the problem with childcare policy is that it "never, ever is first." She fears that childcare reform is "going to be that thing of 'It would be nice to do this, but we're not going to do this right now.'"[17] You have the opportunity to refuse that equivocation. Yes, these programs will cost money. But the point of this sort of spending is that the burden on your everyday life will go down. This is especially true if you're a parent, but if you work at an organization and have seen, firsthand, the burden of unpredictable care on your co-workers, you also understand just how revelatory it could be.

Otherwise, we cue up a nightmare scenario. Childcare becomes even more of a precious, luxury good than it already is, accessible only to the upper middle class and the truly affluent. "We already see women being shoved out of the workplace in droves to provide this care," Haspel said. "So we can revert back to that situation, where mothers are expected to bear the brunt of care in the home, and the cascading effects on family income and stability. And this, of course, will ultimately have effects on people and their decision whether or not to bear children—and we're already at historically low birthrates."

All of it's regressive, all the way down. But there are examples, even just in the United States, of what we could do. Proposed "Common Start" legislation in Massachusetts would fully fund childcare and after-school care across the state, with anyone earning half the state's median income qualifying for free care, while those earning more would pay on a sliding scale, maxing out at no more than 7 percent of their household income.[18] In

Vermont, H.171—which, at the time of this writing, was speeding through the state legislature with around two-thirds of the house of representatives signed on as co-sponsors—promises to fundamentally remake the childcare system in the state: no family would be asked to pay more than 10 percent of their income on care, and the 17.2 percent pay gap between early childhood educators and elementary school teachers would be closed entirely, significantly decreasing the 10.9 percent of Vermont's ECE workforce who lived in poverty.[19]

In 2020, a ballot initiative for universal preschool won 64 percent of the vote in Portland, Oregon, and surrounding Multnomah County. In addition to providing free care for three- and four-year-olds, regardless of family income, the initiative raises preschool teacher salary from $31,000 a year to $74,000, with the aim of making the profession more attractive and sustainable. And they're doing it by taxing the upper echelons of the income bracket: 1.5 percent on single incomes of more than $125,000 and joint filings of more than $200,000.

Two of these models require electing

politicians on the state level who support this sort of change. The other required votes on the municipal level. In each, you, as a voter and/or taxpayer, have the ability to support this paradigm shift. It may or may not directly affect you but could have dramatic, life-altering effects on the overall well-being of your city and state and nation, and a diverse coalition of support, in every sense of the word, is absolutely fundamental to these initiatives' success. This can't just be about your childcare costs, or your sister's, or your friend's. We should support these changes because we don't want work and parenting, no matter your occupation, to feel so impossible or like an impossible burden that's the individual's, alone, to bear.

"We focus so much on the child, and on school readiness, and making sure that a kid develops well and is stable and secure," Haspel told us. "And all of that's so important. But we also have to think about what it takes for parents to actually thrive." Think of what a weight it would lift off you, off parents in different jobs from you, off your neighbors and people across your town, to have the weight of finding affordable, high-quality childcare for their three- and four-year-olds, **regardless** of their employment status, lifted from them. This isn't fantasy; it's very real and in very real practice in countries that aren't the United States. You can give yourself and others in your greater community that gift, even if you will not or no longer be its primary beneficiary. You just need to refuse to shut up about it until it happens.

Worker Solidarity

Writing about the white-collar office worker in 1951, the sociologist C. Wright Mills declared that "whatever common interests they have do not lead to unity."[20] That was true then, and it's true now: office workers have either resisted or given up on efforts to generate solidarity, especially when formalized in a union. As Nikil Saval put it in **Cubed,** white-collar workers "believed ardently in the American dream of relentless upward mobility. They preferred the insecurity of getting promoted based on merit to the steady advance of seniority. Unions promised one thing above all—dignity—which white-collar workers claimed they already had, thanks to the prestige of their professions, the bleached stiffness of their collars."[21]

In short, unions were for people stuck on a certain rung of the American dream, or who couldn't advocate for themselves. For those who'd made it to the office, unions just weren't **necessary.**

Corporations have actively cultivated this attitude for decades. The entire field of human resources is meant to convince workers that the company has their best interests at heart. Even the "good" management that we've extolled in previous chapters can undercut solidarity, because hope for advancement—and tiny shifts in job title and salary—keep employees invested in their **individual** potential, instead of collective protections.

Internal comms—whether in the form of all-company emails, Slack channels, or all hands—highlight and celebrate achievements within an organization but also model the way employees **should** behave, underlining the proper posture toward work and the company as a whole. As the professor of management JoAnne Yates argues in **Control Through Communication,** these types of messaging have long been used to encourage feelings of family, and attendant loyalty, among workers, and you don't form a union with your fellow siblings when you get angry with your parents.[22] That's just disrespectful.

Or at least that's been the enduring, and largely successful, messaging toward office workers. There have been pockets of organizational success, particularly government employees. But private corporations have become experts at keeping organizing efforts at bay. It's not that office workers are **necessarily** anti-union. They just don't think they need the protections a union can offer or are too worried about potential backlash.

But that sentiment has begun to shift. Back in the 1950s, Mills predicted a potential future for the white-collar profession: a large percentage would become proletarianized, which is to say, their wages, overall income, prestige, power, and stability would come to resemble that of the wage worker. "It would be possible," Mills wrote, "for a segment of the white-collar people to become virtually identical with wage-workers in income, property, and skill, but to resist being like them in prestige claims and to anchor their whole consciousness upon illusory prestige factors."[23]

You might have watched this happen in your own organization, or left a profession or company because it did. Or you might be watching it gradually happen in your own office as your company opts to fill more positions with subcontractors who might be doing very similar work but for less pay and with far fewer benefits or with less security. In some organizations, the ongoing precarity has led workers to embrace organizing efforts for the first time: workers in digital media, in museums, at Google and Amazon, in breweries and coffee shops and cannabis production are unionizing (or attempting to) for the first time.

Some of these workers, particularly those outside office environments, are fighting for very simple protections: severance after layoffs, safety protections during COVID, work schedules available with enough time to schedule childcare, and paid sick leave. And some just increasingly recognize themselves as part of the "precariat"—the term the theorist Guy Standing uses to describe a class of worker who feels fundamentally unstable in their work, regardless of education or vocation.[24]

Maybe you don't feel this in your job. Maybe you **do** feel cared for. Maybe your company is great, and authentically trying to be better, and your boss is understanding. That is **great**—for you. But a boss is not a good system. It is a short-term, individual solution. Which doesn't mean you need to say screw you to your company. It means figuring out how you can create scenarios in which the stability and flexibility extended to you don't hinge on happening to have a good, understanding boss. Put differently, it means cultivating cross-class, cross-profession solidarity.

Back in the 1970s, it was incredibly difficult for **any** woman, regardless of her background, to rise above clerical work within an organization. As a result, the coalition that formed to advocate for better clerical protections cut across class, race, and educational background. As that coalition grew, corporations recognized its power, and, as Karen Nussbaum, the woman who helped organize clerical and office workers in the 1970s and 1980s, put it to us, execs got sick of their own daughters complaining about their treatment at the office. They had to figure out some safety valve for the growing dissatisfaction, some way to decrease the pressure before a wave of organizing really took hold. The answer was simple: they started promoting the educated, middle-class women out of the secretarial pool.

"They were so clever about splitting the workforce," Nussbaum said. "If you were an individual woman who had been working at an insurance company, say, and all the sudden they finally promoted you, you thought, well, good! This is what we've been fighting for!" The problem was that it was only "good" for part of the coalition, but once it had been divided, its power was lost. "There was this powerful moment in the 1970s and early '80s when women were having independent lives, when a lot of us were able to become very self-reliant, but we were pretty powerless at the same time," Nussbaum recalled. "We felt pretty good about ourselves: we were divorcing bad husbands, raising our kids, working all the time, advocating for equality. But it wasn't all that great."

A similar phenomenon is happening right now, in many of the workplaces most eager to embrace remote work. In early 2021, more than four hundred Google employees formed the Alphabet Workers Union, a historic years-long effort to elevate worker concerns that go well beyond pay equity to address issues from algorithmic bias to ethical concerns about government contracts. But Google, like so many companies in Silicon Valley, offers an updated version of the white-collar union aversion that Mills described in 1951.

Tech companies are home to some of the most desirable jobs available for the American worker, with the highest starting salaries and seemingly limitless on-site perks. At the same time, many of these companies rely heavily on a temporary and contract labor force—so much so that at Google there are more contract employees than full-time employees.[25] There are few formal protections in place preventing Google from gradually transitioning more and more of its workers to contingent status. So why don't employees unionize? Many just don't think they need it; after all, they have some of the best jobs on the planet.

But that sort of thinking has its limitations, especially as the feasibility of remote work leads companies to outsource developer jobs to whoever's willing to work for less. "A big draw of remote work is being able to expand the pool of hiring talent," Nataliya Nedzhvetskaya, a researcher at the University of California, Berkeley who studies the organization efforts of tech companies, told us. "But this has the potential to intersect with the global labor market in a way that allows these companies to undermine their current workers, especially those who might be trying to build collective action in the industry. Given the opportunity to decrease labor costs by 60 percent by hiring in the global south, I guarantee they're going to look into it very seriously."

Nedzhvetskaya is also concerned that remote work could make some parts of organizing more difficult. "The physical space is helpful," she said. "Being physically present helps you see who is with you and who shares your values and who will take the same stand as you, which can be crucial because organizing in the workplace is still so risky in the United States." Still, she argues, there are templates for remote organizing in the tech space that have helped build solidarity. In 2018, more than twenty thousand employees staged a walkout to protest how Google handled sexual harassment; it which was organized largely online.[26] Nedzhvetskaya also cited the phenomenon of the open letter—now blog post—which tech employees have used to gain media attention to their demands.

But those demands might go only so far without the ability to gather and build trust in person. A collective sense of outrage may get the ball rolling, in other words, but it's still fundamentally different from joining together to spell out workers' rights or put mechanisms in place to hold management accountable. "Formal organization is needed to bring about lasting change," Nedzhvetskaya says, "and remote workers will need to be very intentional to create that."

The reality, no matter where you work and for what level of pay, is that our overall system of labor protections is broken. If you've managed to avoid some form of exploitation, it's almost certainly because you've had enough financial security to quit jobs when they start to tilt that way, or avoid them altogether. But when the system is broken, it doesn't matter how self-reliant you are. It'll still break you, too, if you step off the wheel of work.

Which means that regardless of your current feelings of stability, we have to keep advocating for programs like universal health care, which separate safety nets from place or type of employment. But we also have to think more about what broad forms of worker solidarity look like, in and outside the office. Because unions, at least in our current moment, simply aren't available to everyone. To advise as if they were is unrealistic. But that doesn't mean that you can't start thinking about unions or supporting people who **are** unionizing—including those who work in different sectors of your company. And it means electing leaders who are committed to strengthening our diluted labor protections, which have failed to take the radical changes of the last forty years of the labor market into account.

So ask yourself this: How would your office culture shift if you actually thought of yourself not as a copywriter, or claims adjuster, or software developer, but as a **worker**? How can you focus on what binds you to the other workers in your life, in and outside your own company, instead of what differentiates you? Otherwise, we're just like the women who, perhaps understandably, took the promotions offered to them in the 1970s and 1980s, leaving the remaining secretarial workers' efforts behind.

We've spent the preceding pages trying to give you the strategies to rethink our particular type of laptop-bound work. But moving forward, we also have to figure out how to simultaneously advocate for those whose work does not resemble ours, but is in no way less essential to a functioning society. "We **can** rethink the theory of individual advancement that we've bought for all these years, that's brought us to this place where capitalism has no combatants, nothing to keep it in check," Nussbaum told us. "You just need to have a constellation of forces: people who are fed up, the collapse of institutions, a rupture in the way people work." You just need a moment, in other words, like right now.

Reestablish Networks of Care and Community

Pre-pandemic, we carved hours of time out of our weeks to be with other people in some way. Supervising kids' practice, in meetings, in classes, at playdates, at concerts and performances, at anniversaries and bachelorette weekends and birthday parties, at destination conferences and reunions, we did, indeed, gather together. But many of us secretly found these experiences underwhelming, even if we'd never admit it. "We spent much of that time in uninspiring, underwhelming moments that fail to capture us, change us in any way, or connect us to one another," Priya Parker writes in **The Art of Gathering.** "Much of the time we spend in gatherings with other people disappoints us."[27]

Parker argues that we've lost what's actually meaningful about gatherings, the "crackle and flourish" that allow them to bond people to one another and create networks of care. Pre-pandemic, people had become so fixated on the logistics of gathering that they'd lost sight of why we gather in the first place. Our calendars went from a private analog to digital and semipublic, and in the process an overbooked life became a status symbol. We'd forgotten, in other words, what being with other people is actually for.

So what is it for? Fun, of course, and

diversion, but also genuine care, the sort that stems from reestablishing the kinds of strong and loose ties that distinguished the more collectivist moments of our not-so-distant past. Cultivating those ties doesn't mean you necessarily need to start going to religious services, or navigating the knotty politics of your kids' elementary school PTA. It doesn't mean signing up for five different mailing lists in the hopes of finally getting the gumption to show up for a meeting, or finding another book club of friends of a friend whom you secretly resent. It means finding a network that actually means something to you and figuring out what it might look like for you to care for—and be cared for in return by—others within it.

Mutual aid was the bedrock of so many of the organizations listed in the beginning of this chapter, and it formalized the promise of support and insurance that members could not find outside their own networks. Over the last century and a half, mutual aid has provided a means to build safety nets for one another—as immigrants, as black Americans, as trans people—when the state and established capital either refused or failed. Which is part of why mutual aid, in so many forms, has flourished over the course of the pandemic: when it became clear that the state was failing to protect the vulnerable, people did what many had forgotten was, in fact, second nature. They cared for each other.

All over the world, but especially in the United States, where societal support was hard to come by, groups that had been formed for different functions—Buy Nothing Facebook Groups, political organizing—transformed their focus, while others were built from the ground up. Some had more radical and explicit anticapitalist politics; others, particularly in more conservative areas, centered on meeting requests from those in need.

What distinguishes these groups from traditional charity organizations is their dedication to the **mutual.** As Meera Fickling, one of the leaders of Rocky Mountain Mutual Aid Network, explains, "We don't means test, and we wouldn't even have the resources to means test even if we wanted to. If you say you need help, then you need help. People aren't clients. They are simply people who need help at a specific time. And of course, we hope that this goes two ways."

People who request help come and volunteer. And people who can provide help might, at some point, need it as well. That idea is at the heart of community fridge programs that have popped up across the country: there's always a flow of people stocking, servicing, and taking from the fridge. People who fill it with items from a recent shopping trip might, the next day, come and get something they need for themselves. They're just part of the larger fridge community.

Mutual aid takes **time**—the sort of time that might actually be open to you if the rigidity of your schedule eases, alongside your addiction to work. It's a way to conceive of yourself as someone who doesn't simply give money to organizations, but is an active component of an organization yourself. It's also a significant act of necessary humility: a fundamental precept of mutual aid is that everyone needs aid at one time or another. To depend uniquely on yourself—or what, at this point, remains a broken state and federal government—is to declare yourself immune.

Maybe, because of your age or relative health or financial situation, you don't think you need other people now. But you will. You will fall ill; your body and mind will, at some point, break down; you will temporarily or permanently lose an income stream. You will need advice, or an extra set of hands, or a person willing to unload a new table from your car, or a teaspoon of turmeric, and others will need a different set of advice, and a different set of hands, and you to help them unload a table from their car, and a teaspoon of turmeric. What joy, what balance it can foster, to give and receive in return.

For so many, participation in these groups is an act of resistance and enduring proof that our systems are broken and must be replaced. But even in protest, the experience can be a spiritual balm. In the uncertain early days of March 2020, we profiled a group of young community organizers outside Boston who, in under a week, created a massive digital mutual aid network to funnel money, deliveries, and crucial information to residents. The entire process was documented online, and delving into their spreadsheets, you could watch the bonds of community being formed—an uplifting, real-time document of people helping people. The organization offered not just logistical and financial aid but also hope.

These loose and firm bonds of support can come from something like mutual aid, but they can come from other gatherings, too, organized around a religion, a common community cause, or just proximity. They don't need to have secret handshakes, like so many of the groups of the past, and we'd actually suggest avoiding any group where all the members are the same age, race, vocation, or economic bracket as you. One of the things you'll miss about the office is talking with people who are younger and older than you and forming cross-generational bonds. But the opportunity for those connections doesn't have to disappear simply because you're no longer commuting.

You might be struggling to figure out what that means for you. You might be on a lot of email lists, and get a lot of text alerts, but feel as if you'd never be the sort of person who'd show up for a meeting. You might still feel that committing to anything, truly **anything,** is more than you're able to offer right now. Give it time, while you figure out the new rhythms of your life, but not too much. Because part of what will motivate you to advocate for and maintain a flexible schedule is realizing just how much more time you have for these sorts of connections, particularly when you're able to stop thinking of them as obstacles to rest and start thinking of them as conduits to care.

Try to imagine what might make you feel authentically connected. Maybe it's singing with other people. Maybe it's talking, over the course of hours, on a trail, or learning a new skill, or teaching one to others. It might include some component of ritual that makes the time feel meaningful, or a lot of small talk with people with long, meandering memories. What matters is not limiting yourself to your ideas of what gathering, especially the sort of gathering that you resented, pre-pandemic, looks like. Did your book club suck? Leave it, and start volunteering with your local library. Did your community's Nextdoor page devolve into toxicity? Screw it, go leave a note with your number in the mailbox of the eighty-something-year-old down the street. Do you love card games but never have anyone to play with? There's a bridge club that would **love** to have you, we promise. Does church feel traumatizing, but you miss hymns and being with a random assortment of people who aren't like you? There's another version of that; it just might take some seeking.

Halfway through the pandemic, Devon, who recently finished his PhD in geology and lives in Atlanta, was desperate for a way to connect to and help his community—to the point that he was considering applying to med school. But then he found out about Concrete Jungle, a small urban farm in southwest Atlanta. "I get to do farming work that I already really enjoy and found soothing," he said. "And I also know that what we produce is going directly to people who need and are deeply deserving of healthy fresh food. I've personally picked veggies and then packed those veggies up and delivered them to the door of someone who wouldn't be able to access them any other way." For Devon, the opportunity for direct aid filled a void in his paid work, and, he says, "getting involved in this community has always really opened my eyes to how hard a lot of people are working to make Georgia a better place, which is inspiring, to say the least."

Jackie started volunteering with DC Books to Prisons, which sends books to incarcerated readers in thirty-four states. In 2019 alone, the organization sent more than seven thousand packages. Before the pandemic, they'd meet in a church to coordinate requests, but they were able to shift the work to home. From time to time, she has to look up someone before she sends them a package, to double-check their name and current facility. "That means I often see what they are in prison for and find out they are convicted pedophiles, rapists, and murderers. And I still carefully pick out books that I hope they like," she said. "That is a new experience that has made my empathy grow beyond what it once was." It also, she says, made her a better reader: "We get a huge number of requests for Westerns, so I read **Lonesome Dove** to be more familiar with the genre. What a story. And I would have never checked it out without the people writing us. What a gift."

Cultivating a community of care might also look like reinvesting in connections that have gone fallow, for whatever reason, with time. We don't have children, but have long wanted to be part of the children's lives in our greater friend circle. Before the pandemic, our dedication to work made it difficult to establish any sort of consistent presence in our friends' kids' lives. But the pod we created with another family has allowed us to prioritize those relationships like never before. And spending time with their children is deeply enriching for all parties. Rolling on the floor and playing zombie hide-and-seek and drawing underwater creatures have been welcome, cherished distractions from the seriousness of our adult lives and helped ease our friends' care burden. Others have told us similar stories: of moving home, or to the area where their closest friends live, or even figuring out co-living scenarios with another family. You could blame those moves on the pandemic, or you could just view the pandemic as a catalyst for actually seeking out the intimacy and care we crave.

But you need to cultivate patience, too. We're so used to on-demand everything we've forgotten that community takes **time:** to find, to join, to figure out one's place, to guide. "Community is wonderful, but it's also **awful,**" Casper ter Kuile, author of **The Power of Ritual,** told us. "People are hard! But we need these structures to hold us together, even when it's hard. Because if we engage with our community and spiritual lives as consumers, and we check out when it isn't immediately satisfying, we end up losing the most precious experiences of life."

There are opportunities to create, nurture, and grow these sorts of gatherings, wherever you are, but you need to have the wherewithal to find and commit to them. And that wherewithal is incredibly difficult to come by when work remains the axis of your life. But we've mired ourselves in a circular logic: we live to work because there's so little else in our lives; there's so little else in our lives because we live to work. But it doesn't have to be this way. Consider Obum Ukabam from Tulsa. After spending a decade feeling overextended and rootless, he found that a few intentional changes to his work and living scenario completely changed the context and purpose of his life. But Ukabam's path toward community is just one way forward. Depending on your personality, you could be the catalyst, the behind-the-scenes support, the person who shows up every week to do cleanup. Your role matters so much less than the slow-motion revelation of shared commitment to each other.

This is what networks of care, like all forms of collectivism, do: they weave us into reliance on each other. Instead of ignoring suffering, we are encouraged to address it head-on. Such networks have the potential to cultivate our best and most generous selves, and counteract the turn toward individualism, but only if we continue to seek out groups and initiatives that both challenge and comfort us, that benefit us but even more important benefit those whose situations are nothing like our own.

All the potential solutions and pitfalls above underscore a crucial reality: flexible work is not, in itself, the cure to all that ails our society. But it does open the door to continue the essential work of addressing our bigger problems head-on. Additional time and space and energy make it possible to be far more intentional about how we live in our communities; when we're not constantly triaging our own lives, we can begin to care for others.

But as we've attempted to outline throughout this book, the true benefits of remote work will only arrive if we codify them with real policy—the sort that makes them tenable beyond the world of knowledge work. To put it bluntly: to gain these freedoms for ourselves and call it good will be nothing less than a collective moral failure.

We get it: we're all tired, and we know that the resistance to this sort of reform and this ethos of care is robust. But societal safety nets aren't actually reliable—no matter how much you make today, or how safe you feel in your current position—until they're built strong enough to catch us all, no matter how hard, where, or why we fall. We have made ourselves so unspeakably alone for so long, so desperate in our self-reliance. But there's a different way forward, visible once the haze of overwork has cleared. It's through, and with, each other.

A Final Note to Bosses

There's a fair amount of hubris involved in writing a book about the future of anything. This is doubly true for work, which is a vague term that doesn't begin to adequately describe the universe of industries, jobs, expectations, injustices, and strategies that make up our collective laboring. We are attempting to peer around a corner and offer potential visions of what's to come. It's not lost on us that this is treacherous territory. As Scott Berkun, who wrote a best-selling book on remote work all the way back in 2013, points out, "Books about the future of work make the same mistake: they fail to look back at the history of work or, more precisely, the history of books about the future of work and how wrong they were."[1]

Having read our fair share of those books in preparation for this one, we agree. Which is why we've tried not to offer predictions and focused, instead, on mapping out the potential for a lasting paradigm shift. If there is an underlying mood running through this book, it is a feeling of hopeful caution. We believe that work is occupying more and more of our time, burning us out and conferring few of the spoils on workers. We **also** believe that the pandemic has created a rare pause for reflection and an opportunity to rethink the status quo. Still, we're realists. We understand that the past is full of ponderous "future of work" predictions that feel like hubristic attempts to solve serious problems at scale. Ultimately, these "solves" leave a trail of new, even thornier problems in their wake.

Which is why, behind every suggestion or example in this book, there's a nagging note of caution: cut corners, and risk repeating the mistakes of the past. In other words, don't screw this up.

If you're a manager or executive reading those words, you might be rolling your eyes.

You shouldn't. While much of what we've laid out here is firmly rooted in making working lives better for workers, reimagining how we work isn't merely some altruistic project. If you run a company, there are many reasons you don't want to screw this up, but chief among them is that a remote future is better business.

You might remember Darren Murph, GitLab's head of remote, from a previous chapter. Murph is one of the first—if not **the** first—person whose job is dedicated exclusively to remote work strategy. Since March 2020, his expertise has been in high demand; he spends his days in and out of meetings with big companies, all trying to wrap their heads around the ways in which their businesses will change when the pandemic subsides. In many of the meetings, he told us, executives are stubborn or dubious about fully remote work. And so he puts it in terms they can understand. Specifically, compounding interest.

Murph likes to ask these executives a simple question: If they had the choice, would they rather have invested in Warren Buffett's holding company, Berkshire Hathaway, twenty minutes ago or twenty years ago? The choice, of course, is obvious. There are few investment choices you make in the present that would make up for the compounding interest lost when you chickened out on an investment opportunity. And this is how Murph frames GitLab's investment in a fully asynchronous, distributed workforce. Setting up GitLab's workflows to thrive with no office and with employees scattered across every time zone wasn't easy. It required substantial up-front investment of time and energy and resources. And to the naked eye, the company's exhaustive, open-source documentation process (every meeting, every employee README, every wiki and strategic plan) might look unnecessary and inefficient. But that line of thinking, Murph argues, is dangerously short term.

"Our corporate norms condition us to just put one foot in front of the other," Murph told us. "Everyone is thinking about their jobs in thirty-minute chunks: meeting by meeting, email by email."

We are so focused on getting through the day, he argues, that our idea of working efficiently is actually deeply inefficient. His company's documentation strategy is an example of a new way forward. GitLab's employees spend less time intruding on others in the middle of the day or sending redundant emails because all the information they need—whether they attended a meeting or not—is recorded and easily accessible to all.

"If I ask you to take twenty minutes before a meeting to read my README, that's a short-term sacrifice that will pay dividends over time as our working relationship deepens over the weeks and months and years," he said. "We have built up an eight-thousand-page, easily searchable library from employees documenting their successes and failures. That's eight thousand pages of what not to do. How will you catch up to the compound interest of that? The only way is for companies to start that knowledge journey **now.**" Otherwise, their competitors will, and every year their competitive advantage will increase.

Stop thinking short term. This isn't just Murph's advice. It is **the** recurring theme in our hundreds of conversations with executives, management coaches, urbanists, activists, technologists, and workers. In our reporting, most managerial horror stories can be traced back to a set of hasty decisions made in the convenience of the moment, without stepping back to imagine the broader implications.

Understaffing, for example, might be cheaper in the short term, but it slowly begins to eat away at a company. Morale sinks, productivity and quality drain, and employers struggle to retain workers. A company that burns its workers out quickly can hide turnover issues in a competitive industry, but only for so long. The trends emerge on workplace review sites like Glassdoor. What started as disgruntled whispers at the end of the workday at the bar becomes a solidified reputation. Recruiting high-quality candidates gets harder and harder.

You know this. You know not investing in management training leads to miserable workers and that unhappy workers are more expensive workers. You know that relentless focus on short-term metrics like growth and shareholder value irreparably damages the way workers think about and trust their employers. You know that papering over decreased benefits and pensions with bromides about company culture or ornamental perks engenders good faith loyalty only in the short term, if at all.

And you know that short and shallow efforts to employ quick technological fixes to increase productivity don't work well in the long term, either. You know that employees are overwhelmed with what the Greylock venture capitalist Sarah Guo calls "metawork": endlessly tabbing between programs and projects and constantly navigating or quieting digital distractions.[2] In his book **A World Without Email,** the author Cal Newport describes this as having to work alongside a "hyperactive hive mind" or, as he puts it, "a workflow centered around ongoing conversation fueled by unstructured and unscheduled messages." Newport argues that this is deeply ineffective and "requires that you frequently switch your attention from your work to talking about work and then back again."[3]

Again, you know all of this. But for various reasons, you've become very good at quieting or ignoring that knowledge. But now is the time to act otherwise.

The diminishing returns of overwork are real. Aggregate gains in productivity are happening at less than 40 percent the speed of the previous two decades.[4] That figure is so stark because of just how much **more** we're working: between 1980 and 2000, the average American added on an extra 164 hours of work in the course of a year. We are all burning out—including you. Even when job satisfaction is high, we're quitting our jobs at higher rates than ever before and moving to the next spot. And our early attempts at remote work have largely reproduced that culture inside our living rooms. In the early months of the pandemic, Americans spent more than 22 million extra hours working each workday.[5]

You know this. And here's what we know. Workers are desperate for more autonomy over their lives. They crave more balance and less precarity. They also, crucially, **want** to work. But they want to work for places that treat them as human beings and that invest in them and their futures. They want to be a part of organizations that recognize that meaningful and collaborative work can bring

dignity and create value but that work is by
no means the only way to cultivate satisfaction and self-worth. We know that workers
who are overextended become too tired, frustrated, and anxious to do their best work;
they're too busy trying to tread water, look
busy, and keep poorly communicating bosses
happy. We know this because they've told us.
Hundreds of them.

There is so much overlap between what
workers want and what is actually best for a
company in the long run. You could call this
synergy, or you could call it what it really is:
common sense. But if we are actually going
to have any chance at reimagining the way
we do knowledge work, you, as managers and
executives, have to be on board.

Most executives, Darren Murph says, drastically underestimate the power of signaling
from leaders. If companies reopen their offices when it's safe for all, executives, perhaps
counterintuitively, shouldn't be the first ones
in the door. They should be the last. "As soon
as CEO goes back full-time, it sends a signal
to everyone in the company that 'if I want to
progress, I need to be there with them to rub

shoulders,'" Murph said. Leadership has to model the posture it encourages their workforce to adopt, full stop.

But leaders also chronically underestimate the amount of intentional planning and actual time it will take for the true benefits of these shifts to materialize. Remote or flexible work isn't a line item to add on to your chief people officer's job description, Murph argues. It is a full-time job that requires a leader and dedicated team members to handle the re-architecturing of policies, workflows, and perks. For a comparison, Murph suggests leaders look to the trajectory of the chief diversity officer in many tech companies. What started as a boutique HR initiative was actually a wave of change cascading through not just tech but companies of all sizes. "It seems obvious now to hire a chief diversity officer, even though it really should've been obvious then," Murph said. "But companies refuse to see the obvious."

Nobody can see the future. We can, however, get a sense of what might seem obvious tomorrow, but only if we stop obsessing over short-term gains.

When Murph gets frustrated, he recounts

an anecdote about Amazon's CEO, Jeff Bezos, that's become his remote work parable. A few years back, Amazon announced that it had posted record profits on its quarterly earnings call. An analyst on the call spoke directly to Bezos, offering his congratulations on a spectacular quarter. Bezos thanked him and moved on, but in his head he was thinking something else. The guy didn't get it. What Bezos was really thinking was that "that quarter was baked three years ago."[6]

This, Murph says, is what he's talking about when he talks about remote infrastructure and compounding interest. "I keep telling companies, don't expect savings right away. If you own real estate and have ten- or twenty-year leases, it won't happen quickly," he said. Short-term thinkers will see these leases as a reason not to change their policies, but what happens when the lease expires? "They'll look around and see their competitors," Murph said. "And those competitors invested early in a remote-first approach, and now they're able to easily adapt to whatever's next. Meanwhile, that company will be flat-footed."

Many leaders won't listen, especially in entrenched industries like finance. In early

2021, Goldman Sachs's CEO called remote work "an aberration that we are going to correct as quickly as possible." But, as the office trend analyst Dror Poleg notes, they'll be doing so at their own peril: "Forcing everyone to work in a certain way seems dated in a world where talented employees have more choice than ever."[7] Every year, more and more graduates are opting for more flexible industries over those that remain stubbornly inflexible: between 2008 and 2018, Big Tech went from hiring 12 percent of business school grads to 17 percent. In finance, the percentage dropped from 20 to 13.

And that was before the pandemic. If financial firms don't get on board with flexible work, Poleg predicts, that shift toward tech will only continue. This principle applies far beyond the world of finance. "Executives have had flex **forever,**" Michael Colacino, the head of the commercial real estate firm SquareFoot, told us. "I've been able to work from home on Friday since 1992. People always say that the future is here, it just hasn't been evenly distributed. And that's true: flexibility has just been segregated off into the

C-suite and slightly downstream. So what you have happening now is that no one's going to accept the five-days-in-the-office mentality. Now that they've tasted the forbidden fruit, there's no going back. If you say to a millennial, come back 9:00 to 5:00, five days a week, people are just going to quit."

Finance execs know they should be figuring out new ways to work, but those who rose through the ranks one way, and endured a particular form of suffering and overwork, are reluctant to change their ways, no matter how much evidence is presented of the benefits of abandoning them. It's irrational, it's bad business practice, but after months of fear and instability it feels **safe.** But that sort of comfort will prove fleeting. Because, if history is any guide, the business case for remote work will be made—by the same high-paid consultants and pundits who sneered at it— as soon as the societal pressure for flexible work reaches a tipping point. And this makes sense. What remote work ultimately does is nudge companies to do the things that they know they should be doing anyway. And if you take anything away from this book, maybe it should be that. None of this is really about anything new. It's about what you already knew.

We get it if all of this sounds a bit credulous—that Murph's evangelism or the general arguments in this book treat working from home like some magical cure-all. It's not.

In fact, most of the ideas in this book—including the plea to apply a long-term lens to how businesses are run—aren't really about the nitty-gritty of remote work. They're about opening your eyes to better ways of working. The whole post-pandemic "when and how will we return to the office" debate is, in some ways, just a big distraction. The true issue at hand is not where we will work but **how** we will work.

Remote work forces you to change the how. It is not a cure for shitty management or a bad business model or a bad product. It is merely an organizing principle. Being removed from the luxury of tapping anyone on the shoulder at their desk or bumping into somebody in the elevator means thinking more intentionally about how you work. Stripping out some of the artifice and vestigial norms of the office gives us the chance to see our companies as what they really are, what they've always been: a collection of human beings.

If you are a leader in your organization, then you already know this. But now is a time for leadership and a time to act. It is a time and an opportunity to imagine what might seem obvious tomorrow and to lay the groundwork for that future today. It's an investment, yes. And investments always bring risk. But hopefully we've given you an idea of the compounding interest to come. Go forth and don't screw it up.

Letters to Workers

Over the summer of 2020, a new "challenge," simply called 75 Hard, began circulating on TikTok. The rules were straightforward, if somewhat strange: (1) you had to follow a diet, any diet, so long as it restricted your eating in some "structured" way; (2) you had to complete two, forty-five-minute workouts every day—one of which had to be outside; (3) you could not allow yourself any alcohol or "cheat meals," for example, meals when you break your diet; (4) you must drink a full gallon of water each day; (5) you must also read at least ten pages of a book, with the clear stipulation that audiobooks do not count; (6) every day, you are required to take a progress picture of yourself for documentation.

The goal: fulfill all six components of the challenge, every day, for seventy-five days straight. If you mess up on just one, you have to reset the clock. There can be "NO substitute" and "NO compromise." Like all viral challenges, there's a larger story behind 75 Hard: it was engineered by Andy Frisella, a motivational speaker and self-professed "MFCEO" (motherfucking CEO) who markets a cornucopia of products, supplements, books, and consulting services under the umbrella of 75 Hard, which promises to "build that mental strength and discipline within you."

Sticking with 75 Hard is supposed to teach its participants the value of hard work and self-denial. And it's nothing new: this sort of asceticism has a history that goes back millennia. The difference is that self-flagellating monks in hair shirts led these lives as acts of penitence and in search of salvation, whereas 75 Hard is just about doing hard things to prove that you can do hard things, practicing self-denial as a means to repent for . . . Eating? Living? The rest of your life being too easy?

Unlike other training regimens, there's no event at the end of 75 Hard, or even much in the way of a scientific explanation for why you're doing what you're doing. The challenge vaguely asks you to go to "war with yourself" and then win at all costs. There's very little **there** there, just arbitrary denial and a bunch of overuse injuries and over-priced supplements.

At the bleakest moment in the pandemic, when you felt your most stressed, most scared, least centered, you probably heard some variation of the phrase "This is really hard." Maybe you read it, maybe your manager said it to you, maybe you said it to yourself. But that's the truth: the pandemic year-plus, whatever we want to call it, was **hard.** And like everything else in the United States, that difficulty was not evenly distributed: it was hardest for those on the front lines, those afraid of how customers would react to their request to put on a mask, those out of work and in constant fear of the way COVID was whipping through their communities. It was hard, in different ways, for those attempting to work and supervise school from home, for those in complete isolation, for those increasingly terrified of other people. It was fucking **hard,** in so many intersecting and unfair ways.

All that hard, seemingly never-ending work was worth doing so that others—especially the most vulnerable in our lives—might be safer. Even in your most lonely, over-whelmed, or terrified moments, you could still grasp at that purpose. But within that larger goal of survival—and, if we're honest, long before—many knowledge workers had arrived at what we'll call the 9:00-to-5:00 Hard. We worked far beyond the forty hours of the prescribed workweek, but the goal of all that work had become opaque. It was sel-dom to create work that was meaningful or innovative, even if we could mumble some-thing to that effect when asked what we like about doing our jobs. It wasn't so that we could someday work less overall. We worked hard to prove that we were alert and available for **more work.**

This is the tautological quagmire where we've found ourselves. And as we've researched and reported this book, it's become clear that so many of us are not just conflicted about our work lives but fundamentally confused

about how to define "hard work." Some of
that confusion stems from the subjective nature of work in general. But as we read productivity books and CEO hustle porn against
the backdrop of countless testimonials from
burned-out and deeply unsatisfied workers,
the character and purpose of this particular
approach became less and less clear.

Societally, we are taught to revere and
strive for hard work, even as we internalize
that we're never **quite** doing it. You might
be working long hours, you might feel as if
you were suffocating under the weight of demands on your time and body, but it will always fall short of the venerated hard work of
someone else. Many of our preconceptions of
hard work are still rooted in an agrarian or industrial mindset, especially as the percentage
of the American workforce laboring in those
fields has declined. To labor outside, or in a
factory, or in any way that taxes the body, is
considered good, hard, even patriotic work.
If you work inside, at a computer—even if
it affects the body in ways that don't leave
calluses—it is distinctly less venerable.

Which isn't to say that we should pity or
figure out ways to appreciate knowledge

workers: we already do that, and it's called salaries and benefits. But when this type of worker makes up more than 40 percent of the U.S. workforce, it poses a distinct psychological problem.[1] Culturally, we worship productivity and efficiency, and we value creation and reward knowledge work with high salaries. But we still think of this work as cushy or soft: you might have wrenched your back trying to work from your kitchen table over the last year, but you haven't risked your life. At the same time, we publicly praise the jobs that put people at risk, that take a clear toll on the body, and that focus on care as essential, dignified work. And while we bang pots and pans for such workers—at least for the first few months of the pandemic—their societal value is made clear in their stagnant salaries.

So what work is actually valuable? It's incredibly unclear. Many knowledge workers, ourselves included, find themselves insecure in some capacity about the work they're doing: how much they do, whom they do it for, its value, their value, how it is rewarded, and by whom. We respond to this confusion in pretty confusing ways. Some find themselves deeply

disillusioned or radicalized against the extractive, capitalist system that makes all of this so
muddled. And others throw themselves into
work, making it the defining element of their
self-worth. In response to the existential crisis
of personal value, they jump on the productivity treadmill, praying that in the process of
constant work they might eventually stumble
across purpose and dignity and security.

The treadmill rarely provides the kind of
value and meaning that we hope it will. So
why have we spent all this time detailing the
difficult, time-consuming, and challenging
ways to approach work? Why do we keep
telling you "this isn't going to be easy" like
a broken record? Because all of this is **for**
something, or at least it ought to be. We are
reimagining the way offices work so that we
can finally clear some space to reimagine the
way we participate with our close and extended communities. We are trying to get
off the damn treadmill so we can remember all the purpose and dignity that can come
from the **whole** of our lives.

So ask yourself this: Who would you be
if work ceased to be the axis of your life?
How would your relationship with your

close friends and family change, and what role would you serve within your community at large? Whom would you support, how would you interact with the world, and what would you fight for?

We are so overextended, so anxious, and so conditioned to approach our lives as something to squeeze in around work that just asking these questions can feel indulgent. If you really try to answer them, what you're left with will likely feel silly or fantastical: like a Hallmark movie of your life, if you got to cast people to play you and the rest of your family who were well rested, filled with energy and intentionality and follow-through. Your mind will try to tell you it's a fantasy.

But it's **supposed** to sound amazing, because you need to want it, really **yearn** for it, in a way that will motivate you to shift your life in ways that will make the fantasy a reality. This isn't about doing something hard just to say that you've done it. It isn't torturing yourself to feel something approximating worth. This is about doing the hard, truly foundational work that will shift ourselves and our societies.

First, you have to give yourself space to

explore and commit. That starts with cultivating a work scenario where you can do better, more efficient, and more flexible work, with effective guardrails to protect you from simply working all the time. What follows here is not more reasons why working from home is great. Hell, it's not even about working from home. It is about everything else in your life. It is the why of this entire book—the stuff that's worth fighting for.

Figure Out What You Like

Think back on a time in your life before you regularly worked for pay. Recall, if you can, an expanse of unscheduled time that was, in whatever way, **yours.** What did you **actually** like to do? Not what your parents said you should do, not what you felt as if you should do to fit in, not what you knew would look good on your application for college or a job.

It might be spectacularly simple: you liked riding your bike with no destination in mind, making wild experiments in the kitchen, playing around with eyeshadow, writing fan fiction, playing cards with your grandfather, lying on your bed and listening to music, trying on all your clothes and making ridiculous outfits, thrifting, playing **Sims** for hours, obsessively sorting baseball cards, playing pickup basketball, taking photos of your feet with black-and-white film, going on long drives, learning to sew, catching bugs, skiing, playing in a band, making forts, harmonizing with other people, putting on mini-plays, whatever it is, you did it because **you wanted to.** Not because it would look interesting if you posted it on social media, or because it somehow optimized your body, or because it would give you better things to talk about at drinks, but because you took pleasure in it.

Once you figure out what that thing is, see if you can recall its contours. Were you in charge, were there achievable goals or no goals at all, did you do it alone or with others, was it something that really felt as if it were **yours,** not your siblings', did it mean regular time spent with someone you liked? Did it involve organizing, creating, practicing, following patterns, or collaborating? See if you can actually describe, out loud or in writing, what you did and why you loved it. Now see if there's anything at all that resembles that experience in your life today.

If your answer is your job, that makes sense: a lot of us find something that we're good at and like and then try to make a career out of it in some way. Those who've followed the pernicious advice to "do what you love" know this endgame: it's a burnout trap, and a fantastic way to evacuate all pleasure and passion from an activity. **Do what you love, and you'll work every day for the rest of your life.**

A lot of us have only the faintest traces of those childhood and early adulthood activities in our lives—what we might dare call hobbies. They largely exist as conversational markers and rhetorical placeholders of who we once were. We have so many reasons for neglecting them: we don't have the means, financial or otherwise, to pursue them; we don't have the time; we've neglected them so long that our previous skills have atrophied; we simply don't have the wherewithal to even start thinking about how to start doing them again.

All of those are excuses, most of them valid, that we cling to out of overwork. It just seems so much easier to **not** do something, to not have plans, to not try something new or figure out how to do something you used to love. But that's your exhaustion speaking. When work devours your waking hours, it also devours your will to do things that actually nourish you. The truth is that we don't prioritize these activities, because—other than seeking out ways to optimize ourselves as workers or desirable bodies—we don't actually prioritize ourselves.

A real hobby isn't a way to adorn your personality, or perform to masquerade your class status. It's just something you actually like to do, full stop.

Be patient with yourself as you figure that out. When you first start trying to put the guardrails on a flexible, post-pandemic schedule, you still might want to spend your newly protected time napping or ambiently watching sports. That's totally normal and totally expected: you are essentially in recovery, not just from years of overwork, but from the accumulated, consolidated stress of the pandemic. But just because you've lost sight of who you are, and what you like, outside childcare and Netflix, doesn't mean it's disappeared altogether. Again, be patient and gentle with yourself. This isn't self-care. It's recuperation.

When the haze of burnout begins to clear, fight the urge to feel **productive** and channel that into beginning to explore your own pleasures. When this happened to us, pre-pandemic, it led us down two routes. We started skiing, something that Anne had absolutely loved as a kid but had been reluctant to restart because, well, **everything:** her skis were too old, she didn't have anyone to go with, who would take care of the dogs, she didn't have goggles, it would eat an entire weekend she could spend working, what if she wasn't as good as she used to be?

The story she told herself about why she shouldn't go had so many twists and turns, with a ready, well-rehearsed rebuttal for every argument for why she should just **go.** But then we just **did** it. Charlie got some lessons, we got some rental gear, and, because we live in Montana, we had all sorts of options. It felt **spectacular.** For Anne, it felt like visiting a memory of a younger self and getting to restart it in real time.

Charlie had wanted to relearn how to play the guitar but was reluctant to make the investment in a new one: What if it became yet another hobby he invested in and then neglected? He bought a middle-of-the-line model—just good enough to make the experience feel special—and proceeded to suck. It felt uncomfortable at first. We have so much pressure on us to excel in everything that mediocrity feels wrong. But soon, all the lessons from his youth came streaming back. He began noodling around on new and old chord progressions, learning theory, playing until his fingers regrew old calluses. It turns out that embracing mediocrity means opening yourself up to the wonder of constant little improvements. And, crucially, those improvements are in service only of the joy of learning something new for yourself. The guitar became a lifeline: a means to concentrate fully on something that had absolutely nothing to do with work, or anything, really.

Whatever your **thing** might be—and maybe there are many little things—the most important component should be aiming to make it as little like **work** as possible. This means resisting the very contemporary capitalist urge to commodify it in some way, even when people say to you, "Oh, you're so good at [this thing], you should sell it!" But it also means resisting the urge to master it, or display it in a way that transforms it into some mode of performance. You can want to **improve,** or to make something for others, but that's different from trying to be the best, and beating yourself up (or giving up entirely) because of your inadequacies.

Midway through the pandemic, a subscriber to Anne's newsletter told her that she'd taken up drawing. She'd never drawn before in her life, had no natural skill, and didn't really aspire to cultivate it. She just liked making what she called "shit-tier" renderings of scenes in her life—like her dog, say—and then sending them to her friends as amusement. Her pleasure isn't in the product itself, or trying to perfect it. It was the transportative process, the radical delight of doing something that had no purpose or value other than **you like it,** because it grabs something indescribable of you and refuses to let go.

In **How to Do Nothing,** Jenny Odell conceives of these sorts of activities as a means
of wresting back control of your own attention. You're harnessing a desire and acting on
it, instead of ceding your time and effort to
others' ideas of what's important. Which is
why it's important to try to remove yourself
from ideas of hobbies that are cool or popular
in some capacity, and deflect the voice that
says you should try to find an activity that you
can "share" with your partner or your kid.
They can come along later, if they want, but
focus at first on excavating what **you** like. In
the beginning, that'll mean avoiding pursuits
that require significant investment, time or
financial, which will just place outsize pressure on the activity itself.

Find the path of least resistance to whatever
will create this feeling for you, make time for
it, and then make a promise to yourself for
when you'll find that time again. It might
feel weird, as if you were making a habit out
of selfishness, or scheduling yourself as you
would a child. But shut that voice up. If you
live alone, it's just your work addiction talking; hanging out with your own hobbies is
not selfish. If you have partner or parenting

obligations, this, too, is possible, even if it means being very intentional and collaborative about clearing that space for each other. Sublimating your desire for activities that don't involve your children does not make you a more impressive parent; it just makes you a more exhausted and resentful one.

This maxim holds true for other areas of your life as well. When you get a good night's sleep, you're better at basically everything. When you take rest days, you're a better athlete. The restoration we find in hobbies can make us better partners, better friends, better listeners and collaborators, just overall better people to be around. Hobbies help cultivate essential parts of us that have been suffocated by productivity obsessions and proliferating obligations. The hobby itself ultimately matters far less than what its existence provides: a means of tilting your identity away from "person who is good at doing a lot of work."

We love to talk about kids' personalities, how unique and weird and joyful they are. We don't grow out of those characteristics so much as subsume them with duties. But they remain the building blocks of our humanness, the enduring difference between us and robots. We must preserve those inclinations toward delight and whimsy, toward the ineffable and the unimpressive, the feelings you can't re-create with a machine or optimize for peak productivity. They are worth rediscovering not because they will allow us to rest and, as such, make us better workers but because they anchor us to who, at heart, we've always been.

Remember Who You Value

Now that you've spent this time centering yourself, do the opposite. Think about the happiest moments in your life. Not the milestone events, necessarily, just the times you felt most at home, most yourself, most in love with your life. Now, who was there? It might be hanging out in your early twenties, doing nothing at all. It might be the birth of your child, or just a moment when you felt particularly close with your partner, or a weekend with just you and your dad. This can be a bittersweet process: everyone has people who were a part of those memories who are, in some way, lost to them now. But there are others, still in your life, close or distant. These are the members of your close community who mean the most to you. Our relationships with them are precious and irreplaceable, and so many of us have spent years mourning our inability to treat them accordingly.

We need to start acting as if these relationships were as invaluable as we say they are, which means allocating the time and mental space to nurture them. It means quality, extended, unscheduled time, working to rebalance the relational labor between the two of you, and cultivating the sort of trust that makes people feel nurtured and cared for, and makes you feel nurtured and cared for in return.

If you have a partner, start there. Where are the balances and imbalances in your relationship? In our survey of more than seven hundred workers, we found that those who felt there was an inequitable balance of labor in their home often lamented feeling too overextended to even start to have the conversations that would work toward rebalancing. "My partner is much more identified with her job than I am; she could never stop working,"

Rebecca, a mother of two who works at an insurance company in North Carolina, told us. "So I did most of everything else." We heard so many stories of couples where the tasks were ostensibly evenly distributed, but women nonetheless continued to bear the burden of the mental load: the invisible to-do list of all the things that need to be done to keep the household running, from making plans for leftovers to how to schedule a children's doctor's appointment.

If you had more spare time—or, at the very least, more **flexible** time—how would you reconsider the patterns and divisions of labor that have locked you and your partner in place? What do you want your companionship to look like? Remote work isn't a cure for pernicious gender stereotypes, but many of the people we spoke to noted that the sheer ability to work from home, even under the duress of the pandemic, made the totality of labor visible in a way it never had been before. Seeing all the little things, in other words, makes it easy to share in them.

Now pan out further to your extended family, biological or chosen. Maybe you've been trapped with them for an eternity. If so, what does adequate space from them look like? Conversely, what does quality time with them look like? What would you need to feel present in their lives? How can you protect that time so it feels intentional and not obligatory?

Zoom out once more to your friends. With more time, how would you like to be in their lives? Which relationships have atrophied? Which relationships have grown stronger over time? How might you prioritize the friendships that matter to you, cultivating the sort of intimacy that got swallowed by our frantic, overscheduled lives?

You might be reading this and thinking that everything here sounds a bit self-help-y. Yep! We feel that, too! But it's worth stepping back and thinking about what we're really asking for here. What we've listed above, they're not demands. They're not part of any regime. There's no subscription. You don't have to take any expensive nootropic supplements. You don't have to do very much at all. In fact, the less you do, honestly, the better.

This vague outline is, ultimately, a plea to

inventory what you value: about yourself and about others. It's not luxurious, or selfish, or even radical. It just **feels** that way. What results from that inventory, though, might spark a radical change. At least that's what happened with us. The simple process of taking inventory was profound and disorienting. For Anne, it meant realizing that she had coped with pretty much every struggle in her life by simply working **more** and then dedicating two years to writing about burnout and its causes. For Charlie, it took the form of a pretty terrifying realization that most of his life had been a series of preparations for the next step of his career, both academic and professional. He'd cultivated no real sense of what he valued outside a feeling of continually moving up the ladder. He didn't really know what he liked, in part because he'd cut out so many different experiences in order to pursue a vague goal of success.

Realizing that you've lost touch with parts of yourself can be profoundly sad. But sometimes it gives way to clarity. For us, it didn't mean sublimating our curiosity or swearing off work. It just meant finding ways to redistribute our concern and concentration to areas **outside** work: relationships, hobbies, causes, or just hanging out with our own thoughts. Cultivating this sort of balance, and continuously unlearning your attitudes toward work, is an ongoing struggle. There's no switch to flip or perfect proportion between work and life. But there is real potential in spreading the energy and intention we formerly reserved for work to the rest of our lives.

This is how we ground ourselves and how we open space to care about other people. This is how we build resilience in our communities and begin to prepare for the next pandemic or global catastrophe. This is how we build a foundation to move forward: to advocate for change, to be intentional in how we spend our time and attention and not just our money, to use our distinct privilege and labor power to extend the freedoms of the fullness of flexible work life to others. Is this an optimistic view of the future? Of course. But if we can't envision it, in all its wild hopefulness, we can't make it happen.

In some ways, this book surprised us. It was not quite what we expected or even pitched when we first started writing it. In our heads, we thought its core would be remote work: its procedures, its best practices, and our own experiences. There's some of that in these pages, but significantly less than we imagined. Because over months of reading and reporting, talking to dozens of people about what matters and what doesn't, it became clear that the "remote" part of this equation is actually secondary. What we're actually talking about—what we're scared of and excited about, frantic and weird about—are seismic, destabilizing changes in the place of work, both literally and figuratively, in our lives.

There's nothing easy about building the future you want to live in. The gravity of the status quo can, at times, feel insurmountable. But we hope there's enough in these pages to help you see what you already know to be true: there is a world, and a self, outside the long hours of work and the physical office structures that have long enclosed the expanse of our lives. How invigorated, how terrified, how **fortunate** we should feel, to have the chance to figure out, as if for the first time, who we are and where our lives can lead us.

Acknowledgments

We wrote this book during the height of the pandemic and relied on the help, support, and advice of countless people—many of whom are quoted in this book—to get it done. Special thanks are due to: our agents, Allison Hunter and Mel Flashman; our sharp and compassionate editor, Andrew Miller; our diligent fact-checker Jennifer Monnier; the entire production and publicity team at Knopf but particularly Maris Dyer, who kept the trains running on time; and to Ben Smith, former editor-in-chief of BuzzFeed News, who trusted us to move to Montana, even if he looked at us funny when we asked. Our newsletter readers provided feedback, leads, introductions, and reading recommendations that refined the book and its direction; Beth, Joe, Jack, and Little Charlie kept us fed and entertained. Our parents, even from afar, provided us with love and support and enthusiasm for this project and, most importantly, instilled us with a deep belief to expect and strive for both fulfilling careers and rich personal lives outside of work.

Writing a book with your partner is a potentially fraught endeavor that, in this case, worked out better than we could have hoped. We'd each like to thank the other for tapping into our reserves of love and patience when it came to exchanging drafts and chapters in the middle of lockdown.

Finally, our dogs, Peggy and Steve, provide the guiding rhythms of our day—and gave us the escapes and long walks that made this book possible. Working from home is so much more fun when it's with them.

Notes

Introduction

1. May Wong, "Stanford Research Provides a Snapshot of a New Working-from-Home Economy," **Stanford News,** March 29, 2021.
2. Matthew Haag, "Remote Work Is Here to Stay. Manhattan May Never Be the Same," **New York Times,** March 29, 2021.

1 Flexibility

1. Ken Armstrong, Justin Elliott, and Ariana Tobin, "Meet the Customer Service Reps for Disney and Airbnb Who Never Have

to Talk to You," ProPublica, Oct. 2, 2020.

2. Ibid.

3. Hilary Lewis and John O'Connor, **Philip Johnson: The Architect in His Own Words** (New York: Rizzoli, 1994), 106.

4. Louis Hyman, **Temp: How American Work, American Business, and the American Dream Became Temporary** (New York: Viking, 2018), 6.

5. Louis Uchitelle and N. R. Kleinfield, "On the Battlefields of Business, Millions of Casualties," **New York Times,** March 3, 1996.

6. Ibid.

7. David Weil, **The Fissured Workplace: Why Work Became So Bad for So Many and What Can Be Done to Improve It** (Cambridge, Mass.: Harvard University Press, 2017).

8. Uchitelle and Kleinfield, "On the Battlefields of Business."

9. Nikil Saval, **Cubed: A Secret History of the Workplace** (New York: Doubleday, 2014), 236.

10. See Karen Ho, **Liquidated: An Ethnography of Wall Street** (Durham,

N.C.: Duke University Press, 2009); Hyman, **Temp.**

11. Melissa Gregg, **Counterproductive: Time Management in the Knowledge Economy** (Durham, N.C.: Duke University Press, 2018), 54.

12. **State of the Global Workplace** (New York: Gallup Press, 2019).

13. "Report: State of the American Workplace," Gallup, Sept. 22, 2014; **State of the Global Workplace** (New York: Gallup Press, 2017).

14. Edgar Cabanas Diaz and Eva Illouz, "Positive Psychology in Neoliberal Organizations," in **Beyond the Cubicle,** ed. Allison J. Pugh (New York: Oxford University Press, 2017), 31.

15. Carrie M. Lane, "Unemployed Workers' Ambivalent Embrace of the Flexible Ideal," in Pugh, **Beyond the Cubicle,** 95.

16. Melissa Gregg, **Work's Intimacy** (Oxford: Wiley, 2013), 2.

17. "The Next Great Disruption Is Hybrid Work—Are We Ready?," Microsoft Work Lab, www.microsoft.com.

18. Jessica Grose, "Is Remote Work Making

Us Paranoid?," **New York Times,** Jan. 13, 2021.

19. "Four-Day Week Pays Off for UK Business," Henley Business School, July 3, 2019, www.henley.ac.uk.
20. Joel Gascoigne, "We're Trying a 4-Day Workweek for the Month of May," **Buffer Blog,** May 30, 2020.
21. Nicole Miller, "4-Day Work Weeks: Results from 2020 and Our Plan for 2021," **Buffer Blog,** Feb. 18, 2021.
22. "Do More with Less," **Reuters,** Nov. 5, 2019.
23. Jena McGregor, "Hot New Job Title in a Pandemic: 'Head of Remote Work,'" **Washington Post,** Sept. 9, 2020.
24. Roderick M. Kramer, "Trust and Distrust in Organizations: Emerging Perspectives, Enduring Questions," **Annual Review of Psychology** 50 (Feb. 1999): 569–98.
25. Timothy Ferriss, **The 4-Hour Workweek** (New York: Crown, 2007), 91.
26. Louis Morice, "Mais qui travaille vraiment 35 heures par semaine?," **L'Obs,** Sept. 22, 2016.
27. Luc Pansu, "Evaluation of 'Right to Disconnect' Legislation and Its Impact on

Employee's Productivity," **International Journal of Management and Applied Research** 5, no. 3 (2018): 99–119.

28. Drew Pearce, "The Working World: France Gave Workers the Right to Disconnect—But Is It Helping?," Dropbox (blog), Feb. 26, 2019.

2 Culture

1. Terrence E. Deal and Allan A. Kennedy, **Corporate Cultures: The Rites and Rituals of Corporate Life** (Reading, Mass.: Addison-Wesley, 1982), 5.

2. Sidney Pollard, "Factory Discipline in the Industrial Revolution," **Economic History Review** 16, no. 2 (1963): 255.

3. Shoshana Zuboff, **In the Age of the Smart Machine: The Future of Work and Power** (New York: Basic Books, 1988), 31.

4. Pollard, "Factory Discipline in the Industrial Revolution," 254.

5. Jill Lepore, "Not So Fast," **New Yorker,** Oct. 12, 2009.

6. Zuboff, **In the Age of the Smart Machine,** 46.

7. Lepore, "Not So Fast."
8. "Gilbreth Time and Motion Study in Bricklaying," youtu.be/lDg9REgkCQk?t=51.
9. Lepore, "Not So Fast."
10. Thomas J. Peters and Robert H. Waterman, **In Search of Excellence: Lessons from America's Best-Run Companies** (New York: Harper & Row, 1982), 6.
11. Robert D. Putnam, **The Upswing: How America Came Together a Century Ago and How We Can Do It Again,** with Shaylyn Romney Garrett (New York: Simon & Schuster, 2020).
12. William H. Whyte, **The Organization Man** (New York: Simon & Schuster, 1956), 129.
13. Ibid., 130.
14. Ibid., 154.
15. Deal and Kennedy, **Corporate Cultures,** 4.
16. Amanda Bennett, **The Death of the Organization Man** (New York: Morrow, 1990), 101.
17. Ibid., 48.
18. Ibid., 172.

19. Ibid., 23.
20. Deal and Kennedy, **Corporate Cultures,** 196.
21. Terrence E. Deal and Allan A. Kennedy, **The New Corporate Cultures: Revitalizing the Workplace After Downsizing, Mergers, and Reengineering** (New York: Basic Books, 2008), 1.
22. Peters and Waterman, **In Search of Excellence,** 207.
23. Ibid., 96.
24. Ibid., 319.
25. Ibid., 358.
26. Sara Robinson, "We Have to Go Back to a 40-Hour Work Week to Keep Our Sanity," **Alternet,** March 13, 2012.
27. Ryan Cooper, "The Leisure Agenda," People's Policy Project, www.peoples policyproject.org.
28. Anna North, "The Problem Is Work," **Vox,** March 15, 2021.
29. Joan C. Williams and Heather Boushey, "The Three Faces of Work-Family Conflict," Center for American Progress, Jan. 25, 2010.
30. Caitlyn Collins, "Why U.S. Working

Moms Are So Stressed—and What to Do About It," **Harvard Business Review,** March 26, 2019.

31. "The Next Great Disruption Is Hybrid Work—Are We Ready?," Microsoft Work Trend Index, 2021, www.microsoft.com.

32. "Work-Life Balance," OECD Better Life Index, www.oecdbetterlifeindex.org.

33. **State of the Global Workplace** (New York: Gallup Press, 2017).

34. Jack Zenger and Joseph Folkman, "Why the Most Productive People Don't Always Make the Best Managers," **Harvard Business Review,** April 17, 2018.

35. Ryan Fuller et al., "If You Multitask During Meetings, Your Team Will Too," Microsoft Workplace Insights, Jan. 25, 2018.

36. Richie Zweigenhaft, "Fortune 500 CEOs, 2000–2020: Still Male, Still White," **Society Pages,** Oct. 28, 2020.

37. Sarah Coury et al., "Women in the Workplace," McKinsey & Company, Sept. 30, 2020.

38. "Social Unrest Has Fuelled a Boom for the Diversity Industry," **Economist,** Nov. 28, 2020.

39. Frank Dobbin, Alexandra Kalev, and Erin Kelly, "Diversity Management in Corporate America," **Contexts** 6, no. 4 (2007): 21–27; Frank Dobbin and Alexandra Kalev, "Why Diversity Programs Fail," **Harvard Business Review** 94, no. 7 (2016).

40. Cassi Pittman Claytor, **Black Privilege: Modern Middle-Class Blacks with Credentials and Cash to Spend** (Stanford, Calif.: Stanford University Press, 2020).

41. Chika Ekemezie, "Professionalism Is a Relic of White Supremacist Work Culture," **Zora,** Nov. 1, 2020.

42. Chika Ekemezie, "Why It's Hard for People of Colour to Be Themselves at Work," BBC, Jan. 21, 2021.

3 Technologies of the Office

1. Andrew Pollack, "Rising Trend of Computer Age: Employees Who Work at Home," **New York Times,** March 12, 1981.

2. Carol Levin, "Don't Pollute, Telecommute," **PC Magazine,** Feb. 22, 1994.

3. Joel Dreyfuss, "Inside," **PC Magazine,** Aug. 1992, 4.

4. Benjamin Hunnicutt, **Free Time: The Forgotten American Dream** (Philadelphia: Temple University Press, 2013).

5. Shoshana Zuboff, **In the Age of the Smart Machine: The Future of Work and Power** (New York: Basic Books, 1988), 23.

6. Ibid., 63.

7. Harley Shaiken, "The Automated Factory: The View from the Shop Floor," **Technology Review** 88 (1985): 16.

8. William J. Broad, "U.S. Factories Reach into the Future," **New York Times,** March 13, 1984.

9. Zuboff, **In the Age of the Smart Machine,** 118.

10. John F. Pile, **Open Office Planning: A Handbook for Interior Designers and Architects** (New York: Whitney Library of Design, 1978), 9.

11. Ibid., 21.

12. James S. Russell, "Form Follows Fad," in **On the Job: Design and the American Office,** ed. Donald Albrecht

and Chrysanthe B. Broikos (New York: Princeton Architectural Press, 2001), 60.

13. Clive Wilkinson, **The Theatre of Work** (Amsterdam: Frame, 2019), 44.

14. Nikil Saval, **Cubed: A Secret History of the Workplace** (New York: Doubleday, 2014), 205.

15. Michael Brill, Stephen T. Margulis, and Ellen Konar, **Using Office Design to Increase Productivity** (Buffalo: Workplace Design and Productivity, 1984), 2:51.

16. Joel Makower, **Office Hazards: How Your Job Can Make You Sick** (Washington, D.C.: Tilden Press, 1981).

17. Zuboff, **In the Age of the Smart Machine,** 141.

18. Herbert Muschamp, "It's a Mad Mad Mad Ad World, "**New York Times Magazine,** Oct. 16, 1994.

19. Ibid.

20. Warren Berger, "Lost in Space," **Wired,** Feb. 1, 1999.

21. William H. Whyte, **The Organization Man** (New York: Simon & Schuster, 1956), 63.

22. Wilkinson, **Theatre of Work,** 51.

23. Ibid., 227.

24. Jennifer Elias, "Google Employees Are Complaining the Company Has Changed—This Chart Shows One Reason Why," CNBC, Jan. 2, 2020; Douglas Edwards, **I'm Feeling Lucky: The Confessions of Google Employee Number 59** (Boston: Houghton Mifflin Harcourt, 2011), 90–91.

25. Last stock report had number of Google employees at more than 135,000.

26. Jesse Hicks, "Ray Tomlinson, the Inventor of Email: 'I See Email Being Used, By and Large, Exactly the Way I Envisioned,'" **Verge,** May 2, 2012.

27. Dawn-Michelle Baude, **The Executive Guide to E-mail Correspondence** (New York: Weiser, 2006).

28. Ibid., 154.

29. Abigail J. Sellen and Richard Harper, **The Myth of the Paperless Office** (Cambridge, Mass.: MIT Press, 2002), 13.

30. Ibid., 12.

31. Michael Chui et al., "The Social Economy: Unlocking Value and Productivity

Through Social Technologies," McKinsey & Company, July 1, 2012.

32. Ellis Hamburger, "Slack Is Killing Email," **Verge,** Aug. 12, 2014.

33. Rani Molla, "The Productivity Pit: How Slack Is Ruining Work," **Vox,** May 1, 2019.

34. Ibid.

35. Gloria Mark, Daniela Gudith, and Ulrich Klocke, "The Cost of Interrupted Work: More Speed and Stress," **CHI '08: Proceedings of the SIGCHI Conference on Human Factors in Computing Systems,** April 2008, 107–10.

36. Michael Mankins, "Is Technology Really Helping Us Get More Done?," **Harvard Business Review,** Feb. 25, 2016.

37. Berger, "Lost in Space."

38. Sellen and Harper, **Myth of the Paperless Office,** 193.

39. Dror Poleg, "The Future of Offices When Workers Have a Choice," **New York Times,** Jan. 4, 2021.

40. Paul Ford, "The Secret, Essential Geography of the Office," **Wired,** Feb. 8, 2021.

41. John Herrman, "Are You Just LARPing Your Job?," **Awl,** April 20, 2015.

42. "The New Great Disruption Is Hybrid Work—Are We Ready?," Microsoft Workload, March 22, 2021.

43. Steve Lohr, "Remote but Inclusive for Years, and Now Showing Other Companies How," **New York Times,** Oct. 18, 2020.

44. Crystal S. Carey (associate attorney, Morgan Lewis) to Barbara Elizabeth Duvall (field attorney, National Labor Relations Board, Region 5), Sept. 4, 2018, cdn.vox-cdn.com/uploads/chorus_asset /file/16190209/amazon_terminations _documents.pdf.

45. "Outbound Email and Data Loss Prevention in Today's Enterprise, 2008," Proofpoint, Inc., www.falkensecurenet works.com.

46. Alex Rosenblat, Tamarah Kneese, and Danah Boyd, "Workplace Surveillance," Open Society Foundations' Future of Work Commissioned Research Papers 2014, Oct. 8, 2014.

47. Aarti Shahani, "Software That Sees Employees, Not Outsiders, as the Real Threat," NPR, June 16, 2014.

48. Ben Waber, **People Analytics: How**

Social Sensing Technology Will Transform Business and What It Tells Us About the Future of Work, (Upper Saddle River, N.J.: FT Press, 2003), 77-87.

49. Adam Satariano, "How My Boss Monitors Me While I Work from Home," **New York Times,** May 6, 2020.

50. "How and Why to Transition Your Business to Hubstaff," support.hubstaff.com.

51. "U.S. Employers Flexing for the Future," Mercer, www.mercer.us.

52. "What COVID-19 Teaches Us About the Importance of Trust at Work," Knowledge @ Wharton, June 4, 2020.

53. Thorin Klosowski, "How Your Boss Can Use Your Remote-Work Tools to Spy on You," **New York Times,** Feb. 10, 2021.

4 Community

1. Robert D. Putnam, **The Upswing: How America Came Together a Century Ago and How We Can Do It Again,** with Shaylyn Romney Garrett (New York: Simon & Schuster, 2020), 116.

2. Ibid., 114.

3. Ibid., 46.

4. Noreena Hertz, **The Lonely Century: How to Restore Human Connection in a World That's Pulling Apart** (New York: Currency, 2021), 16–17.

5. Derek Thompson, "Superstar Cities Are in Trouble," **Atlantic,** Feb. 1, 2021.

6. Ben Welle and Sergio Avelleda, "Safer, More Sustainable Transport in a Post-COVID-19 World," World Resources Institute, April 23, 2020.

7. "The Ins and Outs of NYC Commuting," NYC Planning, Sept. 2019, www.nyc.gov.

8. Naida Jordan, "Conquering the Cols: Rehabilitation Through Adventure," **France Today,** Sept. 22, 2017.

9. "14th Street Busway Monitoring," Sam Schwartz, www.samschwartz.com.

10. Farhad Manjoo, "I've Seen a Future Without Cars, and It's Amazing," **New York Times,** July 9, 2020.

11. Matt Kadosh, "Westfield Redevelopment: Council Hears from Lord & Taylor Redeveloper," **Tap into Westfield,** Nov. 18, 2020.

12. Alex Kantrowitz, "Where Tech Workers

Are Moving: New LinkedIn Data vs. the Narrative," **OneZero,** Dec. 17, 2020.

13. Philip Stoker et al., "Planning and Development Challenges in Western Gateway Communities," **Journal of the American Planning Association** 87, no. 1 (2021): 21–33.

14. Patrick Sisson, "Remote Workers Spur an Affordable Housing Crisis," Bloomberg City Lab, Feb. 11, 2021.

15. Anna K. Danziger Halperin, "Richard Nixon Bears Responsibility for the Pandemic's Child-Care Crisis," **Washington Post,** Aug. 6, 2020.

16. Anna North, "The Future of the Economy Hinges on Child Care," **Vox,** Sept. 23, 2020.

17. Tracy Clark-Flory, "This Is What Childcare Could Look Like," **Jezebel,** Jan. 1, 2021.

18. Kathleen McNerney, "Bill Would Create Universal Child Care in Mass.," WBUR, Feb. 16, 2021.

19. "Early Educator Pay & Economic Insecurity Across the States," Center for the Study of Child Care Employment, cscce.berkeley.edu.

20. C. Wright Mills, **White Collar: The American Middle Classes** (New York: Oxford University Press, 1951).

21. Nikil Saval, **Cubed: A Secret History of the Workplace** (New York: Doubleday, 2014), 193.

22. JoAnn Yates, **Control Through Communication: The Rise of System in American Management** (Baltimore: Johns Hopkins University Press, 1989).

23. Mills, **White Collar,** 296.

24. Guy Standing, **The Precariat: The Dangerous New Class** (London: Bloomsbury, 2014).

25. Daisuke Wakabayashi, "Google's Shadow Work Force: Temps Who Outnumber Full-Time Employees," **New York Times,** May 28, 2019.

26. Daisuke Wakabayashi et al., "Google Walkout: Employees Stage Protest over Handling of Sexual Harassment," **New York Times,** Nov. 1, 2018.

27. Priya Parker, **The Art of Gathering: How We Meet and Why It Matters** (New York: Riverhead, 2020), xiii.

A Final Note to Bosses

1. Scott Berkun, **The Year Without Pants: WordPress.com and the Future of Work** (San Francisco: Wiley, 2013).
2. Sarah Guo, "Where Are the Productivity Gains?," personal blog, coda.io/@sarah /where-are-the-productivity-gains.
3. Cal Newport, **A World Without Email: Reimagining Work in an Age of Communication Overload** (New York: Portfolio/Penguin, 2021), xviii.
4. Guo, "Where Are the Productivity Gains?"
5. Jo Craven McGinty, "With No Commute, Americans Simply Worked More During Coronavirus," **Wall Street Journal,** Oct. 30, 2020.
6. Jade Scipioni, "Why Jeff Bezos Always Thinks Three Years Out and Only Makes a Few Decisions a Day," CNBC, Dec. 31, 2020.
7. Dror Poleg, "Remote Bullying," Feb. 26, 2021, drorpoleg.com.

Letters to Workers

1. Jaime Teevan, Brent Hecht, and Sonia Jaffe, eds., **The New Future of Work: Research from Microsoft on the Impact of the Pandemic on Work Practices,** Microsoft, 2021, aka.ms /newfutureofwork.

A NOTE ABOUT THE AUTHORS

Charlie Warzel is an award-winning journalist, covering technology, media, and
politics. He was previously a writer-at-
large for **The New York Times.** He writes
the newsletter **Galaxy Brain** and lives in
Missoula, Montana.

Anne Helen Petersen is a journalist and
the author of three previous books, in-
cluding **Can't Even: How Millennials
Became the Burnout Generation** and
**Too Fat, Too Slutty, Too Loud: The
Rise and Reign of the Unruly Woman.**
She writes the newsletter **Culture Study**
and lives in Missoula, Montana.